2021
2022
年度実施

The United Nations
Association's
Test of English

国連英検
過去問題集

公益財団法人
日本国際連合協会 編著

B級

SANSHUSHA

はじめに
英語コミュニケーション能力の測定と国連英検

国連英検統括監修官　服 部 孝 彦

国連英検は，英語コミュニケーション能力を測るためのテストです。ひとくちにコミュニケーション能力をテストするといっても，「コミュニケーション能力」という概念は複雑です。ここでは，コミュニケーション能力の理論的枠組みをできる限り明らかにし，コミュニケーション能力をより的確に測るためのテストとしての国連英検のあり方について論じます。

1960 年代以降に言語研究に科学的な手法が求められるようになり，「コミュニケーション能力」という概念が生まれました。コミュニケーション能力の概念を最初に示したのはハイムズ（Hymes, 1972）ですが，それ以前に彼は，能力（competence）と運用（performance）の概念を提唱したチョムスキー（Chomsky, 1965）から大きな影響を受けたため，まずチョムスキーの言語理論から考察することにします。

チョムスキーは，従来の学習を習慣形成による刺激と反応の結合が発達したもの，すなわち練習と強化によって形成された習慣とみなす行動主義（behaviorism）の考え方に異論を唱えました。彼は「具体的状況における実際の言語使用」（the actual use of language in concrete situation）を運用（performance）とし，それを「話者―聴者の言語の知識」（the speaker-hearer's knowledge of his language）である能力（competence）と区別しました。

ハイムズはチョムスキーの能力（competence）の概念を発展させ，コミュニケーション能力（communicative competence）の概念を示しました。ハイムズは，文法的な意味に限定したチョムスキーの能力（competence）は不十分であるとし，能力を社会的文化的に拡張すると主張しました。ハイムズのコミュニケーション能力は次の 4 つに分類されます。

(1) Whether (and to what degree) something is formally possible;
(2) Whether (and to what degree) something is feasible in virtue of the means of implementation available;
(3) Whether (and to what degree) something is appropriate (adequate, happy, successful) in relation to a context in which it is used and evaluated;
(4) Whether (and to what degree) something is in fact done, actually performed, and what its doing entails.

ハイムズは，文法的に正しいのか，発話することが現実的に可能か，社会的に適切であるか，実際に遂行されているのか，といった4つの基準を示したわけです。前者2つが文法に関するもので，後者2つが発話としての容認性に関するものであるといえます。

ハイムズのコミュニケーション能力は，ウィドウソン（Widdowson, 1983），バックマン（Bachman, 1990），さらにはバックマンとパーマー（Bachman and Palmer, 1996）へと引き継がれました。「コミュニケーション能力」という用語は，communicative competence, communicative language ability, language ability と表記が変わり，定義も見直されました。コミュニケーション能力理論で最も新しいものは，バックマンの論理，およびバックマンとパーマーの理論です。バックマンとパーマー（Bachman and Palmer, 1996）の理論は，バックマン（Bachman, 1990）の理論を踏襲した改訂版で，テスティングのための理論という色彩を強めたものです。この2つの理論は現在，コミュニケーション理論の中で最も信頼のおけるものとして，言語教育で受け入れられています。

バックマンとパーマーは，コミュニケーション能力に language ability という用語を用いています。そして，その language ability の中にハイムズやカネールとスウェインなどが言う communicative competence の構成要素をすべて含んだ言語知識（language knowledge）という概念を設けました。バックマンとパーマーの言語知識は，組織的知識（organizational knowledge）と語用論的知識（pragmatic knowledge）に分けられます。組織的知識はさらに，文法的知識（grammatical knowledge）とテキスト的知識（textual knowledge）に分類されます。語用論的知識は，機能的知識

(functional knowledge)と社会言語学的知識(sociolinguistic knowledge)に分類されます。バックマンとパーマーは，言語知識以外にトピック知識(topical knowledge)や個人的特徴(personal characteristics)なども language ability の中に含まれる要素としており，これらすべてを結びつける能力として方略的能力(strategic competence)を挙げています。

バックマンとパーマーは次のように述べ，自分たちが提示したコミュニケーションのモデルはテスト開発のためのものである，としています。

> We would note that we conceive of this not as a working model of language processing, but rather as a conceptual basis for organizing our thinking about the test development process.

バックマンとパーマーは，心理的な意味での言語処理モデルではなく，テスト開発のための概念的な枠組みを設定したといえます。

バックマンとパーマーの language ability 理論の基礎になったのが，バックマン(Bachman, 1990)の communicative language ability 理論です。バックマンは，知識(knowledge)ではなく能力(competence)という用語を用いて，語用論的能力(pragmatic competence)と組織的能力(organizational competence)について，次のように述べています。

> Pragmatic competence includes the types of knowledge which, in addition to organization competence, are employed in the contexturalized performance and interpretation of socially appropriate illocutionary acts in discourse.

ここでバックマンは，語用論的能力／語用論的知識は，組織的能力／組織的知識の基盤の上にできあがるものであることを示しました。また，語用論的能力／語用論的知識は，テキストを構成しない一文単位でも発揮されるということを考えますと，組織的能力／組織的知識の中心は文法的能力／文法的知識であることがわかります。

以上のコミュニケーション能力理論に基づき，国連英検では以下のように出題されています。高等学校で学習する英語の範囲内で出題される C 級は，語用論的知識に先行して学習する必要のある組織的知識について問い，加えて組織的知識の基礎となる文法的知識を中心として出題しています。B級では，組織的知識の中の文法的知識に加え，英文エッセイをテーマに沿って“書く”問題も出題され，組織的知識の中のもう1つの力であるテキスト的知識も問われます。さらに，国連英検の特徴である国連に対する理解についての設問も出されます。特A級とA級では，1次試験の筆記試験で文法的知識とテキスト的知識および国連に関する知識が問われ，1次試験合格者を対象に実施される2次試験の面接テストでは，これらに加えて語用論的知識である機能的知識と社会言語学的知識，言語力の要素を統合させる方略的能力，さらには国際事情についての知識も問われます。

以上のように，国連英検ではコミュニケーション能力の研究成果を踏まえ，コミュニケーション能力の基盤をなす力を下の級で測定し，上の級ではそれらの基盤的な力の測定に加え，語用論的な力とメタ認知方略に関する力も測定しています。特に最上級の特A級では，良識ある国際人として持つべき国際常識や国際適応能力についてもテストされます。国連英検は，まさしく総合的英語コミュニケーション能力を測定する試験であるといえます。

参考文献

Bachman, L. F. (1990). *Fundamental considerations in language testing*. Oxford: Oxford University Press.

Bachman, L. F & Palmer, A. S. (1996). *Language testing in practice*. Oxford: Oxford University Press.

Canale, M. (1983). On some dimensions of language proficiency. In J. Oller (Ed.) *Issues in language testing research*. (pp. 333-387). Massachusetts: Newburry House.

Canale, M. & Swain, M. (1980). Theoretical bases of communicative approaches to second language teaching and testing. *Applied Linguistics, 1* (1), 1-47.

Chomsky, N. (1965). *Aspects of the theory of syntax*. Cambridge, M.A.: The MIT Press.

Hymes, D. (1972). On communicative competence. In J. Pride & J. Holmes (Eds.) *Sociolinguistics: Selected readings*. (pp. 269-293). Harmondsworth: Penguin.

Widdowson, H. G. (1983). *Learning purpose and language use*. Oxford: Oxford University Press.

国連英検過去問題集　B 級（2021‐2022 実施）

目次

※本書は，実際の検定試験で使用された試験問題に基づいて編集されておりますが，一部修正されている場合があります。

国連英検とは

■「国連英検」（国際連合公用語英語検定試験）は，1981 年に始まり，長い歴史を持つ英語検定試験です。試験は年に 2 回，全国主要都市で実施されます。特 A 級から E 級まで全部で 6 つの級があり（注：現在 D 級・E 級は休止中），中学生から社会人，シニアエイジまでの幅広い層を対象とし，受験資格は特になく，どなたでも受験できます。

試験を主催するのは，外務省の外郭団体としてスタートした公益財団法人日本国際連合協会です。日本国際連合協会は，国連の A 級諮問民間団体である「国連協会世界連盟」（WFUNA）の有力メンバーで，国内外での国連普及活動を積極的に行っています。

国連英検も国連普及活動の一環として実施されており，国連の理念である「国際協力」「国際理解」をコンセプトに，「真に役立つグローバルコミュニケーション能力」の育成を目標としています。試験内容は国連の活動に沿って，世界平和，地球環境，世界政治，世界経済から，人権，食品，医療などの世界情勢，国際時事問題まで幅広く出題されるため，今まさに地球上で問われている問題を認識し，自分の考えや解決策を論理的に伝達する表現力が求められます。単なる語学力の判定にとどまらず，総合的な国際コミュニケーションスキルが問われます。

■ 国連英検は，資格として多角的にアピールできる検定試験です。多くの大学で推薦入試・編入試験の評価資格として認められ，B 級以上の合格を単位認定している大学もあります。

特 A 級は，成績優秀者に外務大臣賞が授与されるほか，合格者には外務省国際機関人事センターが実施している「JPO 派遣候補者選考試験」において加点が行われます。

この JPO は，国際公務員（国連職員・ユネスコ職員など）になるための登竜門と言えるもので，2 年間の海外派遣を経て国際公務員試験に挑戦できる制度です。

A 級は成績優秀者に国連協会会長賞が授与されます。

C 級以上の合格者は，文部科学省より，高等学校卒業程度認定規則において，英語資格としてレベル認定されています。

また，国際協力機構（JICA）では，C 級以上の合格者を，応募の際に必要となる語学力の評価基準をクリアしたものと認定しています。

なお，警視庁では警察官採用試験（1 次試験）に「資格経歴等の評定」を導入していますが，国連英検 C 級以上の合格者については，1 次試験の成績の一部として評価しています。

■ 国連英検は，コミュニケーションを重視した試験です。B 級～ E 級で出題されるリスニング問題のウェイトは 40％と高く，また B 級以上は国際時事問題をテーマとした英作文（ウェイト 20％）が設けられています。A 級以上は 2 次試験で面接試験を実施し，ネイティブスピーカーと国際時事問題について討論を行います。さらに特 A 級については，ネイティブスピーカーに加え，元外務省大使など外交実務経験者や国際関係を研究する大学教授を面接官として，より深い議論を行います。

●国連英検 D 級・E 級の開催休止について
国連英検では昨今の英語教育における新学習指導要領の大幅な改定に鑑み，主に中学生～高校生を受験対象としている D 級・E 級の試験実施を 2023 年度より休止しています。再開時期・受験形式等は，決定次第国連英検のホームページにて広報致します。

●国連英検受験のための指定テキストについて
国連英検は国連に関する基礎知識を学習するための教材として『新 わかりやすい国連の活動と世界』（三修社）を指定テキストとし，特 A 級～ C 級の出題にも使用しています。級により出題範囲が異なりますので，事前にホームページで確認することをお勧めします。

B級のレベルと審査基準および問題の傾向と対策

レベルと審査基準

問題の形式と内容が異なるため，他の英語検定試験との比較は困難ですが，国連英検B級は実用英語検定準1級とほぼ同じレベルといってよいでしょう。「英語を公用語とする国での日常生活に対処できる英語力」が目標です。英字新聞や雑誌の比較的やさしい記事，日常生活において遭遇する場面を扱った会話文，読みやすい随筆・短編小説などが理解できる読解力や現地での日常生活に対処できる程度の会話力が要求されます。

問題の傾向と対策

試験はまずリスニングテスト（40点）で始まり，マークシートによる客観テスト（40点），英作文（20点）が続きます。（2次試験はありません）。

リスニングテストのトピックには，短い対話や200～250語程度のスピーチや会話が用いられ，大問4題が出題されます。大意が楽に読み取れる程度の英文を多く読み，ラジオやテレビの英語講座や国連英検の過去問題集などで英語を聴き取る練習を数多く行うことが大切です。

客観テストでは5題の大問が出されます。国連に関する大問もありますので，指定テキストの『新 わかりやすい国連の活動と世界』*New Today's Guide to the United Nations*（三修社）を読んでおくことが課題になっています。各級の出題範囲は国連英検のホームページに掲載されています。

その他の大問トピックとしては国際問題や時事問題を中心に，読解力・表現力および文法や語彙の能力がテストされます。

英作文では，日常的な話題や時事問題をテーマにして，約80～100語程度の英文を作成できる知識・思考力・表現力が要求されます。

2021年

第1回試験

問題

B級試験問題用紙

B級

外務省後援

２０２１年度第１回国際連合公用語

英語検定試験（120分）

受験上の注意

1．問題用紙は試験開始の合図があるまで開いてはいけません。その間に、この**受験上の注意を熟読**しておいてください。

2．**受験番号と氏名を２枚の解答用紙（マークシートと作文用紙）**に記入してください。

3．解答用紙の配布は１人１部のみです。複数の配布は致しません。

4．試験開始前は、答案への解答記入は禁止です。

5．マークシートの記入は、１～100までの記入箇所がありますが、この級では１～80までを使います。

6．マークシートの記入は、必ずＨＢ以上の濃い鉛筆を使って該当箇所を黒く塗りつぶしてください。書き間違いの場合は「アト」が残らないように消してください。マークシートは絶対に折ったり曲げたりしないでください。

7．受験級、受験地区、会場番号、受験番号のマークシートへの記入は監督者の指示に従い、間違いなく記入してください。**（裏表紙の「マークシート記入例」参照）**

8．作文は、⑴ 読みやすい文字をペン、ボールペンまたはＨＢ以上の濃い鉛筆で書いてください。⑵ 使用語数の80～100語を目安にしてください。

9．試験問題についての質問は、印刷が不鮮明な場合を除き、一切受けつけません。

10．中途退室の際は、マークシートと作文用紙を持って監督者に渡し、他の受験者の迷惑にならないように静かに退室してください。中途退室後の再入室はできません。

11．試験中は他の受験者の妨げとなる行動は慎んでください。また携帯電話等の電源はお切りください。

12．マークシートと作文用紙は監督者に提出し、問題用紙はご自由にお持ち帰りください。

＊試験問題の複製や転載、インターネットへのアップロード等、いかなる媒体への転用を禁止します。

リスニングテストについて

1．リスニングテストは試験開始後、合図があってから実施されます。（40問あります）

2．リスニングテストが始まる前にリスニング問題の指示と内容を読んで、どういう形式のテストなのか、概要をつかんでおいてください。

3．テスト中の発言は、放送機器の具合が悪く放送された英語の聴き取りができない場合を除いて、しないようにしてください。

試験結果について

1．試験の結果は2021年６月30日㈬頃に受験申込書に記載された住所に郵送で通知します。

2．その間に住所変更をされた方は、郵便局へ住所変更の届け出を忘れずに行ってください。

3．発表前の試験結果のお問合せには応じられません。

公益財団法人　日本国際連合協会
http://www.unaj.or.jp/

I. Directions : You will hear 10 statements or questions. For each statement or question, choose the most appropriate response and mark your answer on your answer sheet.

1. A. Why is it here?
B. Where is it?
C. Oh, thank you!
D. The pleasure is mine.

2. A. That's so sweet of you!
B. He couldn't make it.
C. I'll be there.
D. Don't mention it.

3. A. That's alright.
B. Yes, it is.
C. No, not really.
D. They're too old.

4. A. How exciting!
B. Let me show you.
C. How did it go?
D. Let's go now.

5. A. How much is this?
B. I'll send it over right away.
C. It went really well.
D. Don't even think about it.

6. A. Yes, she's here.
B. I'd love to.
C. Try again.
D. No, go ahead.

7. A. Here you are.
B. Where can I mail this?
C. Not too bad.
D. A four-digit number is fine.

8. A. We're all out.
B. I prefer margarine.
C. They need it.
D. You should eat more.

9. A. I look forward to it.
B. The library closes at 5 p.m.
C. The day after tomorrow.
D. I don't like doing anything.

10. A. I would quit too.
B. There are too many people to count.
C. That's my birthday!
D. But you don't look a day over 40!

II. Directions : You will hear 10 short conversations. Choose the best answer for each follow-up question and mark your answer on your answer sheet.

11. A. Start working for the woman's company
B. Reject the job offer
C. Ask the woman to leave a message
D. Schedule another job interview

12. A. The man will buy a house soon.
B. The man has a solution.
C. The woman wants to rent an apartment.
D. The woman agrees with the man.

13. A. The man changed his opinion.
B. The man gave an answer she didn't expect.
C. The man argued with his teacher.
D. The man voted for a controversial politician.

14. A. Job layoffs due to a bad economy
B. A new economic stimulus
C. Problems with central banking
D. Benefits for single-parent families

15. A. It is delayed. B. It has been shipped.
C. It was cancelled. D. It was received.

16. A. She agrees with him. B. She is indifferent.
C. She disagrees with him. D. She couldn't hear him.

17. A. At school B. At the office
C. At home D. At a remote work space

18. A. Husband and wife B. Researcher and assistant
C. Patient and doctor D. Client and fitness coach

19. A. Ambivalent B. Strongly against
C. Uninterested D. Strongly support

20. A. She feels sad. B. She is excited.
C. She feels inspired. D. She is unimpressed.

Ⅲ. Directions : You will hear five conversations. After each conversation, you will hear two follow-up questions. Choose the best answer for each question, and mark your answer on your answer sheet.

[Conversation 1]

21. A. A police officer B. An actor
C. An academic D. A politician

22. A. To get people's attention
B. To describe his theory in detail
C. To pass an important bill
D. To find the right word

[Conversation 2]

23. A. Watch a lot of movies in Japanese
B. Study grammar three to four times a day
C. Watch the same episode or movie many times
D. Speak to twelve Japanese people every day

24. A. A teacher B. A filmmaker
C. A student D. A translator

[Conversation 3]

25. A. Japanese B. French
C. Chinese D. Korean

26. A. Language differences
B. The woman's cultural identity
C. Living abroad in an Asian country
D. The man's background

[Conversation 4]

27. A. Foreign residents voting
B. Low voter turnout
C. The minimum voting age
D. Voting by politicians

28. A. It has increased. B. It has decreased.
C. More than half vote. D. Less than half vote.

[Conversation 5]

29. A. Grateful B. Disappointed
C. Proud D. Frustrated

30. A. Flooded his yard with sprinklers
B. Cut down his favorite lemon tree with an ax
C. Put up a sign supporting a politician
D. Took fruits from his garden without permission

IV. Directions : You will hear two short talks. After each talk, you will hear five follow-up questions. Choose the best answer for each question, and mark your answer on your answer sheet.

[Talk 1]

31. A. A park ranger B. A tour guide
C. A store clerk D. A zookeeper

32. A. How to care for bears
B. Where to go camping
C. Bear safety tips
D. Recommended camping products

33. A. Inside the tent B. High in a tree
C. Next to the tent D. Buried in the ground

34. A. Moving sideways B. Looking at the bear
C. Making a noise D. Running away

35. A. They are curious.
B. They are strong.
C. They are gentle.
D. They are dangerous.

[Talk 2]

36. A. Feature story
B. Breaking news
C. Weekly forecast
D. Interview

37. A. Science
B. Politics
C. Entertainment
D. Human interest

38. A. The gender gap
B. Universal healthcare
C. Details on her personal life
D. Her economic revival plan

39. A. The special feature
B. The exclusive interview
C. The weather report
D. The day's breaking story

40. A. There was a traffic accident involving a famous athlete.
B. A baseball player got injured in a street fight.
C. The injuries sustained were not life-threatening.
D. The police have identified the cause of the crash.

V. Choose from among the four alternatives the one that best completes each of the following sentences.

41. Today there is growing awareness that languages ( ) in ensuring cultural diversity and intercultural dialogue.
A. play vital a role
B. role a vital play
C. play a vital role
D. role play a vital

42. Japan's Diet on Tuesday enacted a revised road traffic law that will ( ) on drivers involved in road rage incidents.
A. tougher impose penalties
B. impose tougher penalties
C. tougher penalties impose
D. impose penalties tougher

43. Earth's global average surface temperature in 2020 tied with 2016 as the ( ), according to an analysis by NASA.

A. warmest year on record
B. record year on warmest
C. year on warmest record
D. on record year warmest

44. In a study on technology stress, bad tech was found to interfere with employee performance ( ) on average.

A. to 30 percent up by
B. up to 30 by percent
C. by up to 30 percent
D. 30 by percent up to

45. The World Health Organization on Wednesday declared the ( ) a pandemic.

A. coronavirus spreading rapidly outbreak
B. outbreak coronavirus spreading rapidly
C. spreading rapidly outbreak coronavirus
D. rapidly spreading coronavirus outbreak

VI. Choose from among the underlined words or phrases the one that is grammatically or idiomatically incorrect.

46. (A) For the first time in the history of the United Nations, (B) global leaders were not able to meet (C) with person for the General Assembly's (D) annual debate.

47. The UN World Food Programme (WFP), (A) which provides lifesaving food (B) assistance to millions across the world, (C) have been awarded (D) the 2020 Nobel Peace Prize.

48. Fifteen Asia-Pacific economies signed what (A) could become the world's largest free trade agreement on Sunday, (B) covered nearly a third of (C) the global population and about 30% of its global (D) gross domestic product.

49. Myanmar's military seized power (A) on Monday in a coup (B) against the democratically elected government (C) of Aung San Suu Kyi, who was detained along (D) for other leaders of her party in early morning raids.

50. (A) The number of crimes recorded in Japan in 2020 hit (B) lowest level in the postwar era (C) for the sixth straight year, with a sharp decline (D) in street crime.

Ⅶ. Choose the best answer from the choices marked (A), (B), (C), and (D) to fill in the blanks based on the knowledge gained from *New Today's Guide to the United Nations.*

The League of Nations was the precursor of the United Nations. It had its roots in a series of international diplomatic **(51)**__________ held throughout the late nineteenth and early twentieth centuries, but the impetus to set up an organizational structure for international cooperation came from the desire of states to prevent a **(52)**__________ of the First World War. The League was established in 1919 by the Paris Peace Conference, as part of the Treaty of Versailles.

The original members of the League were the **(53)**__________ allies of the war (with the exception of the United States, which never ratified the Treaty of Versailles), and other neutral States.

The Covenant of the League of Nations envisaged the Organization as a mechanism to deal with such issues as the need for disarmament, the formation of a permanent Court of International Justice, the preservation of territorial integrity and the imposition of sanctions against aggressor States. The League **(54)**__________ pioneering work in the fields of drug control, aid to refugees, and international labor relations.

For the first time, within an institutionalized format, countries were trying to achieve, by discussion, negotiation and general compact, something that had never existed before: a lasting world **(55)**__________.

51. A. conferences　B. disagreements
C. elections　D. wars

52. A. buildup　B. destruction
C. repetition　D. signal

53. A. defeated　B. victorious
C. rebellious　D. suspicious

54. A. conducted　B. criticized
C. cancelled　D. ceased

55. A. supply B. environment
C. literacy D. peace

Choose the most appropriate of the four alternatives according to your knowledge and the information gained from *New Today's Guide to the United Nations*.

56. The Charter of the United Nations was signed on 26 June 1945 in
A. Paris
B. London
C. New York
D. San Francisco

57. The official seal and emblem of the United Nations is a map of the world, seen from
A. the North Pole
B. the South Pole
C. the equator
D. the United States

58. Japan joined the United Nations on
A. 24 October 1945
B. 31 October 1947
C. 25 June 1950
D. 18 December 1956

59. The Security Council is composed of five permanent members and
A. 5 non-permanent members
B. 10 non-permanent members
C. 15 non-permanent members
D. 20 non-permanent members

60. Voting in the Economic and Social Council is by
A. simple majority
B. two-thirds majority
C. three-fourths majority
D. four-fifths majority

VIII. Read each of the following passages and answer the questions that follow.

[Passage 1: Questions 61 to 63]

Gender inequalities have increased dramatically in the past year, as women bear the brunt of school closures and working from home. **(A)** Many women scientists are facing closed labs and increased care responsibilities, leaving less time for critical research.

For women in scientific fields, these challenges have exacerbated an already difficult situation. According to UNESCO, women account for only one third of the world's researchers, and occupy fewer senior positions than men at top universities. **(B)**

Meanwhile, artificial intelligence and machine learning developments replicate existing biases. Women and girls belong in science. **(C)**

It is time to recognize that greater diversity fosters greater innovation. Without more women in STEM (Science, Technology, Engineering and Math), the world will continue to be designed by and for men, and the potential of girls and women will remain untapped.

We must ensure that girls have access to the education they deserve, and that they can see a future for themselves in engineering, computer programming, cloud technology, robotics and health sciences. **(D)**

Increasing women's participation in STEM can close the gender pay gap and boost women's earnings by $299 billion over the next 10 years. STEM skills are also crucial in closing the global Internet user gap.

Together, let's end gender discrimination, and ensure that all women and girls fulfill their potential and are an integral part in building a better world for all.

61. Choose the best place from among (A), (B), (C), and (D) where the following sentence can be inserted:

This is critical for our work to achieve the Sustainable Development Goals.

62. Choose the best place from among (A), (B), (C), and (D) where the following sentence can be inserted:

This disparity has led to a lower publication rate, less visibility, less recognition and, critically, less funding.

63. Choose the best place from among (A), (B), (C), and (D) where the following sentence can be inserted:

Yet stereotypes have steered women and girls away from science-related fields.

[Passage 2: Questions 64 to 70]

Experts from around the world who **(64) annually** review information submitted by developed countries on their greenhouse gas (GHG) emissions and removals celebrated the 20-year anniversary of the important **(65) transparency** process last year, while continuing to strengthen transparency efforts going forward with a series of virtual meetings and activities in 2020.

The first reviews took place in 2001. Some of the experts that participated in those reviews are still reviewing GHG **(66) inventories** today. Over the 20 years, the review process has been a key contributing factor to improvements in national GHG inventories, which capture both emissions and their removal resulting from climate action, as well as **(67) enhancing** the capacity of individual expert reviewers.

The importance of transparency was on full display in 2020, as experts and the UN Climate Change secretariat identified innovative ways to ensure the continuity of the review process under **(68) adverse** circumstances of the COVID-19 pandemic with virtual means. The successful work undertaken during the past year can be **(69) attributed to** the dedication and expertise of experts from around the world (in total, 142 individuals from 60 countries). So how does the review process work?

The GHG review process itself takes place over a period of several months, with experts typically engaging approximately over four weeks prior to the review week to **(70) address** preliminary issues identified in the countries' inventory submissions and continues for approximately 20 weeks after the review week as experts finalize their draft report. The work of each team is guided by a pair of experienced lead reviewers, with the support of the secretariat. In addition to leading the review process, the lead reviewers convene annually to identify ways to enhance consistency and effectiveness of the review process over time.

64. In this context, the word "annually" is closest in meaning to

A. accurately
B. in detail
C. yearly
D. by hand

65. In this context, the word "transparency" is closest in meaning to

A. being presented in digital formats
B. being clear and easy to understand
C. being scientifically analyzed by experts
D. being written without prejudice

66. In this context, the word "inventories" is closest in meaning to

A. lists of data
B. lists of goods
C. lists of plans
D. lists of staff members

67. In this context, the word "enhancing" is closest in meaning to

A. assisting
B. changing
C. gathering
D. improving

68. In this context, the word "adverse" is closest in meaning to

A. promising
B. sudden
C. unfortunate
D. worldwide

69. In this context, the phrase "attributed to" is closest in meaning to

A. credited to
B. discussed by
C. prevented by
D. used to

70. In this context, the word "address" is closest in meaning to

A. turn down
B. set aside
C. run into
D. deal with

Ⅸ. Read the following passage and answer the questions that follow.

([1] ~[10] indicate paragraph numbers.)

[1] In October, United Nations secretary-general António Guterres made a series of key appointments. He tasked 15 scientists from around the world with providing policymakers with evidence, as well as their thoughts, on the Sustainable Development Goals (SDGs).

[2] This time last year, the UN's flagship plan to end poverty and guide the world to environmental sustainability by 2030 was already off track. Since then, the pandemic has reversed most of the achievements made in the five years since countries adopted the goals.

[3] The World Food Programme estimates that 270 million people are now at risk of starvation: double the number before the pandemic. And school closures resulting from lockdowns have set back one of the few SDGs that were within reach before the

pandemic — the goal to achieve universal primary education. In December, the UN's science and cultural organization UNESCO estimated that some 320 million children were out of school, an increase of 90 million in just one month.

4 In the 3 months from 1 April last year, working hours equivalent to 495 million full-time jobs were lost to lockdowns around the world, according to the International Labour Organization. And in October, the International Monetary Fund projected that the world economy would contract by more than 4% by the end of 2020, a decrease on a scale not seen in generations.

5 This is the situation facing the researchers whom Guterres has tasked with researching and writing the second UN Global Sustainable Development Report (GSDR) — the first was published in 2019. They have been drawn from all over the world and span a range of disciplines, including climate change, ecology, environmental economics, ethics, health policy, infectious diseases, oceanography, the governance of international organizations and the study of science and development.

6 For this editorial, Nature spoke to individual researchers, government and UN officials, and campaigners from high- and low-income countries. Our advice for the report's authors and for the UN — considering the state of the pandemic and the halting progress made towards the goals so far — is twofold. First, the authors need to work fast — faster than the three-year timeline they have been allocated. Second, they must reach out beyond their usual expert networks as early as possible in the evidence-gathering process and, in particular, look for innovative ways to involve under-represented communities.

7 The GSDR's three-year timetable from commissioning to publication is excessive, considering the urgent need for advice on achieving the SDGs. One way to a shorter timetable is for the UN to commit to releasing an interim or work-in-progress document before the end of this year. That could then be circulated and feedback could be gathered by governments, UN agencies and the many organizations involved in implementing the goals, and this input could be incorporated into an amended second draft.

8 The importance of this partnership between research and action cannot be overstated. At present, UN organizations such as the children's charity UNICEF and the World Food Programme are operating in emergency mode. Research often suffers when budgets are stretched and personnel have to be redeployed — in this case to more pandemic-facing roles. But these organizations still need research. They still need to be able to draw on people who have the time to think and gather evidence; people with the time to reflect on that knowledge before providing advice and answering questions from their colleagues on the frontline, and from policymakers and colleagues in other roles.

9 Such hands-on research will not be for the GSDR authors to do, but they could help UN agencies and countries to think about how to meet their research needs during the pandemic. Researchers need to test different strategies to help children

whose families lack access to smartphones, laptops and broadband. They need to study the effect the pandemic is having on health systems. And, as governments rush to revive economic growth, there is a mountain of research to be done on the pandemic's economic impact and on how to make recovery as green as possible. The SDGs will not be met unless research can shine a light on these and other issues.

10 The UN and its science advisers — on the SDGs especially — need to work at speed, and involve under-represented communities, all of which will require extra resources, including more people and more funding. Without this, it's not realistic to expect them to work differently. But business as usual is not an option. Continued research will be needed to support action to end the current crisis and get onto a pathway to greater well-being and, eventually, prosperity and environmental sustainability. The UN's science advisers have been given a bigger responsibility than many are ever likely to face. Everyone must be ready to work with them and help them succeed.

71. Which of the following is mentioned in Paragraph 1?

A. The UN secretary-general had a meeting with world leaders.
B. A group of scientists were selected to work on a UN project.
C. Policymakers were asked to provide their opinions on the SDGs.
D. Evidence was collected to explain the causes of global warming.

72. Which of the following is mentioned in Paragraph 2?

A. The UN added new goals to the initial SDGs.
B. The situation surrounding the SDGs has worsened.
C. The UN changed part of the SDGs based on current data.
D. The five-year effort to achieve the SDGs has brought success.

73. Which of the following can be inferred from Paragraph 3?

A. Before the pandemic, the number of people at risk of starvation was under 150 million.
B. Many schools around the world closed voluntarily to help stop the spread of the virus.
C. The goal to achieve universal primary education seemed to be a difficult one even before the pandemic.
D. The number of children who were out of school increased gradually over the year.

74. Which of the following is mentioned in Paragraph 4?

A. More part-time than full-time workers lost their jobs due to the pandemic.

B. Nearly 500 million full time workers lost their jobs in three months.

C. The IMF made predictions about global economy for the end of 2020.

D. A global economic recession of 4% is not uncommon.

75. Which of the following is mentioned in Paragraph 5?

A. The first UN GSDR was published in 2019.

B. Researchers in charge of the GSDR come from English-speaking countries.

C. The GSDR is written by UN staff members who specialize in report writing.

D. Some of the GSDR researchers do research on fields other than their specialty areas.

76. Which of the following is NOT mentioned in Paragraph 6?

A. The writer(s) of this article collected information from those who are involved in the GSDR.

B. Considering the current situation, the pandemic is expected to slow down in a few months.

C. The three-year timeline for the GSDR should be shortened.

D. The GSDR researchers should collect data from a wider range of communities.

77. Which of the following is mentioned in Paragraph 7?

A. The GSDR should be written and published in one year.

B. The UN should keep a record of the GSDR researchers' progress.

C. Feedback on the completed GSDR is important for future research.

D. The first draft of the GSDR should be shared and commented on.

78. Which of the following can be inferred from Paragraph 8?

A. There is too much emphasis on research in the United Nations.

B. Fewer numbers of UN staff members are assigned to pandemic-facing roles.

C. UNICEF and the World Food Programme have difficulty finding time to do research now.

D. There are disagreements between UN researchers and policymakers around the world.

79. Which of the following is mentioned in Paragraph 9?

A. The GSDR authors could help UN agencies and countries to do necessary research during the pandemic.

B. Governments should provide children and their families with access to smartphones, laptops and broadbands.

C. There is a lot of research on how to revive economic growth in an environmentally-friendly manner.

D. The United Nations should depend more on the voices of the staff members in the field than researchers.

80. Which of the following best summarizes the message of Paragraph 10?

A. The UN and its advisers should work together to work more efficiently with the given resources.

B. Everyone should provide support so that the UN's science advisers can get the SDGs back on track.

C. The UN's science advisers should be proud of their job because they have been given the biggest ever responsibility.

D. The UN should continue with the current approach to SDGs, and the results will follow.

X. Write a short essay of around 80-100 words in English to answer the following question:

What global issue should Japanese people learn more about? Why do you think so?

(You do not need to write down the number of words.)

マークシート記入例

東京の本会場でB級を受験する、国連 太郎さん、受験番号が「東京01-30001」、生年月日が「1980年10月24日」の場合の記入例です。

【受験番号/氏名】
それぞれ受験票の記載通りに記入してください。

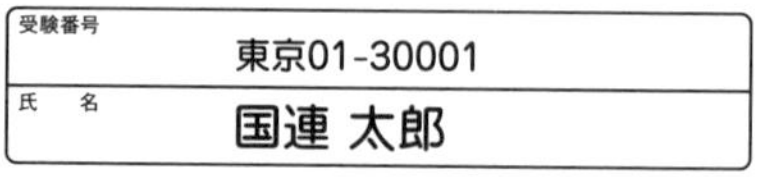

【受験地区】
下段の都道府県部分を塗りつぶしてください。

【会場番号】
都道府県部分に続く2桁の数字を塗りつぶしてください。

【受験番号】
ハイフン（－）以降の5桁の数字を塗りつぶしてください。

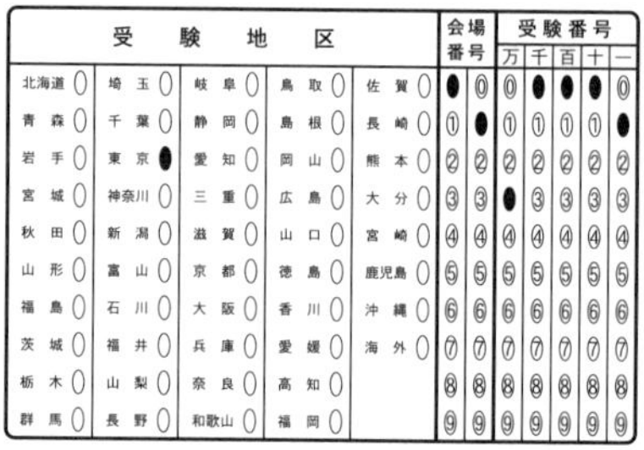

【受験級】
「B」と記入し、下段のB級部分を塗りつぶしてください。

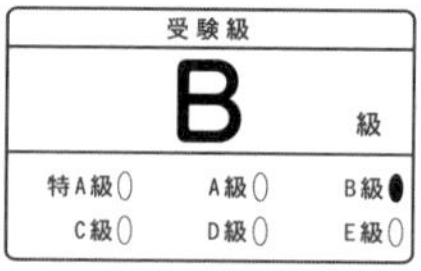

【生年月日】
4桁の西暦・月・日を塗りつぶしてください。
10未満の月・日の十の位は、「0」を塗りつぶしてください。

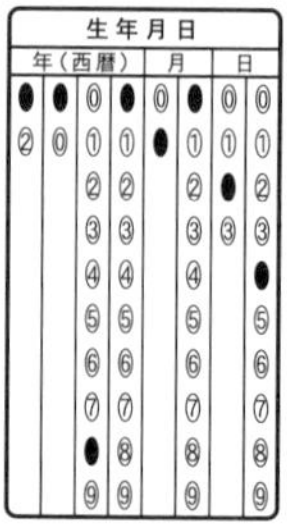

※HB以上の鉛筆を用いてマークをしてください。

※他の地区から会場を変更して受験する場合でも、受験票に記載されている受験地区・会場番号をマークしてください。

2021年
第1回試験

解答・解説

2021年　国連英検B級第1回試験
解答・解説

I 疑問文を含む英文が10題読まれます。
それぞれの英文に対して，最も適切な対応文を選びなさい。

1.　解答：C

解説 相手がコートを褒めているので，Cの "Oh, thank you!"（あっ，ありがとう）が最も適切。

ナレーション　Can I just say, I absolutely love your coat.
「ねえ，あなたのコート本当に素敵ですね」
A. なぜここにあるの？　　B. どこにあるの？
C. あっ，ありがとう。　　D. こちらこそ。

2.　解答：A

解説 何かプレゼントをしてくれているので，お礼を述べているAが最も適切。"That's so sweet of you!"は「あなたは優しいですね」の意味だが，ここでは心をこめてお礼を述べるために使われている。

ナレーション　It's not much, but I hope you like it.
「ちょっとしたものですが，気に入ってもらえるとうれしいです」
A. 本当にありがとう！　　B. 彼はだめでした。
C. そこにいるよ。　　D. どういたしまして。

3.　解答：C

解説 何か面白そうなプロジェクトの計画があるか（= on the horizon），と聞いているので，応答としてはYesもNoもあり得るが，(Are there) any exciting new projects on the horizon? とprojectsが複数形なので，Bは不適。Cが最も適切。

ナレーション　Any exciting new projects on the horizon?
「何か面白そうな新規プロジェクトの計画があるの？」

A. 大丈夫です。　B. はい，それはそうです。
C. いや，別に。　D. それらは古すぎます。

4. 解答：B

解説 I was wondering how to ～「～するにはどうしたらよいでしょうか」と，聞き手に何かのやり方を聞いているので，Bが最も適切。was wondering と過去（進行）形を使うと少し遠慮がちに丁寧に依頼するニュアンスが出る。

ナレーション I was wondering how to input my travel expenses into the system.
「交通費のシステム入力はどうしたらよいのでしょうか」
A. なんて面白い！　B. やり方をお見せします。
C. うまくいきましたか。　D. そろそろ行きましょう。

5. 解答：B

解説 注文をする前に見積もりがもらえるか，という問い合わせなので，Bが最も適切。Could I get ～？は「～をいただけますか」という丁寧な依頼表現。

ナレーション Could I get an estimate before placing the order?
「注文をする前に見積もりをいただくことはできますか」
A. これいくらですか。　B. いますぐにお送りします。
C. とてもうまくいきました。　D. そんなことしては絶対駄目です。

6. 解答：D

解説 立っている人に「列に並んでいるのですか」と話しかけている状況が思い浮かべられるので，選択肢の中ではDが最も適切。

ナレーション Hi, are you in line?
「あの，並んでいるのですか」
A. はい，彼女はここにいます。　B. そうしたいです。
C. もう一度やってください。　D. いいえ，お先にどうぞ。

7. 解答：D

解説 PIN（Personal Identification Number）は「暗証番号」やPINコード

と呼ばれている。暗証番号に文字（letters）と数字（numbers）両方を使うのかという質問なので，応答としてはDが最も適切。

ナレーション For my PIN, do I use letters and numbers?

「PINコードは，文字と数字の両方必要ですか」

A. はい，これをどうぞ。　B. どこでこれを郵送できますか。

C. なかなかいいですね。　D. 4桁の数字で大丈夫です。

8. 解答：A

解説 バターがもっとあるかどうかを聞いているので，応答の中で最も適切なのはAである。Do we haveと聞いていることから，家庭内での家族同士の会話だと想像できる。

ナレーション Do we have any more butter?

「バターもっとある？」

A. もう使い切っちゃったんだ。　B. 私はマーガリンの方が好き。

C. 彼らには必要だ。　D. もっとたくさん食べなきゃ。

9. 解答：C

解説 本のレポート（our book report）がいつ締め切りかを聞いている。クラスメート同士の会話だろう。応答として最も適切なのはCである。

ナレーション When is our book report due?

「私たちの本のレポートの締め切りはいつだっけ？」

A. 楽しみだね。　B. 図書館は午後5時に閉まります。

C. あさってだよ。　D. 何をするのもきらいです。

10. 解答：D

解説 来年定年だと言っている人に対する応答であるから，Dが最も適切である。

ナレーション I'm 59 now so I'll be retiring next year.

「私はいま59才だから来年は定年です」

A. 私も辞職するでしょうね。

B. 数えきれない人がいます。

C. それって私の誕生日です。

D. 40を越えているようには見えないです。

II

10題の対話文が読まれます。
その後に読まれるそれぞれの質問に対して最も適切な答えを選びなさい。

11. 解答：A

解説 女性が電話で男性に伝えたのは，志願している会社への採用が決まったという内容であり，男性も喜んでいることから，正解はAとなる。

A. 女性の会社で働き始める。　B. 採用決定を辞退する。

C. 女性に伝言を残すように頼む。　D. 別の採用面接の予定を立てる。

ナレーション

Woman: I'm calling to announce the results of the job interview. We'd like to offer you the position of senior engineer at our company.

Man: Oh wow, thank you. Thank you so much. I don't know what to say!

Woman: Just say yes!

Question　What will the man most likely do next?

(女)：採用面接の結果をお伝えしたいと思いお電話を差し上げました。あなたに私たちの会社のシニアエンジニアになっていただきたいと考えています。

(男)：えっ，ありがとうございます。本当にありがとうございます。何と言ってよいか。

(女)：ただYesと言ってください！

質問　男性はおそらく次に何をするでしょうか。

12. 解答：D

解説 住宅の購入を考えている男性が，住宅価格の高さについて女性に話している場面である。女性が，I know what you mean.（そうよね）と反応し，不動産価格が庶民には高すぎると述べていることから，Dが正解である。なお，through the roofは「飛び抜けて高い」を意味する。

A. 男性はまもなく住宅を購入するだろう。

B. 男性は解決策を持っている。

C. 女性はアパートを借りたいと思っている。

D. 女性は男性の意見に賛成している。

ナレーション

Man: We want to buy a house here but housing prices in this area have been through the roof these past few years.

Woman: Oh, I know what you mean. Regular folks like us can't afford real estate here anymore.

Man: I wonder what can be done to solve this problem.

Question Which of the following statements is true based on this conversation?

(男)：このあたりで家を買いたんだけどこの周辺の住宅価格はここ数年飛び抜けて高いんだよね。

(女)：本当にそうよね。私たちのような庶民はもうこのあたりでは不動産を買えないわ。

(男)：この問題はどう解決したらいいんだろうね。

質問　会話の内容からして正しいのはどれですか。

13. 解答：B

解説 女性は男性が「原子力発電に賛成だ (for nuclear power)」と授業中に発言するのを聞いて，それが予想しない発言だったので驚いている。したがってBが正解となる。

A. 男性が意見を変えた。

B. 男性が自分の想定しない回答をした。

C. 男性が先生と議論になった。

D. 男性が議論の的となっている政治家に投票した。

ナレーション

Woman: I was really surprised when you said you were for nuclear power in class.

Man: Yeah, I don't mind it as long as it's maintained well. If we had the technology for other alternatives, I'd be for that as well, but at the moment, that's just not a reality.

Woman: Wow, I thought since you are more left-wing, you'd be completely against it. I guess we can't assume a person's opinion just by their political views.

Question Why was the woman surprised?

(女)：あなたが原発に賛成だと授業で発言するのを聞いて驚いたわ。

(男)：まあ，きちんと管理さえしていれば別にいいと思うんだ。他の方法を可能にする技術があればそれに賛成するだろうけれど，現状ではまだ現実的ではないからね。

(女)：えー，あなたはどちらかというと左翼だから，絶対反対なんだと思ったわ。政治的指向性からだけでは個人の意見はわからないのね。

質問　なぜ女性は驚いていたのですか。

14.　解答：B

解説　女性が，政府がまた1つ経済支援法案（another economic relief bill）を可決したことに不満を言っている。家庭に現金支給をすることでインフレを招くのではないかと女性は考えている。問われているのは2人の会話のトピックであるから，Bが正解である。

A. 不況による一時解雇　　B. 新しい経済刺激対策

C. 中央銀行システムの問題　　D. ひとり親家庭への補助金

ナレーション

Woman: I can't believe the government just passed another economic relief bill again.

Man: Wait, isn't that a good thing? Families and households who are struggling can get direct payments.

Woman: Yeah, I know. But I'm scared we will have massive inflation afterwards so even if we have money in our bank accounts, everything will cost more and our buying power will decrease.

Question　What is the main topic of this conversation?

(女)：また政府が経済支援法案を通過させたのは信じられないわ。

(男)：えっ待って。それっていいことじゃないの？　経済的に困っている家族や家庭が直接給付金をもらえるんだから。

(女)：わかっているわ。でも後で深刻なインフレになって，銀行口座にお金はあっても，物価が上がって購買力は下がるんじゃないかと心配なの。

質問　この会話の主なトピックは何ですか。

15. 解答：A

解説 女性は受け取ったEメールに，注文した品物がバックオーダーになっている（an item is on backorder）とあったため，電話でそれが何を意味するのかを問い合わせている。Backorderが「取り寄せ」状態にある旨の説明をしている。女性の注文は遅れることになるので，Aが正解となる。

A. 遅れている。　B. 発送済みである。

C. キャンセルされた。　D. 手元に届いた。

ナレーション

Woman: Hi, I received an email saying an item is on backorder. What does this mean?

Man: It means that there is a temporary delay on your order because we are currently out of stock for that item in our current warehouse. As soon as the item is back in stock, we will ship your order.

Woman: Great, good to know. Thank you very much.

Question　What happened to the woman's order?

（女）：あの，品物がバックオーダーになっているとメールをもらったのですが，どういうことでしょう？

（男）：それはですね，注文された品物が私たちの倉庫で現在在庫切れになっているため一時的に発送作業の遅れが生じているという意味です。入荷が確認され次第，発送いたします。

（女）：よかったです。そうでしたか。ありがとうございます。

質問　女性が注文した品物はどうなりましたか。

16. 解答：C

解説 女性が社内旅行の提案をし，男性が時期について別の提案をしているが，それに対して女性は，But June is our busiest month at the office. と述べているので，Cが正解となる。

A. 彼に同意している。　B. 興味がない。

C. 彼に反対している。　D. 彼の言うことが聞こえなかった。

ナレーション

Woman: I was thinking of holding the company trip at a resort. Maybe sometime in August?

Man: Hmm ... I think August might be a little too hot and humid for some people. How about June? I think the weather is just right then.

Woman: But June is our busiest month at the office.

Question How does the woman most likely feel about the man's suggestion?

(女)：社内旅行はリゾートにしようと思うんだけど。8月あたりはどうかしら。

(男)：うーん。8月はちょっと暑くて蒸し暑いという人もいるんじゃないかな。6月はどう？　気候もちょうどいいし。

(女)：でも6月は会社が一番忙しい時期よ。

質問　女性は男性の提案におそらくどう感じていますか。

17. 解答：C

解説 女性のHey honeyという言葉や，男性の「私はダイニングルームを使うから君はベッドルームを使ったら？」という発言から，この会話が，テレワーク中のオンライン会議を家のどこで行うかを男女が話し合っている場面だとわかるので，正解はCとなる。

A. 学校で　B. 会社で　C. 家で　D. リモートワークスペースで

ナレーション

Woman: Hey honey, I have an on-line work meeting at one o'clock today. What's your schedule like?

Man: I have a team meeting around that time too. I guess I'll use the dining room and you'll use the bedroom?

Woman: No, I want to be in the dining room. It's much warmer there.

Question Where does this conversation most likely take place?

(女)：ねぇあなた，きょう1時からオンライン会議があるんだけど。あなたの方の予定は？

(男)：僕も同じ時間帯にチーム会議があるんだ。僕はダイニングルームを使うから，君はベッドルームを使ったら？

(女)：だめよ。私がダイニングを使いたいわ。だってダイニングの方がずっと暖かいもの。

質問　この会話はおそらくどこで行われていますか。

18.　解答：C

解説 アレルギーに悩む男性が，薬を飲む以外に治す方法はないかと女性に聞いている。女性は具体的な治療方法を示しているので，２人の関係を考えると最も適切なのは，C である。

A. 夫婦　　B. 研究者と助手

C. 患者と医者　　D. 客とフィットネスのコーチ

ナレーション

Man: My allergies have gotten much worse lately and it's affecting my performance at work. Are there any other treatments besides just taking medicine?

Woman: We can give you allergy shots. You have to go in for a shot once a month. This treatment takes about a year but in the long term, it's much more effective than regular prescription medicine.

Man: Anything to get rid of these allergies once and for all. Let's do it.

Question　What most likely is the relationship between the man and the woman?

(男)：アレルギーが最近ひどくて仕事に影響があるんです。薬を飲む以外に何か他の治療法はありますか？

(女)：アレルギー注射もありますよ。1 カ月に一度注射を打ちに通院する必要があります。この治療は 1 年くらいかかりますが，長期的には通常の処方薬よりもずっと効果があります。

(女)：このアレルギーを完全になくすためなら何でもいいです。お願いします。

質問　男性と女性の関係はおそらく何ですか。

19.　解答：B

解説 男性は最近動物実験に疑問を投げかけるドキュメンタリーを見た後，生産過程で動物実験をしない製品だけを買うようになったと言っている。女性は薬などの開発にはやむを得ないと言っているが，男性はそれに対しても反論している。このことから，正解はBとなる。

A. 賛否決めかねている。　B. 強く反対している。

C. 無関心である。　D. 強く支持している。

ナレーション

Man: I recently saw a documentary on animal testing which questions the ethics of this practice. So lately, I've been trying to buy only products that don't test on animals.

Woman: I think for certain products, you can definitely avoid using animals. But I've heard that a lot of research for new drugs and medical treatments require animal models.

Man: But there is just no ethical justification for causing pain and suffering to animals when we have very sophisticated alternatives these days like computer systems and mathematical models.

Question　Which of the following best describes how the man feels about animal testing?

(男)：この間動物実験の倫理的問題をとりあげたドキュメンタリーを見たんだ。それで最近は動物を実験台にしなくて済む製品だけを買うようにしいるんだ。

(女)：製品によっては動物実験を絶対避けることができるものもあると思うわ。でも新薬や新しい治療法などの多くは動物の被験者が必要だと聞いているわ。

(男)：でも，最近はコンピューターシステムや数理モデルなどの高度な代替案もあるんだから，動物たちに痛みや苦しみを与えてよいという倫理的正当性はないと思うんだ。

質問　動物実験について男性の気持ちを最も表しているのはどれですか。

20.　解答：D

解説　展覧会に来ている男女の会話である。女性の方は展示してある作品の意味がわからない（None of these artworks make any sense.）とか，頭痛がする（is giving me a headache）と話していることから，Dが正解である。

A. 悲しい気持ちである。　B. わくわくしている。

C. 刺激を受けた感じである。　D. よいと思わない。

ナレーション

Woman: This is probably one of the weirdest art exhibitions I've ever been to. None of these artworks make any sense.

Man: I don't think they're supposed to. The paintings are supposed to make you question your sense of perspective.

Woman: Well, if that's the purpose, they definitely succeeded. Trying to make sense of anything here is giving me a headache.

Question　How does the woman feel about the art exhibition?

(女)：いままで行ったことのある中でたぶん最も変わった展覧会だわ。作品のどれ 1 つをとっても全く意味不明よ。

(男)：意味を理解してもらおうと思っていないんだよ。絵というのは見る人に自分の感覚に疑問を抱かせるためのものなのさ。

(女)：えー，もしそれが目的なら，大成功だわ。だってここにあるものを理解しようとするだけで頭痛がしてくるもの。

質問　女性は展覧会についてどう感じていますか。

III

5 つの対話文が読まれます。各対話文の後で，それに対する質問が 2 つ読まれます。各質問に最も適切な答えを選びなさい。

Conversation 1

21.　解答：C

解説　女性が男性の発言についてインタビューしていると思われる場面である。また男性が発言の後半で「政治家たちに〜を問いたい」と述べていることから，正解は C となる。

A. 警察官　B. 役者　C. 研究者　D. 政治家

22.　解答：A

解説　「人々にこの潜在的問題に注意を払ってもらうため（= to bring people's attention to this potential problem）にあえて人を挑発するような（provocative）表現を使った」と男性が述べているので，A が正解となる。

A. 人々の注意を引く　B. 自分の理論を細かく説明する

C. 重要法案を可決させる　D. 正しい用語を見つける

ナレーション

Woman: You said automation will create a class of quote-unquote "useless people". Many people have criticized you for using this term. Would you like to clarify for our readers what you meant by that?

Man: Yes, of course. I purposely use provocative terms like "useless" to bring people's attention to this potential problem.

Woman: And what is this problem?

Man: That automation will render a group of people economically useless. Of course, no human being is useless from the point of view of their loved ones. But from an economic perspective, with the widespread adoption of automation and AI, there WILL be a group of people deemed as useless economically, and — as an outsider who has studied this subject extensively — I'm trying to ask policymakers, "What sort of educational policies can the government put in place to prevent this from happening?"

Woman: Okay, thank you for clearing that up.

Questions 21. Who most likely is the man?

22. What was the man's explanation for why he used the term "useless"?

(女)：オートメーションは，「不必要な人々」という階級を作り出すだろうとおっしゃいました。この言葉の使用について多くの方からの批判があります。読者のみなさんへ先生からご説明をいただけますでしょうか。

(男)：もちろんです。私がこの「不必要な」といった挑発的な言葉を意図的に使ったのは，みなさんの注意をこの潜在的な問題に向けたかったからなんです。

(女)：それはどういった問題なのでしょうか。

(男)：オートメーションによってあるグループの人々は経済的に不必要な存在になるのです。もちろん，家族や友人の視点からすれば不必要な人間など1人もいません。しかし経済的な視点からすれば，オートメーションやAIの幅広い普及に伴って，必ず一定のグループの人々が経済的に不必要だと見なされることになるのです。そして，この課題について広範にわたり研究してきた外部の人間として，私は政治家たちに，「この問題が起こることを防ぐために，政府はどのような教育政策を実施できるのか」と尋ねようとしているのです。

(女)：なるほど。ご説明ありがとうございました。

質問　21. 男性はおそらく誰ですか。

22. 男性はなぜ「不必要な」という言葉を使ったと説明しましたか。

Conversation 2

23. 解答：C

解説 男性の2回目の発言の中に "the key is to this exercise is to use the same episode or movie over and over again" とあることからCが正解となる。

A. 日本語でたくさん映画を見る。

B. 1日に3，4回文法を学ぶ。

C. 同じエピソードや映画を何回も見る。

D. 毎日12人の日本人に話しかける。

24. 解答：A

解説 男性が，"One thing I always encourage my students to do is ..."（いつも生徒に勧めているのは）と言っていることから，正解はAとなる。

A. 教師　　B. 映画製作者　　C. 生徒　　D. 翻訳家

ナレーション

Woman: Hey Kevin, what's one of the best language learning techniques you recommend?

Man: One thing I always encourage my students to do is to pick an episode from a drama or movie ...

Woman: Oh, I've heard that before ...

Man: But the key to this exercise is to use the same episode or movie over and over again. And I mean, hundreds of times. When I was studying Japanese seriously, I watched the movie Juninin no yasashii nihonjin three to four times a day.

Woman: Wow, that's pretty intense.

Questions 23. What does the man suggest the woman do?

24. What is most likely the man's occupation?

(女)：ねえケビン，おすすめの最良の言語学習方法ってある？

(男)：僕がいつも生徒に勧めているのは，ドラマの一話や映画を選んで……

(女)：あっ，それは聞いたことがあるけど……

(男)：でもこの練習法で大事なのは，同じドラマの1話や映画を何度も何度も使うことなんだよ。それも，何百回もね。僕が本格的に日本語を勉強していたときは，「10人のやさしい日本人」という映画を1日に3，4回見たよ。

(女)：えーっ。それはすごいわね。

質問 23. 男性は女性にどうするように助言しましたか。

24. 男性の職業はおそらく何ですか。

Conversation 3

25. 解答：B

解説 会話の内容から，男性は，Korean, Chinese, Japanese, English が話せると言っているので，正解は B となる。

A. 日本語　B. フランス語　C. 中国語　D. 韓国語

26. 解答：D

解説 女性の冒頭の発言「えっ，じゃあなたは，国籍は中国だけれど民族的には韓国人なの？」や男性の発言の内容から，D が正解となる。

A. 言語の違い　B. 女性の文化的アイデンティティ

C. アジアの国での海外生活　D. 男性の生い立ち

ナレーション

Woman: Wait, let me get this straight. So your nationality is Chinese, but you're ethnically Korean?

Man: That's right. I'm Korean-Chinese. We are a very small ethnic minority in China. Many of us live in the northeast region of China bordering North Korea.

Woman: Wow, so do you speak both Korean and Chinese?

Man: Yeah, I went to a school for Koreans in China and we learned both languages there. That's why it was easy for me to learn Japanese since Korean and Japanese have similar grammar, and Chinese and Japanese share many similar Chinese characters.

Woman: So you know three of the main Asian languages, AND English?! I'm so jealous!

Questions 25. From the conversation, which language does the man probably NOT speak?

26. What is the main topic of this conversation?

（女）：待って，ということは。あなたは国籍は中国だけど，民族的には韓国人ということ？

（男）：そうだよ。僕は韓国系中国人なんだ。中国ではかなり少数派の民族なんだ。多くは，北朝鮮との国境近くの，中国北東部に住んでいるんだよ。

（女）：へー，じゃ韓国語も中国語も話せるの？

（男）：ああ，僕は中国に住む韓国人向けの学校に通いそこで両方の言葉を学んだんだよ。だから日本語を学ぶのは僕にとっては簡単だったんだ。なにしろ韓国語と日本語は文法が似ているし，中国語と日本語は多くの同じ漢字を使っているからね。

（女）：ということは，あなたは，アジアの3つの主な言語と，さらに英語を話せるのね。羨ましい！

質問 25. 会話から，男性が話せない言語はおそらくどれですか。

26. この会話の主なトピックは何ですか。

Conversation 4

27. 解答：C

解説 アルゼンチンの投票について女性が言及しているのは，投票できる最低年齢，16～18才までの投票権の行使，18才以降の投票義務，71才以降の投票権の行使状況と投票率である。したがって正解はCとなる。
A. 外国人住民の投票　B. 低い投票率
C. 最低選挙権年齢　D. 政治家による投票

28. 解答：D

解説 男性が，“Here, less than half of young voters turn out to vote.”と述べていることから，正解はDである。
A. 増加した。　B. 減少した。
C. 半数より多くが投票する。　D. 投票するのは半数に満たない。

ナレーション

Man: Some people are proposing to lower the voting age to 16 because of all the recent political activism by young people these days.

Woman: I know that in Argentina, the minimum voting age is 16 but it's completely optional to vote between the ages of 16 and 18. After 18 however, voting becomes compulsory. And when you turn 71, then voting becomes optional again. They have something like a 70% voter turnout rate.

Man: I wonder what the voter turnout is like for the younger generation in Argentina. Here, less than half of young voters turn out to vote.

Woman: That's why I doubt changing the voting age would have much of an effect.

Man: Maybe. Who knows? This new generation might surprise you.

Questions 27. Which of the following did the woman mention about voting in Argentina?
28. What is the young voter turnout rate like where the man lives?

(男)：最近の若者の活発な政治活動状況を理由に，選挙年齢を16才に引き下げるべきだと言う人々がいるんだ。

(女)：アルゼンチンでは，最低選挙権年齢が16才だというのは知っているけれど，16才から18才までの間は投票は完全に任意よ。でも18才以降は投票義務があるの。そして71才になるとまた任意になるの。アルゼンチンでは投票率は70％くらいなのよ。

(男)：アルゼンチンでは，若者の投票率はどれくらいなんだろう。ここでは，半分以下だけど。

(女)：だから私は，投票年齢の変更はあまり効果がないと思っているのよ。

(男)：たぶんね。どうなるかは誰にも予想できないね。新しい世代の若者は予期しない動きを見せるかもしれないね。

質問　27. アルゼンチンでの投票について女性が話題にした内容は次のうちどれですか。

28. 男性が住んでいる地域では若者の投票率はどうですか。

Conversation 5

29.　解答：D

解説　男性が，隣人について，“They drive me up the wall.”（本当にイライラする）と言ったり，その原因となる行為について述べたりしていることから，Dが正解となる。

A. 感謝している　　B. がっかりしている

C. 誇りに思っている　　D. イライラしている

30.　解答：B

解説　隣人の行為として男性が例示したのは，散水機の話，自分の庭のレモンの果実を勝手に取っていく話，自分の嫌いな政治家の看板を立てた話，であるから，選択肢からそれ以外を選ぶとBが正解である。

A. 散水機で彼の庭を水浸しにした。

B. 斧で彼のお気に入りのレモンの木を切り倒した。

C. ある政治家を支持する看板を立てた。

D. 許可なく彼の庭の果実を取り去った。

ナレーション

Man:　　I can’t stand my new neighbors. They drive me up the wall.

Woman: Oh no ... I’ve heard this before. What did they do this time?

Man: Last month, their sprinklers flooded my yard. Two weeks ago, I caught them picking the lemons from the lemon tree in our garden without asking. And then just yesterday, they put up a sign for a politician I absolutely hate.

Woman: Well, the first two are indefensible but as for the political sign, how are they supposed to know which politician you like or dislike?

Man: Because I have a sign for his opponent in my yard!

Questions 29. Which word best describes the man's attitude towards his neighbor?

30. Which of the following did the man's neighbor NOT do?

(男)：新しく越してきた隣の住人には我慢できない。本当にイライラする。

(女)：あらあら。この間も言っていたわね。今度は何をしたの？

(男)：先月は，彼らの散水機が私の家の庭を水浸しにしたんだ。2週間前は，許可なく私の庭のレモンの木から，レモンをもぎ取っているところを見つけたんだ。その上昨日は，私が大嫌いな政治家を支持する看板を立てたんだ。

(女)：まあ，最初の2つは言い逃れのしようがないわね。でも政治関連の看板については，お隣さんにとって，あなたがどの政治家を好きか嫌いかなんて，どうしてわかるのかしら。

(男)：私が庭に，その対立候補を支持する看板を立てているからだよ！

質問 29. 隣の人に対する男性の態度を最もよく表している言葉はどれか。

30. 隣の人がしなかったのは次のうちどれですか。

IV (初めに) 2つの短いナレーションが読まれ，そのナレーションの後にそれぞれ5つの質問文が読まれます。最も適切な答えを選びなさい。

Talk 1

31. 解答：A

解説 "This is an important message from the U.S. Forest Service." と話していることから，米国森林局の担当者だとわかる。したがって正解はA

となる。

A. 自然保護官　B. ツアーガイド　C. 店員　D. 動物飼育係

32. 解答：C

解説 “When visiting one of our national parks, you may come across a black bear.” という言葉に続き，一貫してクマに遭遇した際の安全策について話しているので，正解は C となる。

A. クマの世話の仕方　B. おすすめのキャンプ地

C. クマ安全対策情報　D. 推奨するキャンプ用品

33. 解答：B

解説 ゴミや食料，匂いのするものは，トランク，クマ対策用容器，木の高いところに収納するように言っているので，選択肢の中では B が正解である。

A. テントの中　B. 木の高いところ　C. テントの横　D. 地面の中

34. 解答：D

解説 クマに遭遇したらすべきこととして挙げられているのは，「ゆっくり横方向に離れる」「クマから目を離さない」「絶対に走らない」「車や建物の中に隠れる」「声を出す」である。この中にないものを選べばよいので，正解は D となる。

A. 横に動く　B. クマを見る　C. 音を出す　D. 走って逃げる

35. 解答：A

解説 “A standing bear is usually just curious, not threatening.” と話していることから，正解は A となる。

A. 興味を示している　B. 力が強い　C. 優しい　D. 危険である

ナレーション

This is an important message from the U.S. Forest Service.

When visiting one of our national parks, you may come across a black bear. Although this can seem exciting, if the bear rips through your tent to look for food, your carefree camping trip can turn disastrous and even deadly.

To avoid black bear encounters, be sure to store trash, food and scented products, like toothpaste, in your car's trunk, bear-resistant food containers or high up in a tree.

If you happen to encounter a bear, move away slowly and sideways. This allows you to keep an eye on the bear and avoid tripping. Moving sideways is also non-threatening to bears. Do NOT run. If possible, get into a vehicle or a secure building.

Remember to stay calm. Most bears do not want to attack you. Use your voice to make noise so the bear knows you are a human and not a prey animal. The bear may come closer or stand on its hind legs to get a better look or smell. A standing bear is usually just curious, not threatening.

Also, carry bear pepper spray in case you encounter an aggressive bear.

This public service announcement was brought to you by the US Forest Service.

Questions 31. Who most likely is the speaker?

32. What is the main topic of this talk?

33. According to the announcement, where should campers keep their food and trash?

34. Which of the following action is NOT recommended in the announcement?

35. What does the announcement say about standing bears?

語句 come across ～: ～に遭遇する　carefree: 気楽な　disastrous: 悲惨な　bear-resistant container: クマ対策用容器　allow 人 to ～: 人が～することを可能にする　bear pepper spray: クマよけスプレー　in case ～: ～するときに備えて（～するといけないから）

訳例　米国森林サービスからの重要なお知らせです。

米国の国立公園を訪れる際，ブラックベアに遭遇するかもしれません。わくわくする経験に思えるかもしれませんが，このクマが食べ物を探しにテントを破って侵入してきたら，気楽なキャンプの旅が悲惨な，あるいは死にさえ至る旅になるかもしれません。

ブラックベアとの遭遇を避けるため，ゴミや食料，あるいは歯磨きなど匂いのする製品は，必ず，車のトランク，クマ対策用食品容器，あるいは木の高いところに収納しておいて下さい。

もしクマに出くわしたら，ゆっくり横方向に離れてください。こうすることで，あなたはクマから目を離さず，なおかつ転ぶことを防ぐことができます。横に動くことはまた，クマを威嚇しないで済む効果があります。決して走らないで下さい。可能なら，車の中か頑丈な建物の中に入ってください。

冷静でいることを忘れないでください。ほとんどのクマは，あなたを襲いたいとは思っていません。クマが，あなたが人間であって獲物ではないとわかるように，声を使って音を出して下さい。クマは，相手をよく見たり匂いを嗅いだりするために，近づいたり後ろ足で立ったりするかもしれません。クマが立っているのは，ふつうは単に興味を示しているだけで，威嚇しているわけではありません。

また，攻撃的なクマに遭遇したときの備えに，クマよけスプレーを携行してください。

このお知らせは米国森林サービスがお送りしました。

質問　31. 話し手はおそらく誰ですか。

32. この話の主なトピックは何ですか。

33. このお知らせによると，キャンパーたちは，食料やゴミはどこに保管すべきですか。

34. 次の行動のうちお知らせで推奨されていないものはどれですか。

35. 立っているクマについてこのお知らせは何と言っていますか。

Talk 2

36.　解答：B

解説　“But first, today’s breaking story.” と言っているので最初に放送されるのは，「最新ニュース」だとわかる。したがって正解はBとなる。

A. 特報　　B. 最新ニュース　　C. 週間天気予報　　D. インタビュー

37.　解答：D

解説　今晩の特報として “we tell the heartbreaking but inspirational story of a local woman” と話しており，さらに “It’s a story of love, loss, and resilience.” と描写していることから，報道の1つのジャンルである，人物に焦点を当てた物語であるとわかる。したがって正解はDである。

A. 科学　B. 政治　C. 娯楽　D. 人物とその生きざま

38. 解答：D

解説 大統領にインタビューで尋ねたトピックは，経済回復策，ベーシック・インカム戦略，初の女性大統領としての思い，であるから，正解はDである。

A. ジェンダー格差　B. 包括的医療保障

C. 彼女の細かな私生活　D. 彼女の経済回復策

39. 解答：C

解説 “so you definitely do not want to miss this segment”（ぜひここもお聞き逃しなく）と言っているのは，ハリケーン対策情報も得られる週間天気予報のコーナーである。したがって正解はCとなる。

A. 特報　B. 独占インタビュー　C. 天気予報　D. 最新ニュース

40. 解答：A

解説 最新ニュースで報じられたのは，有名な野球選手が自動車事故で重症を負い生死をさまよっており，警察が事故原因を調査中である，という内容であるから，正解はAとなる。

A. 有名なスポーツ選手が交通事故にあった。

B. 野球選手が路上のケンカでけがをした。

C. けがは命の危険があるものではなかった。

D. 警察は事故の原因をつきとめた。

ナレーション

Good evening and welcome to FNC News at six o’ clock. This is Roger Carlson. For our special feature tonight: we tell the heartbreaking but inspirational story of a local woman whose bed and breakfast was destroyed in the tsunami 10 years ago, how she and her husband managed to rebuild their business and community, and the tragic fishing boat accident that took the lives of all her family members. It’s a story of love, loss, and resilience.

Later in the program, we will air our exclusive interview with

President Peterson. We asked about her plans to revive the economy, the details on her new universal basic income initiative, and her thoughts on being the first female president.

Then Kate Summers will bring us the weekly forecast and updates on Hurricane Samuel, including the steps you can take to protect yourself and your family. It's always good to be prepared in advance for natural disasters, so you definitely do not want to miss this segment. Finally, Jose Sanchez will round out the hour with today's latest sports scores and highlights.

But first, today's breaking story. Major league star and pitcher Jackson Lee was involved in a single-car accident today and suffered serious injuries to his arms and legs. He is in serious condition and currently undergoing surgery at UCMA Medical Center. We currently still do not know whether he will make it or not.

According to the Mariner County Sheriff Department, the crash occurred a little after 7 a.m. local time on First Street. Authorities are currently on the scene examining the crash site and officials said it will take several weeks to complete the investigation as to the cause of the crash.

Questions 36. Which story in the program is covered first?
37. What type of news is the special feature?
38. Which topic did they ask the President about?
39. Which section of the broadcast does the newscaster strongly recommend?
40. Which of the following is true about the day's breaking story?

語句 special feature: 特報 bread and breakfast (B & B): 民宿 resilience: 不屈の心，困難から立ち直る力 exclusive: 独占の universal basic income: 包括的最低所得保障 initiative: (政策実現にむけた) 戦略，構想 segment: 部分 round out ～: ～を締めくくる single-car accident: 自損事故 sheriff department: 保安官事務所

訳例 こんばんは。6 時の FNC ニュースです。ロジャー・カールソンがお伝えします。今晩の特報では，心痛む，しかし感動を与えるある地元の女性の物語をお伝えします。10 年前の津波で自らが営む民宿を失い，その後夫とともにい

かに彼女が民宿と地域を建て直したか，そしてまた彼女が家族全員を失ってしまうことになる悲劇的な釣り舟事故。これは愛と喪失と不屈の心の物語です。

プログラム後半では，ピーターソン大統領との独占インタビューを放送します。私たちは大統領に，彼女の経済回復策や，新たな包括的ベーシック・インカム戦略の詳細，そして初の女性大統領としての思いについて尋ねました。

そのあと，ケイト・サマーズが週間天気予報とハリケーンサミュエルについての最新情報，みなさんと家族がご自身を守るためにとるべき行動についてお伝えします。自然災害には事前の備えが大切ですから，ぜひお聞き逃しなく。最後に，ホセ・サンチェスが，最新のスポーツの結果とハイライトをお伝えします。

でもまずは，きょうの最新ニュースから。メジャーリーグのスターでピッチャーの，ジャクソン・リー選手がきょう，車の自損事故で両腕・両足に重症を負いました。彼は重体で，現在 UCMA 医療センターで手術を受けています。一命を取り留められるかどうかはまだわかっていません。

マリナー郡保安官事務所によると，事故は現地時間午前7時過ぎにファーストストリートで起きました。当局が現在現場にいて，衝突現場を調べていますが，担当者の話では事故の原因については調査を終えるのに数週間はかかるとのことです。

質問　36. プログラムのうちどれが最初に放送されますか。
　　　37. どのタイプのニュースが特報になっていますか。
　　　38. 大統領に尋ねたのはどのトピックですか。
　　　39. 放送のどの部分をニュースキャスターは強く勧めていますか。
　　　40. きょうの最新ニュースについて正しいのはどれですか。

V

４つの選択肢の中から，
以下のそれぞれの英文の（　　　　）に入る最も適切なものを選びなさい。

41.　解答：C

解説　play a role で「役割を演じる（果たす）」の意味となり，vital は「重要な」の意味の形容詞であるから，正解は C となる。

訳例　今日，文化的多様性や国際的対話を実現することにおいて，言語が重要な役割を果たしていることへの意識が高まっている。

42.　解答：B

解説　will に続くのは動詞でなければならないから impose が来る。さらに tougher は「より厳しい」の意味であるから penalties を修飾するのが自然である。したがって正解はBとなる。

訳例　日本の議会は火曜日，あおり運転をした運転手に対してより厳しい罰則を課す改正道路交通法を成立させた。

43. 解答：A

解説　theに最も自然につながるのはwarmestであり，文脈上「観測史上最も暖かい年」と考えるのが適切なので，正解はAとなる。

訳例　NASAの分析によると，2020年における地球の世界平均表面温度は観測史上最も暖かい年として2016年と肩を並べた。

44. 解答：C

解説　悪影響の度合が平均どの程度かを表すフレーズが入る。前置詞byはincrease［decrease］by～「～（の割合・量だけ）増加［減少］する」などの使い方をする。up to ～は「最高～まで」の意味。したがってCが正解である。

訳例　テクノロジーストレスの研究によると，粗悪なテクノロジーは，社員の業績を平均で最大30%も低下させていることがわかった。

45. 解答：D

解説　declared ～ a pandemicは，「～をパンデミックと宣言する」の意味であるから，～に入るべき名詞句として適切なのはD（急速に広がっているコロナウイルスの感染）である。

訳例　世界保健機関は水曜日，急速に広がっているコロナウイルス感染を，パンデミックであると宣言した。

VI

下線を引いた単語または語句の中から，
文法的もしくは慣用的に不適切なものを選びなさい。

46. 解答：C

解説　(C) with personは文法的に誤っている。in personとすれば「直接」「対面で」の意味になる。

訳例　国連の歴史上初めて，世界の指導者たちは，国連総会での年に1度の討議を対面で行うことができなかった。

47. 解答：C

解説 この文の主語は，The UN World Food Programなので，(C) have beenはhas beenとしなければならない。

訳例 国連世界食糧計画は，世界の何百万人もの人々に対して人命救助のための食糧支援をしており，このたび2020年のノーベル平和賞を受賞した。

48. 解答：B

解説 (B) のcovered (過去分詞) を，covering (現在分詞) にすることにより，先行するwhat could become the world's largest free trade agreementに，「～の3分の1，そして…の30%を含む」という情報を付け加える表現になる。

訳例 アジア太平洋地域の経済連合諸国15カ国は，日曜日，世界最大規模となる可能性のある貿易協定に調印したが，この協定は世界の人口の3分の1近く，世界の国内総生産のおよそ30%を含むものである。

49. 解答：D

解説 (D) のforをwithにすれば，along with ～「～とともに」の意味となり，文脈上意味の通る文になる。

訳例 ミャンマー軍は月曜日，民主的に選ばれたアウンサンスーチー政府に対するクーデターで同国の権力を掌握し，アウンサンスーチーは早朝の襲撃により彼女の政党の指導者らとともに拘束された。

50. 解答：B

解説 (B) のlowest levelは最上級であるから，the lowest levelとすべきである。

訳例 2020年に日本で記録された犯罪は6年連続で戦後最低となり，路上犯罪は激減した。

VII-A 『新 わかりやすい国連の活動と世界』から得た知識に基づき，(A)～(D) から空欄を埋めるのに最も適切なものを選びなさい。

51. 解答：A

解説 国際連盟は，19世紀後半から20世紀前半にかけて行われた一連の国際外交会議 (conferences) に由来するものである。

A. 会議　B. 意見の相違　C. 選挙　D. 戦争

52.　解答：C

解説　国際連盟の目的は，第 1 次世界大戦の再現（repetition）防止を意図したものであった。

A. 増強　B. 破壊　C. 再現　D. 合図

53.　解答：B

解説　国際連盟創設時のメンバーは，第 1 次世界大戦に勝利した（victorious）国々であった。

A. 敗北した　B. 勝利した　C. 反抗的な　D. 懐疑的な

54.　解答：A

解説　国際連盟は，麻薬取締り，難民救済，国際労働関係の分野において，先駆的な役割を果たした（conducted）。

A. 果たした　B. 批判した　C. 中止した　D. 終えた

55.　解答：D

解説　国際連盟は，永続的な世界の平和（peace）達成を目指す国際社会にとって初めての試みであった。

A. 供給　B. 環境　C. 識字力　D. 平和

訳例　国際連合の前身にあたるのは国際連盟である。国際連盟は，19 世紀後半から 20 世紀前半にかけて行われた一連の国際外交（51）会議に由来するものであるが，この国際協力組織の設置の具体的な意図は，第 1 次世界大戦の（52）再現防止にあった。連盟は，ヴェルサイユ条約の一環として 1919 年，パリ平和会議で創設された。

創設時のメンバーは，第 1 次世界対戦の（53）戦勝国（ヴェルサイユ条約を批准しなかったアメリカ合衆国を除く）と他の中立国であった。

国際連盟規約によれば，この組織は軍備縮小の必要，常設国際司法裁判所の設置，領土保全の保護，侵略国に対する制裁などの問題を扱う機関とされている。麻薬取締り，難民救済，国際労働関係の分野において，連盟は先駆的役割（54）を果たした。

各国は組織化された枠組みの中で議論，交渉および一般的な盟約を通じ，永続する世界（55）平和というかつて存在したことのないものの達成を目指すという初の試みを行ったのである。

『新 わかりやすい国連の活動と世界』p.42

Ⅶ-B 『新 わかりやすい国連の活動と世界』から得た知識に基づき，4つの選択肢から空欄を埋めるのに最も適切なものを選びなさい。

56. 解答：D

解説 国連憲章が調印されたのは，1945年6月26日，サンフランシスコにおいてである。

A. パリ　B. ロンドン　C. ニューヨーク　D. サンフランシスコ

『新 わかりやすい国連の活動と世界』p.43参照

57. 解答：A

解説 国連の公式の印章，標章は北極の上から見た世界地図である。

A. 北極　B. 南極　C. 赤道　D. 米国

同上p.45参照

58. 解答：D

解説 日本が国連に加盟したのは，1956年12月18日である。

A. 1945年10月24日　B. 1947年10月31日

C. 1950年6月25日　D. 1956年12月18日

同上p.45参照

59. 解答：B

解説 国連安全保障理事会のメンバーは，5つの常任理事国と10の非常任理事国である。

A. 5つの非常任理事国　B. 10の非常任理事国

C. 15の非常任理事国　D. 20の非常任理事国

同上p.55参照

60. 解答：A

解説 経済社会理事会の票決は単純多数決による。

A. 単純多数決　B. 3分の2の多数決

C. 4分の3の多数決　D. 5分の4の多数決

同上p.57参照

VIII-A 以下の各英文を読み，下記のそれぞれの質問に答えなさい。
下記の英文を挿入するのに最も適した箇所を，(A)〜(D) から選びなさい。

Passage 1

61.　解答：D

解説 This is critical for 〜「これは〜にとって非常に重要だ」と述べていることから，This は何らかの改善提案を指していることがわかる。直前の内容が具体的改善提案になっている箇所を選べばよいから，正解は D となる。

62.　解答：B

解説 This disparity has led to 〜「この格差が〜につながっている」とあり，〜の部分には研究者としての女性の不利な状況が述べられている。直前の内容が，女性の研究者としての不利な状況を引き起こす格差である箇所を選べばよいから，正解は B となる。

63.　解答：C

解説 Yet stereotypes have steered women and girls away from science-related fields（しかしながら固定観念が女性や女児を科学分野から遠ざけている）とあることから，直前には，女性は科学を研究すべき存在であるという主旨の内容が来ると想像できる。したがって正解は C となる。

語句 bear the brunt of 〜: 〜の矢面に立つ（〜の影響をまともに受ける）　exacerbate 〜: 〜を悪化させる　labs (= laboratories): 研究所　replicate 〜: 〜を再現する　foster 〜: 〜を育む　belong in 〜: 〜にいる（ある）べきだ　remain untapped: 開発されないままでいる　integral part: 不可欠な存在

訳例　男女間の不平等がこの 1 年間で劇的に拡大し，学校閉鎖や在宅勤務などの影響を女性がまともに受けています。(A) 多くの女性科学者が研究所の閉鎖や家族の世話の負担増加といった問題に直面し，重要な研究に使う時間が少なくなっています。

科学分野で働く女性にとって，こうした課題はそれでなくても困難な状況をより一層悪化させています。ユネスコによると，女性は世界の研究者の 3 分の 1 しかおらず，一流大学で上級職に就いている人数は男性よりも少ない状況です。(B) この格差が，男性よりも低い出版率，知名度，認知度，そして決定的な問題として研究費支給度の低さにつながっています。

一方，人工知能や機械学習の発展は，既存の男女格差を再生産する結果となっています。女性や女児は科学を学ぶべき存在です。(C) しかし，固定観念が女性や女児を科学関連分野から遠ざけています。

いまこそ，多様性の拡大がより大きなイノベーションを育むことを認識すべきです。STEM（科学，技術，工学，数学）の分野でより多くの女性が活躍しなければ，世界は男性によって，男性のために設計され続け，女児や女性の可能性は未開発のままでしょう。

私たちは，女児達がふさわしい教育を受けられるようにし，エンジニアリング，コンピューター・プログラミング，クラウド技術，ロボット工学，健康科学などの分野で彼女たちが自分たちの将来を見通せるようにしなければなりません。(D) これは，持続可能な開発目標を達成するための我々の活動にとって非常に重要です。

STEM 分野への女性の参加を増やすことで，男女間の賃金格差を解消し，今後 10 年間で女性の所得を 2,990 億ドル増加させることができます。また，世界のインターネット利用格差の解消にも，STEM スキルは欠かせません。

みんなで協力して，男女差別をなくし，すべての女性と女児が自分の可能性を発揮し，すべての人にとってよりよい世界を築くために不可欠な存在となるようにしましょう。

Ⅷ-B

Passage 2

64. 解答：C

解説 専門家が先進国から提出された温室効果ガスに関する情報を annually に審査する，という文脈で，annually は anniversary（年に一度の記念日）と同様，ラテン語 annus（= year）に由来する。正解は C となる。

A. 正確に　B. 詳細に　C. 毎年　D. 手作業で

65. 解答：B

解説 この文脈における「透明性」とは審査のプロセスが透明である，つまり誰が見てみてもわかる，ということであるから，B が正解である。

A. デジタル形式で示されている

B. 明確で理解が容易である

C. 専門家により科学的に分析されている

D. 偏見のない記述がされている

66.　解答：A

解説 inventory は「一覧表」「在庫」などの意味があるが，この文脈では先進国が調査機関に提出する温室効果ガスに関する一覧表のことであるから，A が正解である。

A. データのリスト　　B. 品物のリスト
C. 計画のリスト　　D. 職員のリスト

67.　解答：D

解説 enhancing the capacity of individual expert reviewers（個々の専門調査官たちの能力を enhance している）とあり，この文が含まれるパラグラフ全体としても，調査プロセスがいかに温室効果ガス一覧の「向上（improvement）」に寄与しているかが述べられている。したがって正解は D である。

A. 助けている　　B. 変えている
C. 集めている　　D. 向上させている

68.　解答：C

解説 adverse circumstances が COVID-19（新型コロナウイルス感染症）によるパンデミックが原因の困難な状況を指していることから，正解は C となる。

A. 有望な　　B. 突然の　　C. 不利な　　D. 世界的な

69.　解答：A

解説 be attributed to は「～に帰する」の意味であり，この文脈では，審査プロセスに関する業務が世界中の専門家の献身的な努力により成功してきたことを述べているから，正解は A となる。

A. ～の功績による　　B. ～により論じられた
C. ～に妨害された　　D. ～するために使われた

70.　解答：D

解説 address には「住所」「～に対して演説する」「～に対応する」などの意

味があるが，ここでは address preliminary issues とあるので，D が正解となる。

A. ～を断る　B. ～を棚上げにする

C. ～に出くわす　D. ～に対応する

語句 greenhouse gass: 温室効果ガス　virtual meeting: 仮想会議　going forward: これからも，引き続き　GHG inventory: 温室効果ガス一覧表（国が1年間に排出・吸収する温室効果ガスの量を一覧にまとめたもの）　on full display: すべて見えている　adverse: 不利な　dedication: 献身的な努力　convene: 集まる

訳例　温室効果ガス（GHG）の排出と除去に関して先進国が提出する情報を（64）毎年審査している世界中の専門家は，昨年，重要な（65）透明性プロセス導入20周年を祝うとともに，2020年も一連の仮想会議や活動により，引き続き透明性への取り組みを強化している。

最初の審査が行われたのは2001年だった。当時の審査に参加した専門家の中には，現在も温室効果ガス（66）一覧表の審査を行っている人もいる。この20年間で，この審査プロセスは，気候変動対策に起因する温室効果ガスの排出とその除去を示す，国の温室効果ガス一覧表の改善に大きく貢献するとともに，個々の専門家審査官たちの能力を（67）向上させる要因にもなってきた。

2020年は，透明性の重要性が十分に示された年だった。COVID-19の大流行という（68）不利な条件下で，専門家と国連気候変動事務局は，仮想手段を用いて審査プロセスの継続を確実に実施する革新的な方法を見いだした。この1年間に行われた作業の成功は，世界中の専門家（60カ国，計142名）の献身的な努力と専門知識（69）に帰するものだと言える。では，審査はどのように行われるのだろうか？

温室効果ガスの審査プロセス自体は数カ月にわたって行われ，専門家は通常，審査週間の約4週間前から各国の一覧表提出で特定された予備的問題（70）に取り組み，審査週間後も約20週間，専門家が報告書の草案を完成させるまで継続する。各チームの作業は，事務局の支援のもと，経験豊富な2人の主任審査官によって指導される。主任審査官たちは審査プロセスを指導するだけでなく，年に一度集まり，審査プロセスの一貫性と有効性を長期的に強化する方法を確認する。

IX 以下の英文を読み，下記のそれぞれの質問に答えなさい。

【長文問題の解答対策】

長文を読む際は，まずトピックは何か，誰が何のために書いているか（スピーチスクリプトの場合は誰がどのような場で話しているのか）を想像する。その上で，各パラグラフの中心的な内容や主張を頭の中で整理しながら読み進める。つまり，「このパラグラフではこういうことを言っているのだな」とそのパラグラフのポイントを一言で要約（あるいは頭の中でイメージ）しながら読むのである。そうすることで，パラグラフからパラグラフへのつながりや，英文の論理展開を大局的に捉え，筆者（話者）の言いたいことのポイントを迅速に捉えることが可能になる。その際，難解な語彙や表現があっても，「何を言っているのだろう？」と自問しながら，想像力を働かせて理解しようとする姿勢が重要である。

今回の英文は，冒頭に In October とあり，続いて国連事務総長が行ったことが事実として書かれている。そのため，事実やそれに対する意見を第三者が論じる英文であり，それが SDGs に関係するものであることが想像できる。

71. 解答：B

解説 第 1 パラグラフでは，グテーレス事務総長が重要な任命を行った（made a series of key appointments）とあり，その対象は科学者であるので，B が正解である。

第 1 パラグラフで述べられているのは次のどれか。

A. 国連事務総長は世界の指導者たちと会議を持った。

B. 科学者のグループが国連のプロジェクトのために選ばれた。

C. 政策立案者達は SDGs についての意見を述べるよう求められた。

D. 地球温暖化の原因を説明するために証拠が集められた。

72. 解答：B

解説 国連の最重要計画である SDGs が，パンデミックの影響で逆風を受けているというのがこのパラグラフの主旨であるから，B が正解である。

第 2 パラグラフで述べられているのは次のどれか。

A. 国連は当初のSDGsに新たな目標を追加した。
B. SDGsに関する状況は悪化した。
C. 国連は最近のデータに基づきSDGsの一部を変更した。
D. 5年間に及ぶSDGs達成の努力が成功をもたらした。

73. 解答：A

解説 現在飢餓のリスクのある人々の数が2億7,000万人であるとされ，それはパンデミック以前の2倍であると述べていることから，Aが正解となる。B～Cについては本文の内容と矛盾する箇所が含まれているため不適切である。

第3パラグラフから言えることは次のどれか。
A. パンデミック以前は，飢餓のリスクのある人々の数は1億5,000万人以下であった。
B. 世界中の多くの学校はウイルスの拡散を止めるために自主的に休校措置をとった。
C. 普遍的初等教育を達成する目標はパンデミック以前でさえも困難に思われた。
D. 学校に通っていない児童の数は年間を通して徐々に増加した。

74. 解答：C

解説 3行目に“And in October, the International Monetary Fund projected ...”とあるように，IMFは世界経済についての予想を出したのであるから，Cが正解である。

第4パラグラフで述べられているのは次のどれか。
A. パンデミックのために，正規雇用者よりも不正規雇用者の方が多く職を失った。
B. 3カ月の間に5億人近くの正規雇用者が職を失った。
C. IMFは2020年末に向けての世界経済について予測を出した。
D. 4%の世界経済不況は珍しくない。

75. 解答：A

解説 GSDR 報告書について，“the first was published in 2019” とあるので，A が正解である。B ～ D についての記述は見当たらないので不適切である。

第 5 パラグラフで述べられているのは次のどれか。

A. 最初の国連 GSDR 報告書は 2019 年に出版された。

B. GSDR 報告書を担当する研究者は英語圏の国々出身である。

C. GSDR 報告書は，報告書を専門とする国連職員により書かれる。

D. GSDR 担当研究者の中には，自分の専門以外の領域の研究をする者もいる。

76. 解答：B

解説 「このパラグラフで述べられていない」ものを選ぶ場合，本文の内容と矛盾しない選択肢を入念に確認する必要がある。A はパラグラフ冒頭にその記述があり，C と D は筆者の 2 つの提言の内容と一致する。B については記述がないので B が正解となる。

第 6 パラグラフで述べられていないのは次のどれか。

A. この記事の著者は GSDR に関係する人々から情報を集めた。

B. 現状を考慮すると，パンデミックは数カ月で落ち着くだろう。

C. GSDR のための 3 年のタイムラインは短縮するべきだ。

D. GSDR 担当研究者はより広範なコミュニティーからデータを集めるべきだ。

77. 解答：D

解説 このパラグラフの中心的主張は，報告書はまずその中間段階で公表しフィードバックを得るべきだ，ということであるから，D が正解である。A ～ C についてはそのような言及はないので不適切である。

第 7 パラグラフで述べられているのは次のどれか。

A. GSDR 報告書は 1 年で書かれ出版されるべきだ。

B. 国連は GSDR 担当研究者たちの進捗を記録すべきだ。

C. 完成されたGSDR報告書へのフィードバックは将来の研究にとり重要である。

D. GSDR報告書の初稿は共有され意見を求められるべきだ。

78. 解答：C

解説 このパラグラフの中心的主張は，ユニセフや世界食糧計画は “operating in an emergency mode” であり，現場優先の状況になっているということであるから，正解はCとなる。A, B, Dに関する言及は見当たらない。

第8パラグラフから言えることは次のどれか。

A. 国連では研究に重きを置き過ぎている。

B. パンデミック関連の役割に任命される国連職員は減っている。

C. ユニセフや世界食糧計画は今研究する時間を捻出しづらい。

D. 国連研究者と世界中の政策立案者達との間に意見の相違がある。

79. 解答：A

解説 冒頭に “... but they (= the GDSR authors) could help UN agencies and countries to think about how to meet their research needs during the pandemic” とある。一方B, C, Dは本パラグラフの内容と矛盾する。したがって正解はAである。

第9パラグラフで述べられているのは次のどれか。

A. GSDRの著者らは国連機関や関係諸国がパンデミックの中で必要な研究をする手助けをすることができるだろう。

B. 政府は子どもたちやその家族に対し，スマートフォン，ラップトップコンピューター，ブロードバンド環境を提供すべきだ。

C. 環境に優しい方法で経済成長を活性化させる方法について多くの研究がある。

D. 国連は研究者よりも現場で働く国連職員の声により耳を傾けるべきだ。

80. 解答：B

解説 このパラグラフでは筆者の結論が述べられている。それは，パラグラフ最後の “Everyone must be ready to work with them (= the UN's science advisors) and help them succeed. の一文である。A については「現在ある資源で」，C については「誇りを持つべきだ」，D については「現在のアプローチを継続すべき」という部分が本文と矛盾する。正解は B である。

第 10 パラグラフの主張を最も適切に要約しているのは次のどれか。

A. 国連とその顧問たちは現在ある資源でより効率的な業務ができるよう協力すべきだ。

B. 国連の科学顧問が SDGs を再度軌道にのせられるよう，皆が支援すべきだ。

C. 国連の科学顧問は，これまでにない責任を与えられているのだから，自らの仕事に誇りを持つべきだ。

D. 国連は SDGs に対する現在のアプローチを継続すべきで，そうすれば結果はついてくるだろう。

語句 task（人）with ...ing:（人）に…する任務を与える　off track: 軌道を外れて　set back ～: ～を遅らせる（妨害する）　project that ～: ～と予測する　span a range of disciplines: さまざまな学問分野に及ぶ　campaigner: 運動家　halting progress: 進捗の遅れ　under-represented:（これまでの報告書に）十分に取り上げられていない　commissioning:（任務の）委託　stretch a budget: 予算をやり繰りする　draw on ～: ～を活用する，頼る　hands-on: 実践の，実地の

訳例 1. 10 月，国連のアントニオ・グテーレス事務総長は，一連の重要な人事を行った。グテーレス事務総長は，世界中から集められた 15 人の科学者に，持続可能な開発目標（SDGs）に関するエビデンスと彼らの考えを政策立案者に提供する任務を与えたのだ。

2. 昨年のいま頃，2030 年までに貧困をなくし，世界を環境において持続可能な状態に導くという国連の旗艦計画は，すでに予定の道筋から外れていた。それ以来，各国がこの目標を採択してから 5 年間に達成した成果のほとんどが，パンデミックによって覆されてしまった。

3. 世界食糧計画では，2 億 7,000 万人が飢餓の危険にさらされていると推定しており，その数はパンデミック前の 2 倍となっている。また，ロックダ

ウンによる学校の閉鎖は，パンデミック以前には手の届くところにあった数少ないSDGsの1つである，普遍的初等教育の達成，という目標を後退させている。国連教育科学文化機関ユネスコは12月，約3億2,000万人の子どもが学校に通っていないと推計し，わずか1カ月で9,000万人も増加した。

4. 国際労働機関によると，昨年4月1日からの3カ月間で，世界中で4億9,500万人の正規雇用に相当する労働時間がロックダウンにより失われたという。また，10月には，国際通貨基金（IMF）が，2020年末までに世界経済は4%以上縮小すると予測し，過去数世代に見られない規模の縮小となるとしている。
5. これが，グテーレス事務総長が第2回国連持続可能な開発報告書（GSDR）──第1回目は2019年に発行された──の調査・執筆を任された研究者たちが直面している状況だ。彼らは世界中から集められ，気候変動，生態学，環境経済学，倫理学，保健政策，感染症，海洋学，国際機関ガバナンス，科学と開発の研究など，さまざまな学問分野にまたがっている。
6. 本論考に向けて本紙では，高所得国および低所得国の研究者，政府および国連関係者，運動家たちに話を聞いた。パンデミックの現状と，これまでの目標に向けた進捗の遅れに鑑み，報告書の著者と国連への助言は2つある。第一に，報告書の執筆者たちは，従来与えられた3年という期限を早めて，迅速に作業を進める必要がある。第二に，エビデンス収集のプロセスのできるだけ早い段階で，通常の専門家ネットワークを超えて情報収集を行い，特に，十分にデータに反映されていない地域の情報も得る革新的な方法を模索する必要がある。
7. SDGs達成のためのアドバイスが緊急に必要であることを考えると，GSDRの委託から出版までの3年間のタイムテーブルは長すぎる。タイムテーブルを短縮する1つの方法は，国連が今年末までに中間または作業進行中の報告文書を発表することに注力することだ。その後，その文書を配布し，各国政府，国連機関，目標の実施に関わる多くの組織からフィードバックを集め，その意見を修正した第2次草案に反映させることができるだろう。
8. このような研究と行動の連携の重要性は，いくら強調してもし過ぎることはない。現在，児童のための慈善機関であるユニセフや世界食糧計画などの国連機関は，緊急事態体制のもとで運営されている。予算をやり繰りし，人員を再配置しなければならない場合，研究にしわ寄せがくることが多い。しかし，これらの組織は依然として研究を必要としている。また，考えたりエビデンスを集めたりする時間のある人材，つまり，最前線にいる同僚や，政策立案者，他の職務にある同僚からの質問に答えたり，アドバイスを提供したりする前に，その知識を熟考する時間を持つ人材を活用する必要がある。

9. このような実地調査はGSDRの執筆者が行うべきものではないが，執筆者たちは，パンデミック時に国連機関や各国に対し，それぞれの研究ニーズを満たす方法を考える援助をすることはできるだろう。研究者は，スマートフォンやラップトップ，ブロードバンドを利用できない家庭の子どもたちを支援するために，さまざまな戦略を検証する必要がある。パンデミックが医療制度に与える影響も調査する必要がある。また，各国政府が経済成長の回復を急ぐ中，パンデミックの経済的影響や，可能な限り環境に配慮した復興方法など，調査すべき内容は山ほどある。研究がこれらの問題やその他の問題に光を当てない限り，SDGsを達成することはできないであろう。

10. 国連とその科学顧問は，特にSDGsに関しては，スピード感をもって取り組み，十分に考慮の対象になってこなかったコミュニティを巻き込む必要がある。これなくして，これまでと異なる活動を期待するのは現実的ではない。だからといって，これまで通りという選択肢はない。現在の危機を終わらせ，より大きな幸福，ひいては繁栄と環境の持続可能性への道筋をつけるための行動を支援するために，継続的な研究が必要である。国連の科学顧問は，多くの科学者が通常持ちうる責任よりも大きな責任を与えられてきた。誰もが彼らと協力し，その成功を支援する態勢を整えねばならない。

X

以下の質問に対して，80～100語の短いエッセイを英語で書きなさい。

質問：日本人がより一層学ぶべき世界的な問題は何か？　なぜそう思うのか？

（語数を記入する必要はありません）

【Essay writing問題の解答対策】

英語で意見文を書く力を高めるには，まずさまざまな問題について自分の考えや意見を持つことが重要である。その上で，それを日本語ではなく英語で行うことに慣れるために，日頃から英文を読み，トピックに特有の重要表現を学び，要約したり意見を書いたりするといった，インプットからアウトプットへの一連のプロセスを英語で行うとよい。自分の考えを直接英語にする練習として，英文日記を書いたり，思ったことを英語でひとり言としてつぶやいたりする練習に加え，解答例に示すような意見文のモデルを多数読み，意見を述べるために必要な定型表現や，Introduction-Body-Conclusionといった基本的論理構成を学ぶとよい。

解答例 I think one of the most important global issues that Japanese people should learn more about is the problem of overfishing.

In recent decades, overfishing has caused the population of certain fish such as the bluefin tuna and unagi to become endangered. Without the necessary global cooperation, future generations will not be able to enjoy these wonderful delicacies. In addition, overfishing also greatly damages the ocean ecosystem.

Seafood is an invaluable part of the Japanese diet. That's why the issue of overfishing is a particularly important issue for Japanese people to learn about now so they can help solve it in the near future.

(104 words)

構成 ① Introduction: 質問に対する回答を明確に述べる。ここでは次のようになっている。
- 日本人が学ぶべき最も重要な国際問題の 1 つは漁業における乱獲である。

② Body: 短めのエッセイ課題の場合できるだけ簡潔に論を展開する必要がある。ここでは，次のようになっている。
- 特定の魚が絶滅の危機に瀕《ひん》している。
- 国際的な協力がなければこれらの魚は食べられなくなる。
- さらに，乱獲は海の生態系にも悪影響を及ぼす。

③ Conclusion: この問題についてなぜ日本人が学ぶ必要があるかについて触れながらまとめている。ここでは，次のようになっている。
- 日本人の食生活にとり海産物が重要である。
- 将来解決できるよう，海の乱獲について学ぶ必要がある。

2021年B級第1回試験　正解一覧

I
1. C　2. A　3. C　4. B　5. B　6. D　7. D　8. A　9. C　10. D

II
11. A　12. D　13. B　14. B　15. A　16. C　17. C　18. C　19. B　20. D

III
21. C　22. A　23. C　24. A　25. B　26. D　27. C　28. D　29. D　30. B

IV
31. A　32. C　33. B　34. D　35. A　36. B　37. D　38. D　39. C　40. A

V
41. C　42. B　43. A　44. C　45. D

VI
46. C　47. C　48. B　49. D　50. B

VII-A
51. A　52. C　53. B　54. A　55. D

VII-B
56. D　57. A　58. D　59. B　60. A

VIII-A
61. D　62. B　63. C

VIII-B
64. C　65. B　66. A　67. D　68. C　69. A　70. D

IX
71. B　72. B　73. A　74. C　75. A　76. B　77. D　78. C　79. A　80. B

2021年

第2回試験

問題

UNA-JAPAN

B級試験問題用紙

B級

外務省後援

２０２１年度第２回国際連合公用語

英語検定試験（120分）

受験上の注意

1．問題用紙は試験開始の合図があるまで開いてはいけません。その間に、この**受験上の注意を熟読しておいてください。**

2．**受験番号と氏名を２枚の解答用紙（マークシートと作文用紙）**に記入してください。

3．解答用紙の配布は１人１部のみです。複数の配布は致しません。

4．試験開始前は、答案への解答記入は禁止です。

5．マークシートの記入は、１～100までの記入箇所がありますが、この級では１～80までを使います。

6．マークシートの記入は、必ずＨＢ以上の濃い鉛筆を使って該当箇所を黒く塗りつぶしてください。書き間違いの場合は「アト」が残らないように消してください。マークシートは絶対に折ったり曲げたりしないでください。

7．受験級、受験地区、会場番号、受験番号のマークシートへの記入は監督者の指示に従い、間違いなく記入してください。**(裏表紙の「マークシート記入例」参照)**

8．作文は、⑴ 読みやすい文字をペン、ボールペンまたはＨＢ以上の濃い鉛筆で書いてください。
⑵ 使用語数の80～100語を目安にしてください。

9．試験問題についての質問は、印刷が不鮮明な場合を除き、一切受けつけません。

10．中途退室の際は、マークシートと作文用紙を持って監督者に渡し、他の受験者の迷惑にならないように静かに退室してください。中途退室後の再入室はできません。

11．試験中は他の受験者の妨げとなる行動は慎んでください。また携帯電話等の電源はお切りください。

12．マークシートと作文用紙は監督者に提出し、問題用紙はご自由にお持ち帰りください。

＊試験問題の複製や転載、インターネットへのアップロード等、いかなる媒体への転用を禁止します。

リスニングテストについて

1．リスニングテストは試験開始後、合図があってから実施されます。(40問あります)

2．リスニングテストが始まる前にリスニング問題の指示と内容を読んで、どういう形式のテストなのか、概要をつかんでおいてください。

3．テスト中の発言は、放送機器の具合が悪く放送された英語の聴き取りができない場合を除いて、しないようにしてください。

試験結果について

1．試験の結果は2021年11月24日㈬頃に受験申込書に記載された住所に郵送で通知します。

2．その間に住所変更をされた方は、郵便局へ住所変更の届け出を忘れずに行ってください。

3．発表前の試験結果のお問合せには応じられません。

UNA-JAPAN
公益財団法人 日本国際連合協会
http://www.unaj.or.jp/

I. Directions : You will hear 10 statements or questions. For each statement or question, choose the most appropriate response and mark your answer on your answer sheet.

1. A. What time? B. It's okay.
C. No way. D. Me neither.

2. A. How about next Friday? B. I'll arrive next week.
C. Most definitely. D. Here you go.

3. A. The restaurant is too far. B. Who is it?
C. She's at home. D. Your name, please?

4. A. Sounds good. B. What a shame!
C. Don't mention it. D. Today's the day!

5. A. Where are you? B. It's not mine.
C. It's your turn. D. Let's leave now.

6. A. Hurry up! B. Don't bother.
C. Sure thing. D. No idea.

7. A. I'm afraid not. B. Are you sure?
C. How many are there? D. They're coming.

8. A. It's quite expensive. B. I got it online.
C. You can't smoke here. D. No, that's all.

9. A. He's the worst. B. Better than I expected.
C. As much as you can. D. This is going to be fun!

10. A. The sooner the better. B. Watch your step!
C. I'll do it tomorrow. D. What a beautiful house!

Ⅱ. Directions : You will hear 10 short conversations. Choose the best answer for each follow-up question and mark your answer on your answer sheet.

11. A. The man likes his job.
B. The man works nineteen hours a week.
C. The woman is twenty-one.
D. The woman is a student.

12. A. He partially disagrees.
B. He thinks she is right.
C. He thinks she is wrong.
D. He doesn't understand her.

13. A. His company went bankrupt.
B. His partner is quitting the company.
C. Too many people want to talk to him.
D. False rumors are being spread about him.

14. A. Her parents live too close.
B. Daycare costs are too high.
C. She can't contact government officials.
D. Her daughter doesn't like to go to school.

15. A. She said it's hard to match. B. She said it's too old.
C. She said it's too expensive. D. She said it's dirty.

16. A. Water crisis B. Deforestation
C. Plastic straws D. Overfishing

17. A. Bank clerk B. Cashier
C. Math teacher D. Receptionist

18. A. She pities him. B. She looks down on him.
C. She envies him. D. She is not interested.

19. A. She is worried. B. She doesn't care.
C. She is forgetful. D. She feels dissatisfied.

20. A. Compassionate B. Resentful
C. Irritated D. Thankful

Ⅲ. Directions : You will hear five conversations. After each conversation, you will hear two follow-up questions. Choose the best answer for each question, and mark your answer on your answer sheet.

[Conversation 1]

21. A. At a hotel　B. At a post office
C. At a restaurant　D. At an online retailer

22. A. He is glad.　B. He is angry.
C. He is confused.　D. He is indifferent.

[Conversation 2]

23. A. Adopt solar energy　B. Reduce carbon emissions
C. Invest in more research　D. Implement a carbon tax

24. A. Climate change is not that important to them.
B. Natural disasters will destroy their homes.
C. They don't believe that climate change exists.
D. They are worried about their children's future.

[Conversation 3]

25. A. Political activism
B. Freedom to protest
C. Evolutionary biology
D. The cancellation of an event

26. A. He thinks it sets a bad example.
B. He thinks few students support it.
C. He thinks it wouldn't cause damage.
D. He thinks it would protect many students.

[Conversation 4]

27. A. She thinks they are too slow.
B. She thinks their priorities are wrong.
C. She thinks they spend too much money.
D. She thinks they should hire more people.

28. A. To save children's lives
B. To help pharmaceutical companies
C. To improve their influence abroad
D. To promote their medical technology

[Conversation 5]

29. A. Her colleagues B. Her commute
C. Her salary D. Her manager

30. A. It takes her four hours to get to work.
B. Her boss seems to act as if she is not capable.
C. Her male coworkers make more money than she does.
D. She has a bad relationship with the people in her team.

Ⅳ. Directions : You will hear two short talks. After each talk, you will hear five follow-up questions. Choose the best answer for each question, and mark your answer on your answer sheet.

[Talk 1]

31. A. A chef B. A singer
C. An actor D. A professor

32. A. A musical performance
B. A classroom lecture on film
C. A personal development seminar
D. A university graduation ceremony

33. A. Becoming a successful comedian
B. Running his own restaurant
C. Graduating high school
D. Making movies

34. A. 5 B. 99 C. 150 D. 500

35. A. Do what you love.
B. Never doubt yourself.
C. You can fail, but don't quit.
D. Your loved ones always come first.

[Talk 2]

36. A. A city mayor B. A company president
C. A newscaster D. A teacher

37. A. A press conference B. A weather report
C. A news interview D. A speech on natural disasters

38. A. Hospitals B. Gymnasiums
C. Residents' houses D. Community centers

39. A. 25 B. 100 C. 587 D. 1200

40. A. Stay inside B. Evacuate to high places
C. Prepare an emergency bag D. Pay attention to local notices

V. Choose from among the four alternatives the one that best completes each of the following sentences.

41. An advisory panel urged the government on Thursday to ( ) with fewer students at junior high schools.

A. having consider classes
B. consider classes having
C. having classes consider
D. consider having classes

42. Currently all retail outlets across Japan ( ) customers for the use of plastic bags.

A. charge to required are
B. to charge are required
C. are required to charge
D. required to charge are

43. People across the nation observed ( ) at 2:46 p.m. to remember the people who died from the 2011 Tohoku Earthquake.

A. of a silence moment
B. a moment of silence
C. silence of a moment
D. moment of a silence

44. Greenland and Antarctica both recently showed all-time low levels of ice mass, and glaciers are melting ( ) they did just 15 years ago.

A. 31 percent faster than
B. percent 31 than faster
C. faster than 31 percent
D. than 31 percent faster

45. **For the first time in two decades, the number of children (　　　　　) has risen to 160 million worldwide.**

A. work to put being　　B. to being put work
C. put to work being　　D. being put to work

VI. Choose from among the underlined words or phrases the one that is grammatically or idiomatically incorrect.

46. **The Delta variant is (A) the most contagious coronavirus mutant (B) so far in the pandemic, but COVID-19 vaccines still (C) provide strong protection (D) with it.**

47. **Against the backdrop of a (A) rapidly changing global climate, (B) water-relating hazards top the list of (C) natural disasters with the highest human losses (D) in the past 50 years, according to a new report by the World Meteorological Organization.**

48. **Around one in eight nations (A) spending more on debt than on (B) social services, according to (C) a new report from the UN Children's Fund (UNICEF) (D) launched on Thursday.**

49. **At least 1,146 people died (A) attempt to reach Europe (B) by sea in the first six months (C) of 2021, according to a new briefing (D) released today by the International Organization for Migration.**

50. **Underlining UN commitment to achieving (A) a nuclear-free world, Secretary-General António Guterres has urged (B) government to strengthen (C) efforts to make this goal (D) a reality.**

VII. Choose the best answer from the choices marked (A), (B), (C), and (D) to fill in the blanks based on the knowledge gained from *New Today's Guide to the United Nations*.

The Charter of the United Nations was signed on 26 June 1945 in San Francisco, at the conclusion of the Conference. Its Preamble expresses above all the determination of the peoples of the United Nations "to save humanity from the scourge of **(51)** ________." It also reaffirms their faith in human rights and "in the equal rights of men and women and of nations large and small" as well as their intention to establish conditions under which justice and respect for international law could be **(52)** _________ and "to promote social progress and better standards of life in larger freedom."

The Organization officially came into existence on 24 October 1945, after the Charter of the United Nations had been **(53)** _________ by China, France, the Soviet Union, the United Kingdom, and the United States (the five permanent members of the Security Council), and by a majority of the other 46 nations which had signed it.

The purposes of the United Nations are set forth in Article 1 of the Charter. They are: to maintain international peace and **(54)** _________ ; to develop friendly relations among nations; to cooperate in solving international economic, social, cultural and humanitarian problems and in promoting respect for human rights; and to be a center for harmonizing the actions of nations towards those **(55)** _________ goals.

51. A. hate B. destiny
C. poverty D. war

52. A. destroyed B. maintained
C. restricted D. solved

53. A. ratified B. rectified
C. investigated D. invented

54. A. approval B. consent
C. security D. language

55. A. limited B. common
C. personal D. tentative

Choose the most appropriate of the four alternatives according to your knowledge and the information gained from *New Today's Guide to the United Nations.*

56. One of the threats to world peace that Secretary-General António Guterres mentioned in his address to the General Assembly on 19 September 2017 is
A. medical revolution B. free trade
C. terrorism D. artificial intelligence

57. One of the official languages of the United Nations is
A. Arabic B. Dutch
C. German D. Japanese

58. The United Nations' main source of funds for the regular budget is the contributions of

A. Member States

B. the Security Council members

C. the Economic and Social Council members

D. major conglomerates in the world

59. The General Assembly appoints the Secretary-General for a term of

A. two years B. three years

C. four years D. five years

60. The Japanese government established an SDGs Promotion Headquarters in the Cabinet in

A. 1995 B. 2001 C. 2016 D. 2020

Ⅷ. Read each of the following passages and answer the questions that follow.

[Passage 1: Questions 61 to 63]

Almost 75 years since the adoption of the first General Assembly resolution in 1946 committed the United Nations to the goal of nuclear disarmament, our world continues to live in the shadow of nuclear catastrophe.

Relationships between States possessing nuclear weapons are characterized by division, distrust and an absence of dialogue. **(A)**

This International Day highlights the need to reverse course and return to a common path to nuclear disarmament.

The use of nuclear weapons would affect all States, meaning that all States have a responsibility to ensure that such deadly armaments are never used again and are eliminated completely from national arsenals. **(B)**

COVID-19 has exposed a wide range of global fragilities, from pandemic readiness and inequality to climate change to lawlessness in cyberspace; our preparedness to address the threat of nuclear weapons is one of those vulnerabilities. We need a strengthened, inclusive and renewed multilateralism built on trust and based on international law that can guide us to our shared goal of a world free of nuclear weapons.

Those States that possess nuclear weapons must lead. They must return to real, good-faith dialogue to restore trust and confidence, reduce nuclear risk and take tangible steps in nuclear disarmament. **(C)** They should take steps to implement the commitments they have undertaken.

The death, suffering and destruction caused by the atomic bombing in Hiroshima and Nagasaki must not be repeated. **(D)** The United Nations stands ready to work with all States to achieve this shared goal.

61. Choose the best place from among (A), (B), (C), and (D) where the following sentence can be inserted:

The only guarantee against the use of these abhorrent weapons is their total elimination.

62. Choose the best place from among (A), (B), (C), and (D) where the following sentence can be inserted:

As they increasingly choose to pursue strategic competition over cooperation, the dangers posed by nuclear weapons are becoming more acute.

63. Choose the best place from among (A), (B), (C), and (D) where the following sentence can be inserted:

They should reaffirm the shared understanding that a nuclear war cannot be won and must not be fought.

[Passage 2: Questions 64 to 70]

Devastating floods destroyed towns in Germany and Belgium. A ruthless heat wave broiled the Western U.S. and Canada. Heavy rains paralyzed a Chinese industrial **(64)** hub home to 10 million people. These recent weather phenomena are being **(65)** intensified by the changing climate.

But the link between these **(66)** far-flung extremes goes beyond warming global temperatures. All of these events are touched by jet streams, strong and narrow bands of westerly winds blowing above the Earth's surface. The currents are generated when cold air from the poles **(67)** clashes against hot air from the tropics, creating storms and other phenomena such as rain and drought.

"Jet streams are the weather—they create it and they **(68)** steer it," said Jennifer Francis, a senior scientist at the Woodwell Climate Research Center. "Sometimes the jet stream takes on a very **(69)** convoluted pattern. When we see it taking big swings north and big dips southward, we know we're going to see some unusual weather conditions."

Meteorologists worry whenever those swings and dips form omega-shaped curves that look like waves. When that happens, warm air travels further north and cold air penetrates further south. The result is **(70)** a succession of unusually hot and cold weather systems along the same latitude. Under these conditions, winds often weaken and dangerous weather can remain stuck in the same place for days or weeks at a time—rather than just a few hours or a day—leading to prolonged rains and heat waves.

64. In this context, the word "hub" is closest in meaning to

A. center
B. factory
C. wheel
D. machine

65. In this context, the word "intensified" is closest in meaning to

A. heated
B. observed
C. prevented
D. worsened

66. In this context, the phrase "far-flung extremes" is closest in meaning to

A. long periods of bad weather in a few areas
B. different kinds of severe natural disasters
C. unexpected connections between two events
D. radical opinions about how climate change happens

67. In this context, the phrase "clashes against" is closest in meaning to

A. exceeds
B. hits
C. contradicts
D. weakens

68. In this context, the word "steer" is closest in meaning to

A. break
B. predict
C. control
D. follow

69. In this context, the word "convoluted" is closest in meaning to

A. simplified
B. changed
C. mysterious
D. twisted

70. In this context, the phrase "a succession of" is closest in meaning to

A. a series of
B. a small piece of
C. a large amount of
D. an instance of

Ⅸ. Read the following passage and answer the questions that follow.

(1 ～ 10 indicate paragraph numbers.)

1 The last year has been a dark one for families all over the world, but the rapid development of COVID-19 vaccines provided a hopeful light at the end of the tunnel. At long last, the COVAX Facility begins to make good on its promise to make sure that light shines for all. And we are off and running. Vaccine doses have arrived in West Africa and Asia, with many more countries to follow in the coming days and weeks. We've now seen Africa's first vaccinations with COVAX doses in Ghana and Ivory Coast, in truly moving ceremonies in both countries yesterday.

2 But what took place Monday is more than a feel-good story that speaks to our collective best natures; it is a necessary first step that speaks to our collective best interests. The only way out of this pandemic is to ensure vaccination is available around the globe, and that people from less wealthy countries are not left behind in the race to be protected.

3 At UNICEF, we are committed to making this happen. Last week's momentous arrivals are just the first batches of vaccines that UNICEF will ship through the COVAX Facility as part of this historic effort to deliver close to 2 billion doses of COVID-19 vaccines to around 190 countries and territories. To date, more than 1.1 million doses have been delivered, with more than 20 more countries expected to receive hundreds of thousands of doses this week.

4 I would like to thank Serum Institute of India (SII) for being the first to help deliver vaccines to Advance Market Commitment (AMC) countries and for working around the clock to package and make vaccines available in record time, as well as to the Government of India for their immense support. We have a lot of work ahead of us.

5 In terms of delivery, UNICEF is also working closely with airlines and other partners to find innovative solutions to help us deliver COVAX vaccines as quickly as possible. We've already seen tremendous partnership. I would like to thank freight forwarders and Emirates Airlines for helping UNICEF with shipments to Ghana and Ivory Coast in record turnaround time. Only today we have 5 shipments including to DRC, Angola and Nigeria where, we are delivering COVID-19 vaccines consolidated with syringes and routine vaccines insuring children are also protected, among many other 20 countries receiving vaccines this week.

6 We have also supported governments in developing national vaccination plans and preparing for the arrival of vaccines. Along with our partners, we have mapped out existing cold chain equipment and storage capacity. And we have delivered and installed thousands of new fridges to keep vaccines at the right temperature in health facilities this past year. In Ghana, for example, we have delivered 2,500 fridges since May of last year. But much work still remains.

7 With each of these steps, we move closer to the moment when we can start to

return to normal for the billions of children and families affected around the world. And this is, obviously, our focus at UNICEF. Over the next couple of weeks, we will be talking a lot about how this pandemic has impacted the lives of children, starting later today when we will be issuing estimates of the number of children who have been unable to attend class in person for almost the entire past year.

[8] So, when we talk about vaccines arriving in countries, we need to recognize what this also represents for children—it is hope. Their access to education, health and protection services has been severely disrupted by the pandemic. As vaccinations roll out, this will help to bring the pandemic under control so that we can start the work to build a better, safer, and healthier future for everyone.

[9] Lastly, I want to just pause just for a moment on exactly where we are. What has happened in the span of less than a year is nothing short of astounding. There are no miracles in public health, but if there were, this would be one. Not even 12 months have passed since most of the world began locking down, closing up, and socially distancing to prevent the spread of COVID-19. And in that time, not only did the world's scientists rally to do the impossible—identify, test and mass-produce vaccines to treat the virus; but procurement and distribution of vaccines began because the world's humanitarians rallied to do that together. And not just for wealthy countries—they have now arrived, and will continue to arrive, in the world's least wealthy countries as well.

[10] These are remarkable efforts, and the work we all—the private sector, UN and development agencies, governments, donors, and other partners—will doubtlessly continue to do more moving together, and will stand for generations to come as proof of what the world can do, when we do it together. It is history in the making.

71. Which of the following is mentioned in Paragraph 1?

A. The development of COVID-19 vaccines slowed down the pandemic.
B. The COVAX Facility has finally started to distribute COVID-19 vaccines.
C. COVID-19 vaccines have arrived in all parts of Africa and Asia.
D. Ghana and Ivory Coast welcomed additional doses of COVID-19 vaccines.

72. Which of the following is mentioned in Paragraph 2?

A. The project was made possible by volunteers from around the world.
B. The call for help needs to be spread to as many countries as possible.
C. Worldwide vaccination is the only way to overcome the current crisis.
D. People from less wealthy countries tend to have more racial problems.

73. Which of the following can be inferred from Paragraph 3?

A. The COVAX Facility sends doctors to vaccinate people around the world.

B. The COVAX Facility encouraged UNICEF to deliver more vaccines.

C. UNICEF has shipped the vaccines to about 190 countries and territories.

D. UNICEF collaborates with the COVAX Facility in vaccine deliveries.

74. Which of the following is mentioned in Paragraph 4?

A. SII is helping deliver COVID-19 vaccines to AMC countries.

B. SII is behind schedule in distributing COVID-19 vaccines.

C. The Government of India offered financial support to UNICEF.

D. The Government of India has a future joint project with UNICEF.

75. Which of the following is mentioned in Paragraph 5?

A. Trucks and trains are the primary means of transportation for UNICEF.

B. UNICEF included vaccines for children in the COVID-19 shipments.

C. Three African countries will receive vaccines within a month.

D. In Africa, children are the first to receive COVID-19 vaccines.

76. Which of the following is NOT mentioned in Paragraph 6?

A. UNICEF has supported countries in making their vaccination plans.

B. UNICEF examined if countries were ready to receive and store vaccines.

C. UNICEF has helped countries to repair their old refrigerators.

D. UNICEF provided refrigerators to help store vaccines properly.

77. Which of the following is mentioned in Paragraph 7?

A. The lives of children and families in the world are returning to normal.

B. The pandemic's impact on children's lives will be reported.

C. Ninety percent of the children surveyed were unable to attend class in person.

D. Children around the world are afraid to go to school due to the pandemic.

78. Which of the following is mentioned in Paragraph 8?

A. Vaccinations will provide children with a better and healthier life.

B. The pandemic will be under control soon after the vaccines arrive.

C. If children's health improves, adults can get back to work as before.

D. Adults' well-being leads to that of children in the long run.

79. Which of the following is mentioned in Paragraph 9?

A. We should not depend on miracles but learn to work together.

B. It took more than a year for the world to take action against the pandemic.

C. The world's scientists and humanitarians did something that seemed impossible.

D. COVID-19 vaccines will be distributed to less wealthy countries first.

80. Which of the following best summarizes the message of Paragraph 10?

A. Private and public sector collaboration is the key to solving the world's toughest challenges.

B. In order to tackle future global issues, the UN and the world's nations should continue to work together.

C. It is certain that the world's leaders will continue to work together to fight against common threats.

D. This historic fight against the pandemic is proof that the world can work together for the common good.

X. Write a short essay of around 80-100 words in English to answer the following question:

What is one negative effect of social media and how can it be solved?

(You do not need to write down the number of words.)

マークシート記入例

東京の本会場でB級を受験する、国連 太郎さん、受験番号が「東京01-30001」、生年月日が「1980年10月24日」の場合の記入例です。

【受験番号/氏名】
それぞれ受験票の記載通りに記入してください。

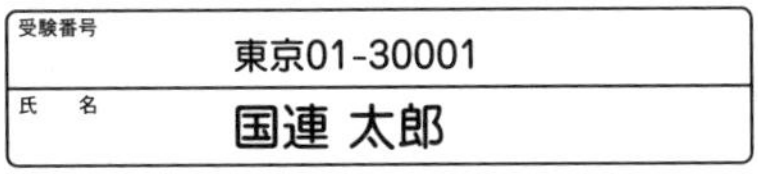

【受験地区】
下段の都道府県部分を塗りつぶしてください。

【会場番号】
都道府県部分に続く2桁の数字を塗りつぶしてください。

【受験番号】
ハイフン（－）以降の5桁の数字を塗りつぶしてください。

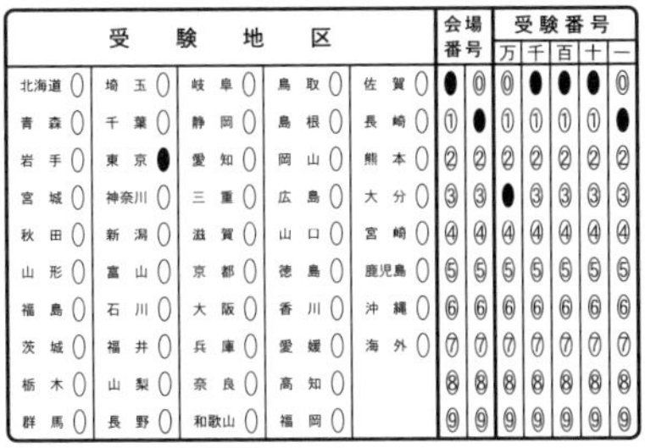

【受験級】
「B」と記入し、下段のB級部分を塗りつぶしてください。

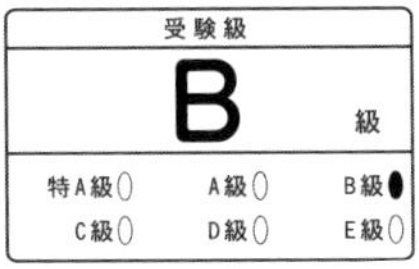

【生年月日】
4桁の西暦・月・日を塗りつぶしてください。
10未満の月・日の十の位は、「0」を塗りつぶしてください。

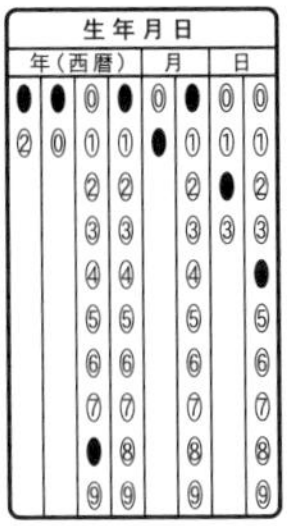

※HB以上の鉛筆を用いてマークをしてください。

※他の地区から会場を変更して受験する場合でも、受験票に記載されている受験地区・会場番号をマークしてください。

2021年 第2回試験

解答・解説

2021年　国連英検B級第2回試験
解答・解説

I　疑問文を含む英文が10題読まれます。
それぞれの英文に対して，最も適切な対応文を選びなさい。

1.　解答：B

解説　遅れてきて謝っている人に対する応答なので，最も適切なのはBである。

ナレーション　Sorry to have kept you waiting.
「待たせてしまってごめんなさい」

A. 何時に？　B. 大丈夫ですよ。
C. うそでしょ。　D. 私もしていません。

2.　解答：A

解説　make itは，「できる」「間に合う」などさまざまな意味があるが，ここではcan't make it todayで「きょうは行けない（出席できない）」の意味になる。したがって最も適切な応答はAである。

ナレーション　I can't make it today.
「きょうは無理です」

A. 来週の金曜日はどう？　B. 私は来週到着します。
C. ほとんど確実です。　D. はいどうぞ。

3.　解答：D

解説　予約をした，と言っているので，予約の相手は病院，レストラン，美容院などさまざまな可能性があるが，選択肢の中で最も適切な応答はDである。選択肢のBは，玄関やドアの向こう側にいる相手に使う。ちなみに，用件不明の電話などに対して「どなたですか」というときは，Who is this? を使う。

ナレーション　I have an appointment at six.
「6時に予約をしたのですが」

A. そのレストランは遠すぎます。　B. 誰ですか。

C. 彼女は家にいます。　D. お名前をお願いできますか。

4. 解答：C

解説 take ～'s shift は誰かの（仕事の）シフトを代わってあげるという意味で，ここでは，自分のシフトを代わってくれたことに対する感謝をしている。最も適切なのは C である。

ナレーション　Thanks for taking my shift yesterday.

「昨日シフトを代わってくれてありがとう」

A. いいですね。　B. それは残念。

C. どういたしまして。　D. きょうこそがその日です。

5. 解答：B

解説 前を歩いている人が何かを落としたりしたときに言う表現である。そう声をかけられたときの応答として，選択肢の中で最も適切なのは B である。

ナレーション　Hey, I think you just dropped this.

「あの，これ，いま落としましたよ」

A. どこにいるの？　B. それは私のではありません。

C. あなたの番です。　D. もう帰りましょう。

6. 解答：C

解説 食卓での場面でよく交わされそうな会話である。想定される応答としては「はいどうぞ」という趣旨の表現であるので，C が最も適切である。

ナレーション　Could you pass the salad, Jason?

「ジェイソン，サラダ取ってくれる？」

A. 急いでよ。　B. わざわざいいよ。

C. はいよ。　D. さっぱりわからないな。

7. 解答：A

解説 come with ～ は「～が一緒に付いてくる」の意味。骨董品《こっとうひん》店で，客が店員（店主）に対して骨董品が保証付きかを尋ねているので，応答として最も適するのは A である。

ナレーション Do these antiques come with a warranty?
「ここにある骨董品は保証付きですか」
A. 残念ながら付いていません。 B. 本当ですか。
C. いくつありますか。 D. 彼らが来ます。

8. 解答：D

解説 レストランなどでよく交わされるやり取りである。ウエイターが注文は他にないかと聞いているので，それに対する応答として最も適するのは，Dである。

ナレーション Would you like anything else with your order?
「ご注文は何か他にありますでしょうか」
A. とても値段が高いですね。 B. オンラインで買いました。
C. ここは禁煙です。 D. いいえ，それで全部です。

9. 解答：B

解説 How'd (How did) you do on ～？は「～の出来栄えはどうだった」の意味であるから，応答として最も適切なのは，Bである。

ナレーション How'd you do on the final exam?
「あなたは期末テストどうだった？」
A. 彼が最低でした。 B. 思ったよりよかったです。
C. できるだけ頑張って。 D. これは面白くなるよ。

10. 解答：C

解説 家庭で，親子の間で交わされそうな会話である。応答として最も適切なのはCである。選択肢のAは「早くやればやるほどよい」と掃除を命じる側が使いそうな表現である。

ナレーション Did you clean your room like I told you to?
「言われた通り部屋の掃除をしたのかい？」
A. 早い方がいいよ。 B. 足元，気をつけて。
C. 明日やるよ。 D. 何て美しい家なんだ！

II

10題の対話文が読まれます。
その後に読まれるそれぞれの質問に対して最も適切な答えを選びなさい。

11. 解答：D

解説 女性が，今学期は21単位取っている（I'm taking 21 credits this semester.）と言ったのに対し，男性が19単位でも相当に大変な重荷（a crazy workload）と応答しているので，大学生同士の会話だと想像できる。Dが正解である。

A. 男性は自分の仕事が好きだ。　B. 男性は週に19時間働いている。
C. 女性は21才である。　D. 女性は学生である。

ナレーション

Woman: I'm taking 21 credits this semester.
Man: Wow, and I thought I had a crazy workload with 19 credits. Anyway, don't burn yourself out!
Woman: Yeah, well it's the only way I can graduate on time since I switched majors halfway through.
Question Which of the following statements is true based on this conversation?

（女）：今学期は21単位取っているのよ。
（男）：えー，僕なんか19単位でもひどく重荷だと思っていたのに。とにかく燃え尽きないようにね。
（女）：そうね。まあ私途中で専攻を変えたので予定通りに卒業するにはこれが唯一の方法なのよ。
質問　この会話の内容に照らして正しいのはどれですか。

12. 解答：B

解説 女性が政治家は選挙公約を守らないと不満を述べたのに対し，男性は“(I) can't argue with you there.”（その点では君に反論できないね）と応答しているので，Bが正解である。

A. 部分的に反対である。
B. 彼女は正しいと思っている。
C. 彼女は間違っていると思っている。
D. 彼女の言っていることが理解できない。

ナレーション

Man: Did you watch the presidential debate?

Woman: What's the point? They all say one thing when they're running for office but never keep their promises once they're actually in office. I'd trust my life with my cat before I'd trust a politician.

Man: Can't argue with you there.

Question What does the man think about the woman's opinion?

（男）：大統領候補者ディベート見た？

（女）：見て何になるの？　あの人たち選挙戦で言っていることを当選した後守ったためしがないわ。政治家を信じるくらいなら私のネコを頼りにするわ。

（男）：君の言うとおりだね。

質問　女性の意見について男性はどう思っていますか。

13. 解答：D

解説 女性が「何人かの人が話しているのを偶然聞いた（overheard)」と話していることから，D が正解である。

A. 彼の会社が倒産した。

B. 彼の同僚が会社を辞める。

C. 彼と話をしたい人が多すぎる。

D. 彼について間違ったうわさが流れている。

ナレーション

Woman: Are you really quitting at the end of the month?

Man: What? No! Who told you that?

Woman: I just overheard some people talking. Anyway, glad to know you'll still be with us.

Question Why was the man surprised?

（女）：今月末で本当に会社を辞めるの？

（男）：えっ？　まさか！　誰がそんなこと言ったの？

（女）：誰かが話しているのをたまたま聞いちゃったのよ。とにかくあなたがまだ一緒にいてくれてうれしいわ。

質問　なぜ男性は驚いているのですか。

14. 解答：B

解説 女性が不満の原因として挙げているのは，daycare（託児施設）の料金が高いことと，両親が遠くに住んでいて子育ての援助を頼めないこと，政府による子育て援助が手薄いことであるから，選択肢の中ではBが正解である。

A. 両親が近くに居すぎる。　B. 託児施設の料金が高すぎる。

C. 政府の担当者に連絡がつかない。　D. 娘が学校に行きたがらない。

ナレーション

Woman: My daughter just started daycare and I can't believe how expensive it is!

Man: Tell me about it. My wife and I could barely afford to send all three of our kids. Fortunately, my parents agreed to look after them for us.

Woman: Yeah, too bad my parents live in a different state. Times like these make me wonder what the government is using our tax money for.

Question Why is the woman frustrated?

(女)：娘を託児所に預けるようになったんだけど，料金が信じられないくらい高くて。

(男)：本当だよね。妻と私では，子どもを３人とも預けるのはほぼ無理だと思うよ。運良く，私の両親が面倒を見てくれると言ってくれたんだ。

(女)：そうね。運悪く私の両親は別の州に住んでいるのよ。こんな時，政府が私たちの税金をいったい何に使っているのかって考えちゃうわ。

質問 女性はなぜ不満を募らせているのですか。

15. 解答：A

解説 男性が"How does this look?"と尋ねたのに対し，"It's going to be hard to find any clothes to match that hat."と答えていることから，正解はAである。

A. 合わせるのが難しい。　B. 古すぎる。

C. 高すぎる。　D. 汚れている。

ナレーション

Woman: I love secondhand clothing stores like this. Sometimes you can find some amazing vintage pieces. Look at this beautiful dress!

Man: This place has some awesome cowboy hats from the 70's, too. How does this look?

Woman: It's going to be hard to find any clothes to match that hat. How about this baseball cap instead?

Question What did the woman say about the cowboy hat?

（女）：私，古着屋さん大好き。ときどき驚くようなビンテージ物が見つかるし。このきれいなドレス見て！

（男）：ここの店は 70 年代の最高にかっこいいカウボーイハットもあるんだよ。これなんかどうかな？

（女）：その帽子に合う服を見つけるのが大変そうね。この野球帽の方はどうかしら。

質問 女性はカウボーイハットについてどう言いましたか。

16. 解答：C

解説 男性と女性が共通して話題にしているのは，plastic straws であるから C が正解である。

A. 水の危機　　B. 砂漠化

C. プラスチックのストロー　　D. 魚の乱獲

ナレーション

Man: I am all for reducing plastic waste in our oceans and everything, but do we really have to ban plastic straws?

Woman: Haven't you seen that turtle video, where the turtle has a plastic straw stuck up its nose?

Man: Yeah, I've seen it. And yes, I do feel sorry for the turtle. I'm just complaining because I hate paper straws. Guess I need to carry my own reusable straws from now on.

Question What is the main topic of this conversation?

（男）：海のプラスチックゴミを減らしたりとかは全く賛成なんだけど，プラスチックのストローを禁止する必要は本当にあるのかな？

(女)：あのウミガメのビデオ見たことないの？　鼻にプラスチックのストローが刺さった状態でいるあの映像。

(男)：見たことあるさ。もちろんウミガメは可哀相だよ。ただ僕は，紙のストローが嫌いだから文句を言っているだけなんだ。これからは，再利用できるマイストローを持ち歩くしかないかな。

質問　この会話の主なトピックは何ですか。

17.　解答：A

解説　日本では馴染みがないが，海外では口座を持っているだけで「口座維持手数料」がかかる場合がある。ここでは，女性が男性にその手数料について尋ねているので，答えている男性の職業として正しいのはAである。男性の説明の中に，the fee will be waivedという表現があるが，これは「手数料を請求する権利は放棄されます」つまり「手数料は適応されない」の意味である。

A. 銀行員　　B. レジ係　　C. 数学教師　　D. 受け付け係

ナレーション

Woman: Is there a monthly service fee with this account?

Man:　Yes, it's 12 dollars but if you have at least $1,500 in the account, the fee will be waived.

Woman: I see. Thank you.

Question　What is most likely the man's job?

(女)：この口座は月額手数料が必要ですか。

(男)：はい，月に12ドルですが，口座に最低1,500ドルの預金があれば料金は無料になります。

(女)：なるほど，ありがとうございます。

質問　男性の仕事はおそらく何ですか。

18.　解答：C

解説　男性の話を聞いて，女性は “I wish we had relatives overseas.” と言っていることから，正解はCである。

A. 気の毒に思っている。　B. 見下している。

C. 羨ましく思っている。　D. 興味がない。

ナレーション

Woman: Are you putting your kids into international school?

Man: I originally wanted to but when I looked up how much it costs a year, I decided not to. I'd rather use that money to visit our families abroad and have my kids learn the language naturally.

Woman: That sounds like a good idea. I wish we had relatives overseas.

Question　How does the woman feel about the man's situation?

(女)：お子さんたちをインターナショナルスクールに入れるの？

(男)：最初はそう思ったんですが，年間の費用を調べた結果やめました。そのお金を使って，海外にいる家族を訪れて，子どもたちに自然に言葉を学ばせようと思って。

(女)：それはいい考えね。私たち夫婦にも海外の家族がいるといいんだけれど。

質問　女性は男性の状況についてどう感じていますか。

19.　解答：B

解説　男性が女性に，「売る側の口車にのって買わされているんだよ」と言っているにもかかわらず，The funny thing is ...「面白いのは…」と言いながら，気にしいない様子なので，B が正解となる。

A. 心配している。　B. 気にしていない。

C. 忘れがちである。　D. 不満に思っている。

ナレーション

Woman: Look at these awesome new tech gadgets I just bought! They were all on sale!

Man: Let me guess ... for a limited time only? You know they just say that to get you to buy their products ...

Woman: The funny thing is, I know what they're doing, yet I still fall for it every time!

Question　What is the woman's attitude towards her spending habits?

(女)：この買ったばかりのすごい新作ハイテク機器を見てみて！　みん

なバーゲンセール品だったの！

(男)：当ててみようか……期間限定ってやつだろ？　自分たちの製品を買わせるためにみんなそうやって宣伝するんだよ。

(女)：面白いことにね，私もわかっているのよ。でも毎回それに乗っちゃうのよ。

質問　女性は自分の購買癖に対してどのような態度をとっていますか。

20.　解答：D

解説　昇進面接に際して男性が助言してくれたことに対して，女性は“I couldn’t have done it without you”（あなたがいなければそれを成し得なかったでしょう）などと感謝の気持ちを述べているので，D が正解である。

A. 同情的である。　B. 憤慨している。

C. イライラしている。　D. 感謝している。

ナレーション

Man:　I heard you got the promotion! Congratulations!

Woman: Thank you! I couldn’t have done it without you. Your tips for the interview were a lifesaver.

Man:　I’m glad to hear that. You’ve worked so hard for this. You totally deserve it.

Question　How does the woman feel towards the man?

(男)：昇進したそうだね！　おめでとう！

(女)：ありがとう！　あなたがいなかったら昇進できていなかったわ。面接のための助言は本当に助かったわ。

(男)：それはよかった。君が一生懸命頑張ったんだから。当然の結果だよ。

質問　女性は男性に対してどう感じていますか。

III

5 つの対話文が読まれます。各対話文の後で，それに対する質問が 2 つ読まれます。各質問に最も適切な答えを選びなさい。

Conversation 1

21.　解答：C

解説　女性が電話で “Amelia’s Diner” と言い，注文を早く届けてもよいかと言ったことに対し，男性が「空腹なのでちょうどいい」と返答していることなどから，正解はCとなる。Dのretailerは「小売業」つまり物を売る店のことだからここでは当てはまらない。

A. ホテル　B. 郵便局　　C. レストラン　　D. オンラインショップ

22.　解答：A

解説 男性は女性の提案を歓迎しているので，正解はAとなる。

A. 喜んでいる。　B. 怒っている。

C. 混乱している。　D. 興味がない。

ナレーション

Man:　Hello?

Woman: Hi, this is Amelia's Diner. I believe you placed an order with us online to be delivered at 6pm.

Man:　Yes, that's right ...

Woman: I'm really sorry about this but we're a little short on staff today. Would it be okay if we delivered your order a little earlier, say at 5:30pm?

Man:　Oh, that's actually even better. I was getting pretty hungry already. See you guys soon!

Questions　21. Where does the woman most likely work?

22. How does the man feel about the woman's proposal?

(男)：もしもし。

(女)：こんにちは，アメリアダイナーですが。オンラインで6時に配達のご注文をいただいたと思いますが。

(男)：はい，そうです。

(女)：申し訳ございませんが，現在スタッフが少し手薄になっておりまして。少し早めの，たとえば5時30分とかにお届けしてもよろしいでしょうか？

(男)：ああ，それならその方が都合がいいですよ。もうお腹がすいてきたところでした。じゃ，よろしくお願いします！

質問　21. 女性はおそらくどこで働いていますか。

22. 女性の提案について男性はどう感じていますか。

Conversation 2

23. 解答：B

解説 男性が，“Governments need to start drastically reducing carbon emissions.” と述べていることから，B が正解である。

A. 太陽光エネルギーを採用する。　B. 二酸化炭素排出量を減らす。
C. より研究に投資する。　D. 炭素税を導入する。

24. 解答：A

解説 女性は，一般の人は気候変動よりももっと身近な問題で悩みを抱えていると主張しているので，A が正解である。

A. 気候変動は一般の人々にとってそれほど重要な問題ではない。
B. 自然災害は一般の人々の家を破壊するだろう。
C. 一般の人々は気候変動は存在しないと思っている。
D. 一般の人々は子どもたちの将来を心配している。

ナレーション

Man: All these reports about extreme weather events make me feel we're not doing enough to address climate change. Governments need to start drastically reducing carbon emissions.

Woman: Oh, give me a break. Sure, climate change is a real problem but it's just not what the average person is worried about. There are issues that matter much more.

Man: Like what?

Woman: Umm ... education, health, good jobs, a government that's not corrupt, clean water ... I mean these may seem like basic things but there are people who still don't have access to them. We can afford to care about climate change because we live in comfortable developed countries, but that's not the reality for most people.

Man: Gee, I never thought of it that way ...

Questions 23. What does the man say governments need to do to deal with climate change?

24. What does the woman say about the average person in the world?

(男)：こうした異常気象現象について耳にすると，気候変動について僕たちは十分な対応をしていないと感じるね。政府は二酸化炭素排出をより劇的に削減しはじめる必要があるよ。

(女)：ちょっと待って。確かに気候変動は現実の問題だけど，一般の人が心配するような問題じゃないわ。もっと重要な問題がたくさんあるでしょ。

(男)：例えば？

(女)：そうね……教育，健康，よい仕事，腐敗していない政治，きれいな水……こういうことが基本のように思えるのに，これさえ手に入らない人たちがいるのよ。私たちが気候変動について心配する余裕があるのは，私たちが快適な先進国に住んでいるからだけど，それが多くの人にとっての現実ではないのよ。

(男)：えー。そんな風に思ったことはなかったな。

質問　23. 気候変動について政府は何をする必要があると男性は言っていますか。

24. 世界の平均的な人について女性はどうだと言っていますか。

Conversation 3

25.　解答：D

解説　ある生物学の教授の講演が，匿名の活動化による暗殺予告のために中止になったことが話題の中心であるので，D が正解である。

A. 政治活動化　　B. 抗議の自由
C. 進化生物学　　D. あるイベントの中止

26.　解答：A

解説　男性は，学校が脅しに屈することは，“a horrible precedent to set”（最悪の前例を作ること）だと言っているので，正解は A となる。

A. 悪い前例を作ることになる。　B. 支持する学生はほとんどいない。
C. 悪影響は及ぼさないだろう。　D. 多くの学生を守るだろう。

ナレーション

Man: Are you going to Jordan Rogan's talk?

Woman: That controversial biology professor? Didn't you hear? The event's been cancelled because some anonymous activists sent death threats to the school administrators.

Man: That's ridiculous. I thought we lived in a society that values freedom of speech.

Woman: Yeah, but it's the school's responsibility to maintain the safety of their students.

Man: Still, they should have found some other way. By cancelling the event, the school is sending the message that whenever activists threaten to use violence, they'll always get their way. That's a horrible precedent to set.

Questions 25. What is the main topic of this conversation?
26. What does the man think about the school's decision?

(男)：ジョーダン・レーガンの講演聞きに行く？

(女)：あの物議を醸している生物学教授の？　聞かなかったの？　あの講演はどこかの匿名の活動家が学校の経営陣に暗殺予告を送りつけたので，中止になったのよ。

(男)：それは馬鹿げているよ。僕たちは言論の自由を尊重する社会に生きていると思っていたけど。

(女)：そうよ。でも学校には学生たちの安全を守る責任があるのよ。

(男)：でも，何か他の方法を見いだすべきだったよ。講演を中止することで，学校は，活動家が暴力行使をちらつかせる行為に出れば，思い通りになるんだというメッセージを送っていることになるんだよ。それは，最悪の前例を作ることになる。

質問 25. この会話の主なトピックは何ですか。
26. 学校の決定について男性はどう思っていますか。

Conversation 4

27. 解答：B

解説 自国の国民よりも近隣諸国を優先していて「わけがわからない」(It makes no sense.) と述べていることから，B が正解である。

A. 政府は対応が遅すぎる。　B. 政府の優先順位は誤っている。
C. 政府は予算を使い過ぎだ。　D. 政府はもっと人員を雇用すべきだ。

28.　解答：C

解説 周辺領域における地政学的（geopolitical）優位を保つためだと説明していることから，C が正解である。

A. 子どもたちの命を守るため
B. 製薬会社を支援するため
C. 海外での自国の影響力を高めるため
D. 自国の医療技術を向上させるため

ナレーション

Woman: I saw on the news that our government is donating millions of vaccine doses to our neighboring countries. Meanwhile, we still don't have enough for the people here. It makes no sense.

Man: Why? It makes perfect sense to me. They're engaging in classic vaccine diplomacy.

Woman: I never realized vaccines could be used for diplomacy.

Man: It's a way for us to expand our influence in other countries and maintain our geopolitical interests. We have to make sure our rival countries don't become too influential.

Woman: Okay, that's all well and good but I wish they'd focus on maintaining geopolitical interests after taking care of folks at home first.

Questions 27. How does the woman feel about her government's actions?
28. What is one reason the man gives for his government's actions?

(女)：ニュースで，私たちの政府が何百回分ものワクチンを近隣諸国に寄付しているって見たけど。一方で，私たちはまだ自分の国の人々に十分なワクチンがないのよ。意味がわからないわ。

(男)：なぜだい？　僕には理解できるよ。政府は常套《じょうとう》手段であるワクチン外交をしているのさ。

(女)：ワクチンが外交に使われるなんて知らなかったわ。

(男)：僕たちの国が他国への影響力を高めて地勢学的権益を維持するための方法なのさ。

(女)：なるほど，まあそれはそれでよしとして，まず自国の国民の手当てをしてから地勢学的権益を維持することに集中してくれればいいのに。

質問　27. 政府の行動について女性はどう感じていますか。

28. 政府の行動について男性が挙げた1つの理由は何ですか。

Conversation 5

29. 解答：B

解説　彼女が言及したのは，同僚（colleagues），福利厚生（benefits）や給料（salary）のよさと上司（manager）への不満であるから，言及していないものはBである。

A. 同僚　B. 通勤　C. 給料　D. 上司

30. 解答：B

解説　仕事上の問題として彼女が話したのは，上司が自分の能力を正当に評価してくれていないことであるから，正解はBとなる。

A. 通勤に4時間かかる。

B. 上司が自分のことを能力不足だと見なす。

C. 同僚の男性の方が自分よりも給料が高い。

D. チームの人たちとの人間関係が悪い。

ナレーション

Man: How's the new job?

Woman: My coworkers are pretty nice and the benefits and salary are great. The problem is my manager.

Man: What's wrong with your manager?

Woman: I feel he doesn't think I'm qualified for the job. He probably thinks if a woman is hired as lead engineer, it's because she's a woman and not because of her skills and experience. I mean, I understand why he would think this way since there aren't that many women in this field to begin with ... but still.

Man: Did he not see your resume and all the patents under your name? I think he probably just feels threatened.

Questions 29. Which of the following does the woman NOT mention about her new job?

30. What is the woman's problem at work?

(男)：新しい仕事はどう？

(女)：同僚はとっても親切だし福利厚生や給料もすごくいいわ。問題は上司よ。

(男)：上司がどうしたの？

(女)：あの人は私にいまの仕事に必要な能力がないと思っているのよ。女性が主任エンジニアに採用されるのは，能力や経験があるからではなく，女性だからだって思っているの。まあ，そう思うのも理解できるわ。そもそもこの領域には女性があまりいないから。でもね。

(男)：彼は君の履歴書や君が取得した特許などの情報を見なかったのかな？　たぶん彼は君を脅威に感じているんだと思うよ。

質問 29. 新しい仕事について女性が話さなかったのは次のどれですか。

30. 女性の仕事上の問題は何ですか。

IV

（初めに）２つの短いナレーションが読まれ，そのナレーションの後にそれぞれ５つの質問文が読まれます。最も適切な答えを選びなさい。

Talk 1

31.　解答：C

解説 "Although today, I am known for my superhero films ..." と述べていることから，正解は C となる。

A. シェフ　　B. 歌手　　C. 俳優　　D. 教授

32.　解答：D

解説 冒頭の，"President Smith, faculty, proud parents, graduates" という挨拶や，"to be giving the commencement speech here" などから，大

学の卒業式の式辞をしているとわかる。したがって正解はＤとなる。

A. 音楽発表会　B. 映画に関する講義

C. 自己啓発セミナー　D. 大学の卒業式

33. 解答：A

解説 “I was known as the least funny comedian in New York City.” や “I realized I wasn’t meant to be a comedian.” などの発言から，コメディアンとしては失敗だったことがわかる。正解はＡとなる。

A. コメディアンとして成功すること

B. 自分のレストランを経営すること

C. 高校を卒業すること

D. 映画を制作すること

34. 解答：D

解説 “two years and 500 shows later” に，コメディアンに向かないことを悟りニューヨークを後にし，自分の故郷に帰ったのであるから，正解はＤとなる。

A. 5回　B. 99回　C. 150回　D. 500回

35. 解答：C

解説 スピーチの最後に “It’s okay to fail, as long as you never quit.” とあることから，正解はＣとなる。

A. 自分が好きなことをしなさい。

B. 自分の力を決して疑わないように。

C. 失敗はしてよいが，あきらめてはいけない。

D. あなたの愛する人がいつも最優先であるべきだ。

ナレーション

President Smith, faculty, proud parents, graduates. I am honored for the invitation to be with you today. It may seem ironic for someone like me, who was rejected from this university, to be giving the commencement speech here two decades later.

Although today, I am known for my superhero films, before any of my box office successes, I was known as the least funny comedian in New York City. I would go on stage, say my lines and 99% of the time, I would get booed off stage in less than one minute. The longest I managed to stay onstage for was 5 minutes, and that was because my girlfriend was the only audience member that day.

Needless to say, two years and 500 shows later, I realized I wasn't meant to be a comedian. So I packed my bags and went home. I worked at my parents' restaurant in the day, and at night, I'd experiment with making videos online. One year and 200 videos later, I got a casting call from Hollywood. So my message to you today is, "It's okay to fail, as long as you never quit."

Questions 31. What is the speaker's current job?
32. Where is the speaker speaking at?
33. According to the talk, what did the speaker fail at?
34. How many shows did the speaker do in New York?
35. What is the speaker's main message to the audience?

語句 proud parents: [式辞等での呼びかけ]（ご子息ご息女のお祝いのために）ご列席の保護者　commencement speech: 卒業式でのスピーチ　box office: 興行収入　get booed off stage: ブーイングをうけてステージを退場する　casting call:（映画などの）役者募集案内

訳例 スミス学長，教員各位，ご列席の保護者の皆様，卒業生の皆様。きょうお招きいただいたことを光栄に存じます。私のようにこの大学から退学になった人間が，20年後に卒業式でスピーチをしているのは皮肉に思えるかもしれません。

今日私はスーパーヒーロー映画で有名になりましたが，興行収入で成功をおさめる以前は，ニューヨークで最も面白くないコメディアンとして知られていました。ステージに上がり，話しはじめると，99%の割合で，ブーイングを受けて1分もしないうちに退場という状況でした。ステージにとどまっていた最長記録は5分でした。それもそのときは私のガールフレンドが唯一の観客だったのです。

言うまでもなく，2年の月日と500回のショーを経て，私はコメディアンには向いていないと悟りました。それで私は荷造りをして実家に戻りました。昼間は両親のレストランで働き，夜はオンラインビデオの制作をいろいろ試しました。1年の月日と200本のビデオ制作を経て，私はハリウッドから配役の打診をもらいました。ですから，きょうみなさんへお伝えしたいメッセージは，

「失敗してもいい。あきらめない限りは」ということなのです。

質問　31. 話し手の現在の仕事は何ですか。

32. 話し手はどのような場で話をしていますか。

33. 話によると，話し手は何に失敗しましたか。

34. 話し手は，ニューヨークで何回ショーに出演しましたか。

35. 話し手の，聴衆への主なメッセージは何ですか。

Talk 2

36. 解答：A

解説 “Before I take any questions, let me just update you on the status of our rescue efforts.” とあることから，救出作戦について責任のある地位の人物だとわかる。選択肢から選ぶとすれば，正解は A となる。

A. 市長　B. 会社社長　C. 報道キャスター　D. 教師

37. 解答：A

解説 災害時の救出作戦や，住民の避難状況についての説明があり，その場の参加者からは質問も受け付ける，というところから，正解は A となる。

A. 記者会見　B. 天気予報

C. ニュースインタビュー　D. 自然災害に関するスピーチ

38. 解答：C

解説 住民は体育館やコミュニティーセンターに設置された避難所に避難し，病院では電気・水道は復旧していると述べる一方，“we are moving as quickly as possible to restore electricity and water to all residential housing within the next 48 hours” と話していることから，未だ電気・水道の復旧が完了していないのは，一般の住宅であることがわかる。したがって正解は C となる。

A. 病院　B. 体育館　C. 住民の住宅　D. コミュニティーセンター

39. 解答：D

解説 “We currently have about 1,200 rescue workers on scene” と述べていることから，正解は D となる。

A. 25 名　B. 100 名　C. 587 名　D. 1,200 名

40. 解答：B

解説 市長が住民に対して推奨した行動は，最大限の警戒をする，外に出ない，地元の通告をよく聞く，非常用持ち出し袋を家族一人ひとりに用意する，ことであるから，この中にないBが正解となる。

A. 建物の中にいる　B. 高台に避難する

C. 非常用袋を用意する　D. 地元の通告に注意を払う

ナレーション

Good morning. Before I take any questions, let me just update you on the status of our rescue efforts.

587 of our residents have been evacuated to temporary shelters at local gymnasiums and community centers. We have managed to restore electricity and water to all the hospitals in the city, and we are moving as quickly as possible to restore electricity and water to all residential housing within the next 48 hours.

As of Tuesday, our search teams have rescued 25 people. Fortunately, there have been no reports of any deaths and I pray it stays that way. However, we still have at least 100 people missing. The President has dispatched members of the military to help us in our rescue efforts. We currently have about 1,200 rescue workers on scene working tirelessly day and night to find those still missing. I would like to personally extend my gratitude to them.

Unfortunately, the meteorological agency is forecasting heavy rains again next week. We urge all residents to be on high alert. Stay indoors, pay attention to local notices, and prepare an emergency bag for each member of your family in case you have to evacuate.

Questions 36. Who most likely is the speaker?

37. What kind of talk is this?

38. According to the talk, which places still do not have electricity and water?

39. How many rescue workers are on the scene?

40. Which of the following did the speaker NOT recommend residents do?

語句 evacuate ～: ～を避難させる　shelter: 避難所　pray ～: ～であることを祈る　dispatch ～: ～を派遣する　extend my gratitude: 感謝の気持ちを表す　meteorological agency: 気象局・気象庁　urge 人 to ～: 人に～するよう勧告する　be on high alert: 厳戒体制をとる

訳例　おはようございます。ご質問を受ける前に，まず我々の救出活動の状況をお伝えします。

住民の方々 587 名が，地元の体育館やコミュニティーセンターに設けられた仮設避難所に避難しています。町のすべての病院の電気と水道は復旧させることができました。また今後 48 時間以内には，すべての住民の住宅における電気・水道の復旧を完了すべく，できる限り迅速に作業を進めています。

火曜日現在，我々の救出チームが，25 人の方々を救出しました。幸い，いまのところ死者が出たとの報告は入っておりませんし，引き続きそうであることを祈ります。しかしながら，いまだに少なくとも 100 人の方が行方不明の状況です。大統領は，我々の救出活動を支援するために軍隊を派遣しました。現在我々は，現場に 1,200 名の救出隊員を配置し行方不明者の発見に向けて昼夜休みなく作業に当たっております。私個人としても救出隊員たちに心から感謝を述べたいと思います。

あいにく，気象局は来週大雨の予想を出しています。住民のみなさんすべての方におかれましては，最大限の警戒をお願いします。外に出ず，地元の避難情報をよく聞き，避難する際の備えとして，家族の一人ひとりに非常用持ち出し袋を用意してください。

質問　36. 話し手はおそらく誰ですか。
37. これはどのような種類の話ですか。
38. 話によると，未だ電気と水が止まったままなのはどこですか。
39. 現場には何人の救急隊員がいますか。
40. 話し手が，住民に対して推奨していないのは次のどれですか。

V　４つの選択肢の中から，
以下のそれぞれの英文の（　　　　）に入る最も適切なものを選びなさい。

41.　解答：D

解説 urge ～ to ... (～に…するように勧告する) に続くのは動詞の原形であり，さらに consider ～ ing で「～することを考慮する」の意味となるので，D が正解である。

訳例　諮問委員会は木曜日，政府に対し中学校でより少人数のクラスを採用することを検討すべきと勧告した。

42.　解答：C

解説　be required to ～ で「～することが求められている」の意味となるので，C が正解である。

訳例　現在では日本中の小売店が，レジ袋の使用に対して利用客に料金を課すよう求められている。

43.　解答：B

解説　a moment of silence は「黙祷《もくとう》」の意味である。したがって B が正解である。

訳例　日本全国の人々が，午後 2 時 46 分，2011 年の東北大震災で亡くなった人々を追悼して黙祷を捧げた。

44.　解答：A

解説　～ percent faster than ... で「…に比べて～パーセント速く」の意味となるので，A が正解である。

訳例　最近，グリーンランドと南極の両方で，氷床量が史上最低を記録し，15 年前に比べて 31％も急速に氷河が溶け続けている。

45.　解答：D

解説　「働かされている児童」が話題になっている。「働かされている」の意味の後置修飾語句として適切なのは，being put to work であるので，正解は D である。

訳例　20 年ぶりに，労働をさせられている児童の数が増加に転じ，世界的で 1 億 6,000 万人に達した。

VI　下線を引いた単語または語句の中から，文法的もしくは慣用的に不適切なものを選びなさい。

46.　解答：D

解説　(D) の with は against に修正することで，protection against ～「～に対する予防」の意味となる。

訳例　デルタ株は，現在のところパンデミックの中で最も感染力の強いコロナ変異ウイルスであるが，COVID-19 (新型コロナウイルス感染症) ワクチンは依然としてそれに対する最強の予防である。

47. 解答：B

解説 (B) を「水に関する災害」の意味にするためには，water-related としなければならない。

訳例 世界気象機関によると，急速に変化する地球の気候という背景において，過去50年間，水に関する災害が最も多くの人間の命を奪う自然災害となっている。

48. 解答：A

解説 このままでは，Around one in eight nations (8つに1つの国が) を受ける主動詞がない。(A) の spending は spends としなければならない。

訳例 木曜日に発表された国連世界児童基金の最新の報告によると，8つに1つの国が社会保障よりも負債の返済に予算を費やしている。

49. 解答：A

解説 died の次の (A) を，attempting と修正することにより，「〜しようとして命を落とした」の意味になる。

訳例 国際移住機関が本日発表した最新の報告によると，2021年の前半6カ月の間に，少なくとも1,146人が，海路でヨーロッパに渡ろうとして死亡した。

50. 解答：B

解説 (B) の government は，各国の政府を意味する場合は複数形にする必要がある。

訳例 核のない世界の実現に向けた国連の強い決意表明の中で，アントニオ・グテーレス国連事務総長は，各国政府に対し，この目標を現実のものとするよう一層の努力を求めた。

VII-A

『新 わかりやすい国連の活動と世界』から得た知識に基づき，
(A)〜(D) から空欄を埋めるのに最も適切なものを選びなさい。

51. 解答：D

解説 国連憲章前文には「戦争 (war) の惨害から将来の世代を救う」決意がうたわれている。

A. 憎悪　B. 運命　C. 貧困　D. 戦争

52.　解答：B

解説　国連憲章前文はさらに，正義と国際法遵守が維持される（maintained）ことを可能にする（＝維持できる）条件の確立を目指すと述べている。

A. 破壊される　　B. 維持される　　C. 制限される　　D. 解決される

53.　解答：A

解説　国際連合が正式に発足したのは，国連憲章が調印国の過半数によって批准された（ratified）1945年10月24日である。

A. 批准された　　B. 是正された　　C. 調査された　　D. 発明された

54.　解答：C

解説　国際連合の目的には，国際平和と安全（security）の維持が含まれている。

A. 是認　　B. 同意　　C. 安全　　D. 言語

55.　解答：B

解説　国連憲章に示された国際連合の目的は，加盟国にとって共通の（common）目的である。

A. 限られた　　B. 共通の　　C. 個人的な　　D. 暫定的な

訳例　国連憲章は，連合国会議の最終日である1945年6月26日にサンフランシスコで調印された。その前文は，なによりもまず加盟した各国国民の「（51）戦争の惨害から将来の世代を救う」決意をうたっている。同時に，人権ならびに「男女および大小各国の同権」に関する信念を確認するとともに，正義と国際法遵守が（52）維持できる条件を確立し，「より大きな自由の中で社会的進歩と生活水準の向上を促進する」意図を表明している。

国連が正式に発足したのは，国連憲章が安全保障理事会の常任理事国である中華民国（現在は中国），フランス，ソ連（現在はロシア連邦），イギリス，アメリカ合衆国および他の46調印国の半数によって（53）批准された同年10月24日である。

国連の目的は，国連憲章第1条に記されており，その主旨は次の通りである。すなわち，国際平和と（54）安全を維持すること，諸国間の友好関係を発展させること，経済的，社会的，文化的及び人道的問題を解決し，人権および基本的自由の尊重をはかるため国際協力を行うこと，これら（55）共通の目的を達成するにあたり，諸国間の活動の調和をはかるための中心的存在となること，である。

『新 わかりやすい国連の活動と世界』p.43

VII-B 『新 わかりやすい国連の活動と世界』から得た知識に基づき，４つの選択肢から空欄を埋めるのに最も適切なものを選びなさい。

56. 解答：C

解説 アントニオ・グテーレス国連事務総長は 2017 年 9 月 19 日の国連総会演説で世界平和を脅かす 7 つの脅威に言及した。選択肢の中でその 1 つに含まれていたのは，テロリズムである。

A. 医療革命　B. 自由貿易　C. テロリズム　D. 人工知能

『新 わかりやすい国連の活動と世界』p.25 参照

57. 解答：A

解説 国連総会では国連公用語としてアラビア語，中国語，英語，フランス語，ロシア語，スペイン語の 6 つの言語が指定されている。

A. アラビア語　B. オランダ語　C. ドイツ語　D. 日本語

同上 p.45 参照

58. 解答：A

解説 国連の運用資金の主な財源は各加盟国の分担金である。

A. 国連各加盟国　B. 安全保障理事会の加盟国
C. 経済社会理事会の加盟国　D. 世界の主たる巨大企業

同上 p.62 参照

59. 解答：D

解説 国連総会が任命する国連事務総長の任期は 5 年である。

A. 2 年　B. 3 年　C. 4 年　D. 5 年

同上 p.61 参照

60. 解答：C

解説 日本政府は 2016 年に「持続可能な開発目標推進本部」を設置した。

A. 1995 年　B. 2001 年　C. 2016 年　D. 2020 年

同上 p.170 参照

VIII-A

以下の各英文を読み，下記のそれぞれの質問に答えなさい。
下記の英文を挿入するのに最も適した場所を，(A)～(D) から選びなさい。

Passage 1

61. 解答：D

解説 the use of these abhorrent weapons の these weapons を指すものが前にあり，「その防止のための唯一の保証となるものは完全撤廃（their total elimination）である」という目標を受けたひと言が後に続く箇所は，D である。

62. 解答：A

解説 As they increasingly ... に注目すると，「彼ら」が協調よりも戦略的な競争をますます追求する中で（＝追求するにつれて）状況が悪くなっていることを述べている。前後に核保有国の関係悪化が述べられている箇所をさがすことにより，A が正解だとわかる。

63. 解答：C

解説 挿入文はThey should ... という，提言の形となっている。この文が文脈上もっとも入りやすいのはどこかを考える。すると，Those States that possess nuclear weapons must lead. で始まるパラグラフの英文がmustや should で始まり，核保有国がすべきことが列挙されていることがわかる。したがって正解は C となる。

語句 adoption: 採択　commit ～ to ...: ～に…を付託する　catastrophe: 惨禍，大惨事　acute: 深刻な　eliminate ～: ～を取り去る　arsenal: 兵器庫　COVID-19: 新型コロナウイルス感染症　fragility: 脆弱性《ぜいじゃくせい》　multilateralism: 多国間主義（課題に対し多数の国家で取り組むこと）　good-faith dialogue: 誠実な対話　tangible steps: 具体的な（実体的な）方策　commmitment: 公約　undertake ～: ～を約束する　abhorant: 忌まわしい　stand ready to ～: ～する用意がいつでもできている

訳例　1946 年，初の総会決議の採択によって国連に核軍縮という目標が課されてからほぼ 75 年が経ったいまも，私たちの世界は核による惨禍の影の下に生きています。

核兵器保有国間の関係は分断と不信，対話の欠如という様相を呈しています。(A) 核保有国が協調よりも戦略的な競争を追求する中で，核兵器がもたら

す脅威はますます深刻化しています。

今年の国際デーは，この流れを逆転させ，核軍縮へと向かう共通の道へ戻る必要性をあらためて強調しています。

核兵器が使用されれば，すべての国に影響が生じます。つまり，このような殺戮《さつりく》兵器が二度と用いられることなく，各国の兵器庫から完全に取り払われるようにするための責任が，すべての国にあるのです。(B)

COVID-19は，パンデミックに対する準備態勢と不平等の問題から，気候変動，サイバー空間の無法状態に至るまで，広範に及ぶ世界の脆弱性を露呈させました。核兵器の脅威に取り組むための準備態勢も，こうした脆弱性の1つです。私たちは，信頼を基盤とし，核兵器のない世界という共通目標の達成に向けた指針となりうる国際法に基づいた，より強く，より包摂的な，新しい多国間主義を必要としています。

核兵器保有国は，この取り組みの先頭に立たなければなりません。これらの国々は実質的で誠実な対話に戻ることで，信頼と信用を回復し，核のリスクを削減し，核軍縮に向けて具体的なステップを踏まなければなりません。(C) こうした国々は，核戦争ではだれも勝利することはできず，これを決して起こしてはならないという共通の理解も再確認すべきです。そして，自分たちが約束した公約を履行するための措置も講じるべきです。

広島と長崎への原爆投下によって引き起こされた死や苦痛，破壊を繰り返してはなりません。(D) これら忌まわしい兵器の不使用を保証する唯一の道は，その全面的な廃絶以外にないのです。国連はこの共通目標を達成するために，すべての国とともに連携する用意がいつでもできています。

Ⅷ-B

Passage 2

64.　解答：A

解説　hubは車輪の軸の意味であるが，比喩的に何かの中心，中枢の意味がある。ここは文脈から後者の意味であるから，正解はAである。

A. 中心　　B. 工場　　C. 車輪　　D. 機械

65.　解答：D

解説　intensifyは「強める」の意味である。この文脈では，最近の異常気象が，気候変動によって「強められて」いると述べている。したがってここでのintensifiedに最も意味が近いのはDである。

A. 熱せられて　　B. 観察されて

C. 妨げられて　　D. 悪化させられて

66.　解答：B

解説　far-flung は「広範囲に及ぶ」の意味であるから far-flung extremes は「広範囲に及ぶ異常な状況」である。この文脈では，この表現は第 1 パラグラフで述べられた異常気象を指しているので，正解は B である。

A. いくつかの地域での長期的な悪天候

B. さまざまな種類の過酷な自然災害

C. 2 つの出来事の予期せぬ関連性

D. 気候変動の原因に関する過激な意見

67.　解答：B

解説　この文脈では clashes against は冷たい空気が暖かい空気にぶつかるという意味で使われているので，これに最も近い意味である B が正解である。

A. 越える　　B. ぶつかる　　C. 矛盾する　　D. 弱める

68.　解答：C

解説　steer とは，steering wheel（車のハンドル）に見られるように，「舵取りをする」という意味である。この文脈では，ジェット気流が天候の舵取りをする，すなわち天候をコントロールするという意味で用いられているので，正解は C である。

A. 壊す　　B. 予想する　　C. 左右する　　D. 後を追う

69.　解答：D

解説　convoluted は「入り組んだ」「複雑な」の意味で，この場合はジェット気流が入り組んだパターンを呈するといった文脈で使われている。本来は西から東に直線的に吹くものが，次のパラグラフで言及されているように，Ω（オメガ）型の流れ（北にそれて南に下がる）になるという具合である。したがって最も意味の近いものは，D となる。

A. 単純化した　　B. 変化した

C. 不可解な　　D. 曲がりくねった

70. 解答：A

解説 a succession of は「一連の」の意味であり，この文脈でも，猛暑と極寒の天候が一連の流れの中で入れ替わる様子を表現している。したがって正解は A である。

A. 一連の　B. 小さな断片の　C. 多量の　D. 一事例としての

語句 devastating: 破壊的な　ruthless: 情け容赦のない　paralyze ～: ～を麻痺《まひ》させる　far-flung: 広範囲に及ぶ　be touched by ～: ～に影響を受ける　take on ～:（形など）を帯びる　omega-shaped curves:（ギリシャ語の）オメガ（Ω）型をしたカーブ　penetrate: 貫通する，広がる　latitude: 緯度

訳例　ドイツとベルギーでは大洪水が町を破壊した。アメリカ西部やカナダには猛烈な熱波が襲いかかった。1,000 万人が住む中国の産業の（64）中心地は豪雨により麻痺状態に陥った。これら最近の気象現象は，気候の変化により，（65）激化している。

しかし，このような（66）広範に及ぶ極端な気象現象の原因は，地球の気温が上昇していることだけにとどまらない。これらの現象はすべて，地表を吹き抜ける強く細い帯状の偏西風であるジェット気流の影響を受けている。ジェット気流は，両極域の冷たい空気が熱帯域の暖かい空気と（67）ぶつかり合うことで発生し，嵐や雨，干ばつといった現象を引き起こす。

ウッドウェル気候研究センターのシニアサイエンティストであるジェニファー・フランシス氏は，「ジェット気流は天候そのもの，つまりジェット気流は天候を作り出し，その（68）舵取りをするものです。ジェット気流はときどき，非常に（69）複雑なパターンになります。ジェット気流が大きく北に進路を変えたあと大きく南へと蛇行する形になるときは，異常気象が起こると予測することができます」と語る。

気象学者は，これらの揺れや落ち込みが波のように見えるオメガ型のカーブを形成するたびに心配する。そうなると，暖かい空気はさらに北上し，冷たい空気はさらに南下する。その結果，同じ緯度に沿って（70）一連の猛暑と極寒の天候が現れる。このような状況では，風も弱まり，数時間や 1 日ではなく，数日から数週間も危険な天候が同じ場所にとどまり，長雨や熱波が発生することがある。

IX

以下の英文を読み，下記のそれぞれの質問に答えなさい。

【長文問題の解答対策】

長文を読む際は，まずトピックは何か，誰が何のために書いているか（スピ

ーチスクリプトの場合は誰がどのような場で話しているのか）を想像する。その上で，各パラグラフの中心的な内容や主張を頭の中で整理しながら読み進める。つまり，「このパラグラフではこういうことを言っているのだな」とそのパラグラフのポイントを一言で要約（あるいは頭の中でイメージ）しながら読むのである。そうすることで，パラグラフからパラグラフへのつながりや，英文の論理展開を大局的に捉え，筆者（話者）の言いたいことのポイントを迅速に捉えることが可能になる。その際，難解な語彙や表現があっても，「何を言っているのだろう？」と自問しながら，想像力を働かせて理解しようとする姿勢が重要である。

今回の英文は，第1パラグラフでweが2回使われており，COVID-19などのキーワードがあることから，コロナウイルスのワクチンに関する何らかの業務に携わる人の文章（ないしはスピーチのトランスクリプト）だと想像できる。

71. 解答：B

解説 第1パラグラフは，COVAXファシリティーを通じ，懸案であったワクチンの配布を開始したことが中心的な内容である。このプロジェクトが始まったばかりだということを理解すると，A, C, Dは不適切だとわかる。正解はBである。

第1パラグラフで述べられているのは次のどれか。

A. COVID-19ワクチンの開発はパンデミックの勢いを弱めた。

B. COVAXファシリティーはついにCOVID-19ワクチンの配布をはじめた。

C. COVID-19ワクチンはアフリカとアジアの全ての地域に到着した。

D. ガーナとコートジボワールはCOVID-19ワクチンの追加の提供を歓迎した。

72. 解答：C

解説 3行目からの“The only way out of this pandemic is ...”の一文がこのパラグラフで筆者が最も言いたいことである。正解はCである。

第2パラグラフで述べられているのは次のどれか。

A. プロジェクトは世界中からのボランティアたちにより実現した。

B. 援助要請をできるだけ多くの国に求める必要がある。
C. 現在の危機打開唯一の解決策は世界規模のワクチン接種だ。
D. 豊かでない国々の人々はより人種問題に苦しむ傾向にある。

73. 解答：D

解説 第3パラグラフからわかるのは，話者がUNICEFの代表的立場の人物であり，ユニセフはCOVAXファシリティーを通じてワクチンを世界各国に送る（ship through the COVAX facilities）という協力関係にあるということである。したがって正解はDである。

第3パラグラフから言えることは次のどれか。
A. COVAXファシリティーは世界中の人々へのワクチン接種のために医師を派遣している。
B. COVAXファシリティーはユニセフに，より多くのワクチンを届けるよう促した。
C. ユニセフはおよそ190の国と地域にワクチンを送った。
D. ユニセフはワクチンを届けるに当たりCOVAXファシリティーと協力している。

74. 解答：A

解説 話者は，SII社の迅速な対応に感謝の意を述べている。インド政府にも謝意を示しているがC, Dにあるような内容にまでは言及していない。したがって正解はAである。

第4パラグラフで述べられているのは次のどれか。
A. SII社はAMC諸国にCOVID-19ワクチンを届ける支援をしている。
B. SII社はCOVID-19ワクチン配布において予定より遅れている。
C. インド政府はユニセフに対して資金援助を申し出た。
D. インド政府は将来ユニセフと共同プロジェクトの計画がある。

75. 解答：B

解説 下から3行目に“we are delivering COVID-19 vaccines consolidated with syringes and routine vaccines insuring children are also protected" とあるから，B が正解となる。A, C は本文と矛盾があり，D は本文に言及されていない。

第5パラグラフで述べられているのは次のどれか。
A. ユニセフにとってトラックと列車が主な輸送手段である。
B. ユニセフは COVID-19 ワクチン配送に子ども用ワクチンも含めた。
C. 3つのアフリカ諸国が1カ月以内にワクチンを受け取るだろう。
D. アフリカでは子どもたちが最初に COVID-19 ワクチンを受け取る。

76. 解答：C

解説 A, B, D については第7パラグラフで言及されている。冷蔵庫については，3行目に "we have delivered and installed thousands of new fridges" とあるが，修理の援助をしたとは述べていないので，C が正解である。

第6パラグラフで述べられていないのは次のどれか。
A. ユニセフは各国がワクチン接種計画を立てる支援をしてきた。
B. ユニセフは各国がワクチンを受け取り貯蔵する準備ができているかを調べた。
C. ユニセフは各国が自国の冷蔵庫を修理するための援助をした。
D. ユニセフはワクチンを適切に貯蔵できるよう冷蔵庫を提供した。

77. 解答：B

解説 3行目以降に "Over the next couple of weeks, we will be talking a lot about how this pandemic has impacted the lives of children, ..." また "we will be issuing estimates of the number of children who ..." と述べているから，正解は B である。

第7パラグラフで述べられているのは次のどれか。
A. 世界の子どもたちや家族の生活は通常に戻りつつある。
B. パンデミックの子どもたちへの影響について報告される予定だ。
C. 調査を受けた子どもの 90%が対面の授業に出席できていなかった。
D. 世界中の子どもたちはパンデミックのために学校に行くことを恐れている。

78. 解答：A

解説 ワクチンの到着は子どもたちに希望を与え，教育，健康，保護サービスを子どもが得られるようになると述べていることから，Aが正解となる。Bの「到着後まもなく」，Cの「仕事に復帰できる」，Dの「大人の生活の質」については本文と矛盾しているか言及がない。

第8パラグラフで述べられているのは次のどれか。

A. ワクチンは子どもたちによりよい健康的な生活を与えるだろう。

B. ワクチン到着後まもなくパンデミックは収束するであろう。

C. 子どもたちの健康が改善すれば，以前のように大人は仕事に復帰できる。

D. 長期的に見れば，大人の生活の質が子どものそれにつながる。

79. 解答：C

解説 このパラグラフでは，話者は一貫して，パンデミックから1年も経たないうちにいかに世界が協力して偉業を成し遂げてきたかを述べている。2行目からの“There are no miracles in public health, but if there were, this would be one.”という一言が話者の主張を凝縮している。したがって正解はCとなる。

第9パラグラフで述べられているのは次のどれか。

A. 私たちは奇跡に頼るのではなく協働することを学ぶべきだ。

B. 世界がパンデミックへの対応に向けた行動をとるのに1年以上かかった。

C. 世界の科学者や人道主義者は不可能と思われることを成し遂げた。

D. COVID-19ワクチンはまず豊かでない国々に配布されるだろう。

80. 解答：D

解説 このパラグラフで話者は，パンデミックに対する世界のあらゆる機関と関係者の協力が，歴史的な協働作業により大きな業績を残したことを述べている。A, B, Cは「世界のあらゆる機関と関係者」を包括する表現となっていない。したがってこのパラグラフの主張を最も適切に要約しているのはDとなる。

第 10 パラグラフの主張を最も適切に要約しているのは次のどれか。

A. 民間部門と公的機関の協働が世界で最も困難な問題解決の鍵だ。

B. 将来の世界的問題に対処するには，国連と世界の国々が協力すべきだ。

C. 世界の指導者たちは，必ず，協働の脅威に対して協力して立ち向かい続けるだろう。

D. パンデミックに対するこの歴史的戦いは，世界が公共の利益のために協力できることの証である。

語句 COVID-19: 新型コロナウイルス感染症　make good on one's promise: 約束を守る　off and running: 開始して　dose:（投薬の）1 回分　COVAX Facility (COVID-19 Vaccine Global Access Facility): COVID-19 ワクチンを複数国で協働購入し，公平に分配する国際的な枠組み　Ivory Coast: コートジボワール共和国　speak to ～:（人の心）に訴える　be committed to ～: ～に尽力している　batch: 一回分　AMC (Advance Marketing Commitment): 途上国へのワクチン調達のための事前買取制度　freight forwarder: 貨物輸送事業者　turnround time: 往復所要時間　DRC: Democratic Republic of Congo（コンゴ民主共和国）　consolidated with ～: ～と同時に荷積みされた　cold chain: 生産・輸送・消費の過程で医薬品などを低温に保つ物流システム　map out ～: ～を計画する　roll out: 開始する　rally to ～: ～するために集まる　procurement: 調達

訳例

1. 昨年は世界中の家族にとって暗い 1 年でしたが，COVID-19 ワクチンの急速な開発は，トンネルの終わりに希望の光をもたらしました。そしてついに，COVAX ファシリティーは，その光をすべての人に届けるという約束を果たすために動き出しました。そして，私たちは走り出したのです。ワクチンは西アフリカとアジアに到着し，今後数日，数週間のうちにさらに多くの国々にも届く予定です。ガーナとコートジボワールでは，アフリカ初の COVAX ワクチン接種が行われ，昨日，両国で感動的なセレモニーが行われました。
2. しかし，月曜日に行われたことは，私たち人間の良心に訴える単に心温まるお話ではなく，私たち人間の最善の利益のために必要な第一歩なのです。このパンデミックから抜け出す唯一の方法は，世界中でワクチン接種ができるようにすること，そして，裕福ではない国の人々が，人を守るための競争から取り残されないようにすることなのです。
3. ユニセフでは，これを実現するために尽力しています。先週到着した重要な意味を持つワクチンは，ユニセフが COVAX ファシリティーを通じて出

荷するワクチンの最初の出荷分にすぎず，この歴史的な取り組みでは，約20億回分のCOVID-19ワクチンを約190の国と地域に届ける予定です。現在までに110万人分以上のワクチンをお届けしており，今週中にはさらに20カ国以上で数十万人分ものワクチンをお届けする予定です。

4. AMC各国へのワクチン配送をいち早く支援し，記録的な速さでワクチンの梱包と配送を24時間体制で行っているインドのセラム社（SII）と，多大な支援をいただいているインド政府に感謝します。私たちの前には，たくさんの仕事が待っています。

5. 配送に関しても，ユニセフは航空会社やその他のパートナーと緊密に連携し，COVAXワクチンをできるだけ早く届けるための革新的な解決策を探っています。私たちはすでに，多大なパートナーシップを得ています。ガーナとコートジボワールへの出荷を記録的な速さで支援してくれた貨物輸送事業者とエミレーツ航空に感謝したいと思います。きょうは，コンゴ民主共和国，アンゴラ，ナイジェリアを含む5つの国への発送があり，COVID-19ワクチンと注射器，そして子どもたちを守るための定期接種ワクチンを，他の20カ国と同様，今週お届けします。

6. また，私たちは，各国政府による国家予防接種計画の策定や，ワクチンの到着に向けた準備も支援してきました。パートナーとともに，既存の低温物流装置と保管能力に関する計画を作成しました。そしてこの1年，医療施設でワクチンを適温に保つための新しい冷蔵庫を何千台も納入・設置しました。例えばガーナでは，昨年5月以来，2,500台の冷蔵庫を納品しました。しかし，まだ多くの課題が残っています。

7. こうした一歩一歩の積み重ねにより，私たちは，世界中で影響を受けている何十億人もの子どもたちや家族が元通りの生活を取り戻す瞬間に近づいているのです。そして，これこそが私たちユニセフの取り組みの焦点なのです。今後数週間，私たちはこのパンデミックが子どもたちの生活にどのような影響を及ぼしてきたかについて多くを語る予定ですが，本日後半には，この1年間ほとんど授業に出席できなかった子どもたちの数の推定値を発表する予定です。

8. ですから，ワクチンが各国に届くということは，子どもたちにとって希望につながるということを認識する必要があります。パンデミックによって，教育，保健，保護サービスを子どもたちが得られる機会が大きく損なわれています。ワクチン接種が開始されれば，パンデミックを抑制し，よりよい，より安全で健康的な未来をすべての人々のために築く作業を開始することができます

9. 最後に，私たちはいま，どのような状況にあるのか，少し考えてみたいと思います。1年足らずの間に起こったことは，まさに驚異的としか言いようがありません。公衆衛生に奇跡はありませんが，もしあるとすれば，こ

れはその1つでしょう。COVID-19の蔓延を防ぐために，世界の
が封鎖，閉鎖，社会的距離を置き始めてから，まだ12カ月も経っ
のです。その間に，世界の科学者が結集して，ウイルスを治療する
ワクチンを特定し，臨床試験をし，大量生産するという不可能を可
ただけでなく，世界の人道主義者が結集して，ワクチンの調達と配布
始したのです。そして，裕福な国だけでなく，世界で最も経済的に貧しい国々にもワクチンは届いていますし，これからも届き続けることでしょう。

10. これらは驚くべき努力であり，民間企業，国連機関，開発援助機関，各国政府，資金援助者，その他のパートナーなど，私たち全員が力を合わせれば，間違いなくさらに前進を続け，世界が力を合わせれば何ができるかを証明するものとして，後世の世代まで語り継がれるでしょう。まさにいまが，歴史が作られている瞬間なのです。

X

以下の質問に対して，80～100語の短いエッセーを英語で書きなさい。

質問：ソーシャルメディアの悪影響の1つは何か？　どうしたら解決できるか？

（語数を記入する必要はありません）

【Essay writing 問題の解答対策】

英語で意見文を書く力を高めるには，まずさまざまな問題について自分の考えや意見を持つことが重要である。その上で，それを日本語ではなく英語で行うことに慣れるために，日頃から英文を読み，トピックに特有の重要表現を学び，要約したり意見を書いたりするといった，インプットからアウトプットへの一連のプロセスを英語で行うとよい。自分の考えを直接英語にする練習として，英文日記を書いたり，思ったことを英語でひとり言としてつぶやいたりする練習に加え，解答例に示すような意見文のモデルを多数読み，意見を述べるために必要な定型表現や，Introduction-Body-Conclusion といった基本的論理構成を学ぶとよい。

解答例 In the past decade, the number of social media users has increased exponentially. However, this growth comes with a host of problems, with online mob harassment being one of the most serious.

Online mob harassment is when many online users attack an individual who they think has done something wrong. Often, they do this by sending hateful messages or even death threats. This type of harassment has even led to some individuals committing suicide.

Although this problem cannot be easily solved, social media companies can lessen the impact of these online mobs by introducing text filters to block hateful messages or comments. (102 words)

構成 ① Introduction: 質問に対する回答を明確に述べる。ここでは，次のようになっている。

- ここ 10 年で SNS の利用者は急激に増えてきた。
- しかし問題も多く，特にオンライン上の集団の嫌がらせは深刻だ。

② Body: 短めのエッセイ課題の場合できるだけ簡潔に論を展開する必要がある。ここでは，次のようになっている。

- オンライン上の集団の嫌がらせとは群衆（mob）が 1 人を攻撃することだ。
- 多くの場合，憎しみに満ちたメッセージや殺害予告を送りつけてくる。
- これにより何人かが自殺に追い込まれる事件が起きた。

③ Conclusion: この問題をどう解決すべきかについての意見を述べ，締めくくっている。具体的には次のようになっている。

- 簡単には解決できないが，SNS 関連企業は，フィルター機能を導入して嫌悪に満ちたメッセージなどを遮断することで，炎上に加担する人々の影響を抑えることができるだろう。

2021年B級第2回試験　正解一覧

Ⅰ

1. B　2. A　3. D　4. C　5. B　6. C　7. A　8. D　9. B　10. C

Ⅱ

11. D　12. B　13. D　14. B　15. A　16. C　17. A　18. C　19. B　20. D

Ⅲ

21. C　22. A　23. B　24. A　25. D　26. A　27. B　28. C　29. B　30. B

Ⅳ

31. C　32. D　33. A　34. D　35. C　36. A　37. A　38. C　39. D　40. B

Ⅴ

41. D　42. C　43. B　44. A　45. D

Ⅵ

46. D　47. B　48. A　49. A　50. B

Ⅶ-A

51. D　52. B　53. A　54. C　55. B

Ⅶ-B

56. C　57. A　58. A　59. D　60. C

Ⅷ-A

61. D　62. A　63. C

Ⅷ-B

64. A　65. D　66. B　67. B　68. C　69. D　70. A

Ⅸ

71. B　72. C　73. D　74. A　75. B　76. C　77. B　78. A　79. C　80. D

2022年

第1回試験

問題

B級試験問題用紙

B級

外務省後援

２０２２年度第１回国際連合公用語

英語検定試験（120分）

受験上の注意

1．問題用紙は試験開始の合図があるまで開いてはいけません。その間に、この**受験上の注意を熟読しておいてください。**

2．**受験番号と氏名を２枚の解答用紙（マークシートと作文用紙）**に記入してください。

3．解答用紙の配布は１人１部のみです。複数の配布は致しません。

4．試験開始前は、答案への解答記入は禁止です。

5．マークシートの記入は、１～100までの記入箇所がありますが、この級では１～80までを使います。

6．マークシートの記入は、必ずＨＢ以上の濃い鉛筆を使って該当箇所を黒く塗りつぶしてください。書き間違いの場合は「アト」が残らないように消してください。マークシートは絶対に折ったり曲げたりしないでください。

7．受験級、受験地区、会場番号、受験番号のマークシートへの記入は監督者の指示に従い、間違いなく記入してください。**（裏表紙の「マークシート記入例」参照）**

8．作文は、⑴ 読みやすい文字をペン、ボールペンまたはＨＢ以上の濃い鉛筆で書いてください。
⑵ 使用語数の80～100語を目安にしてください。

9．試験問題についての質問は、印刷が不鮮明な場合を除き、一切受けつけません。

10．中途退室の際は、マークシートと作文用紙を持って監督者に渡し、他の受験者の迷惑にならないように静かに退室してください。中途退室後の再入室はできません。

11．試験中は他の受験者の妨げとなる行動は慎んでください。また携帯電話等の電源はお切りください。

12．マークシートと作文用紙は監督者に提出し、問題用紙はご自由にお持ち帰りください。

リスニングテストについて

1．リスニングテストは試験開始後、合図があってから実施されます。（40問あります）

2．リスニングテストが始まる前にリスニング問題の指示と内容を読んで、どういう形式のテストなのか、概要をつかんでおいてください。

3．テスト中の発言は、放送機器の具合が悪く放送された英語の聴き取りができない場合を除いて、しないようにしてください。

試験結果について

1．試験の結果は2022年6月29日㈬頃に受験申込書に記載された住所に郵送で通知します。

2．その間に住所変更をされた方は、郵便局へ住所変更の届け出を忘れずに行ってください。

3．発表前の試験結果のお問合せには応じられません。

UNA-JAPAN
公益財団法人 日本国際連合協会
http://www.unaj.or.jp/

I. Directions : You will hear 10 statements or questions. For each statement or question, choose the most appropriate response and mark your answer on your answer sheet.

1. A. How much is it? B. Unfortunately not.
C. May I take your order? D. That's impressive.

2. A. Yes, I have it. B. It's half past ten.
C. In five minutes. D. Not right now.

3. A. Like what? B. It'll never work.
C. Don't remind me. D. How many people?

4. A. There you are. B. Who's that?
C. Here you go. D. What time?

5. A. Well, not really. B. I think so.
C. Yes, it's here. D. Not at all.

6. A. Will do! B. That's no fun.
C. Oh, it was nothing. D. It really depends.

7. A. How beautiful! B. Yeah, why not?
C. No, that's everything. D. Where was that?

8. A. At least it's over. B. Anything else?
C. The sooner the better. D. Did you make copies?

9. A. Suit yourself. B. You're probably right.
C. What about me? D. Is there a problem?

10. A. I appreciate it.
B. Let's give it a try.
C. Good point.
D. I beg your pardon.

II. Directions : You will hear 10 short conversations. Choose the best answer for each follow-up question and mark your answer on your answer sheet.

11. A. Her store is too small.
B. Her store's rent is too high.
C. She doesn't have enough time.
D. She can't compete with large companies.

12. A. Change her son's mind
B. Pay for her son's tuition
C. Find a college close to home
D. Help her child graduate high school

13. A. Start playing a new sport
B. Watch some Olympic events
C. Follow the artistic swimming event
D. Spend more time with his daughter

14. A. He thinks it's a waste of money.
B. He thinks it isn't possible for him.
C. He thinks it's bad for the environment.
D. He thinks too many people are going to space.

15. A. His cost of living is too high.
B. The roof of his house was destroyed.
C. He has to wait a long time to get a new car.
D. The car parts he wanted are out of stock.

16. A. He thinks he isn't paid enough.
B. He feels the woman disrespected his art.
C. He thinks the woman asks too many questions.
D. He feels the woman doesn't value him or his time.

17. A. The lessons are in person.
B. The class is held once a week.
C. Online lessons are not popular with students.
D. Class attendance is 20% of the student's grade.

18. A. A reporter B. A politician
C. A police officer D. A store manager

19. A. At a cafeteria B. At a daycare
C. At the dentist's office D. At the therapist's office

20. A. Husband and wife B. Director and actor
C. Parent and teacher D. Boss and employee

Ⅲ. Directions : You will hear five conversations. After each conversation, you will hear two follow-up questions. Choose the best answer for each question, and mark your answer on your answer sheet.

[Conversation 1]

21. A. She loves her job. B. She will get fired.
C. She needs the money. D. She has an important deadline.

22. A. Take over her work. B. Talk with the manager.
C. Pay for her living expenses. D. Help her meet the deadline.

[Conversation 2]

23. A. Middle Eastern conflicts B. Health outcomes in Asia
C. A declining population D. Global prosperity

24. A. Poverty rates B. Number of deaths from wars
C. Life expectancy D. Infant mortality rates

[Conversation 3]

25. A. A homeless person B. A new hire
C. Their best friend D. Their old boss

26. A. Tyler has an apartment. B. Tyler is saving up money.
C. Tyler worked for two months. D. Tyler never takes out the trash.

[Conversation 4]

27. A. An administrative assistant B. A café barista
C. A supermarket cashier D. A business owner

28. A. He thinks it's fun. B. He thinks it's easy.
C. He thinks it's hard. D. He thinks it's boring.

[Conversation 5]

29. A. His daughter wants a smartphone.
B. His daughter is addicted to her phone.
C. His daughter always forgets her passwords.
D. His daughter is talking with strangers online.

30. A. She thinks they use too many apps.
B. She thinks they're not cynical enough.
C. She thinks they're very good at technology.
D. She thinks they don't go outside enough.

Ⅳ. Directions : You will hear two short talks. After each talk, you will hear five follow-up questions. Choose the best answer for each question, and mark your answer on your answer sheet.

[Talk 1]

31. A. A chef B. A tour guide
C. A student D. A restaurant owner

32. A. In the kitchen of a house B. In the kitchen of a school
C. In the kitchen of a company D. In the kitchen of a restaurant

33. A. Storage space B. Student housing
C. Staff housing D. Office space

34. A. A type of food B. A type of currency
C. A type of table D. A type of metal

35. A. Hot water B. Charcoal
C. Electricity D. Woodsmoke

[Talk 2]

36. A. A nurse B. A medical doctor
C. A researcher D. A former patient

37. A. To share her experience
B. To advertise a new drug
C. To advocate for cheaper treatments
D. To protest unequal access to healthcare

38. A. Losing her ability to walk
B. Finding a high school nearby
C. Being rejected from a clinical trial
D. Going bankrupt from medical bills

39. A. Psychotherapy　B. Stem cell transplant
C. Organ transplant　D. Chemotherapy

40. A. Money　B. Family
C. Hope　D. Courage

V. Choose from among the four alternatives the one that best completes each of the following sentences.

41. Japanese billionaire Yusaku Maezawa returned to Earth on Monday, (　　　　) on the International Space Station.
A. days after spending 12　B. 12 days after spending
C. after spending 12 days　D. spending 12 days after

42. The Omicron variant, which is dominating the surge around the world, accounts for (　　　　) reported daily.
A. almost all new cases　B. all new almost cases
C. cases all new almost　D. new all cases almost

43. The United Nations offices in the Pacific are closely monitoring the situation in Tonga and are (　　　　) support if requested.
A. to standby on provide　B. standby to provide on
C. provide on to standby　D. on standby to provide

44. Natural gas prices have risen to seasonal record highs as global gas demand is expanding and supply is (　　　　).
A. to not keep able up　B. not able to keep up
C. able not up to keep　D. up not to keep able

45. The UN expert reiterated the urgent need for the Security Council to (　　　　) the Myanmar military and significantly increase financial pressure on the junta.
A. an embargo on arms impose　B. impose an arms embargo on
C. arms on an embargo impose　D. embargo an impose on arms

VI. Choose from among the underlined words or phrases the one that is grammatically or idiomatically incorrect.

46. (A) With more children and young people spending time online, cyberbullying is the top concern for their safety (B) when use the internet, (C) according to a survey conducted (D) by the International Telecommunication Union.

47. The Philippines on Friday said it (A) would start (B) accepting fully (C) vaccinating tourists from Feb. 10, as the country (D) seeks to accelerate economic recovery from the pandemic.

48. The Olympic Truce is intended to secure safe passage (A) for athletes (B) during the Games and, (C) in the long term, promote the idea of working (D) from world peace.

49. People's sense of (A) safe and secure is at a low in almost (B) every country, with (C) six in seven worldwide plagued by feelings of insecurity, according to new (D) data and analysis by the UN Development Programme (UNDP).

50. The World Health Organization (WHO) estimates (A) at least one billion people globally have a near or distance (B) vision impairment that (C) could have prevented, or has (D) yet to be addressed.

VII. Choose the best answer from the choices marked (A), (B), (C), and (D) to fill in the blanks based on the knowledge gained from *New Today's Guide to the United Nations*.

Membership in the United Nations is open to all peace-loving countries that accept —and in the judgement of the Organization are able and willing to carry out—the obligations of the Charter. Any country wishing to become a Member must submit an application to the Security Council, including a **(51)** ________ that it accepts the obligations set forth in the Charter. If the Council recommends admission of the new Member, the application is passed to the General Assembly, which must accept it by a two-thirds **(52)** ________. Membership becomes effective on the date the Assembly accepts the application.

United Nations staff members speak some 170 languages. To **(53)** ________ a Babel of tongues in the Organization, a handful of languages have been designated as "official" or "working" languages. The General Assembly uses six official languages —

Arabic, Chinese, English, French, Russian and Spanish—into which its speeches and documents are translated. The languages which the Secretariat uses in its daily work are English and **(54)** ________, and staff members may use either one in written communications. Professional staff are strongly encouraged to be **(55)** ________ in at least two official languages.

51. A. conclusion B. declaration
C. submission D. translation

52. A. election B. number
C. population D. majority

53. A. avoid B. defend
C. build D. master

54. A. Chinese B. French
C. Russian D. Spanish

55. A. aware B. certain
C. proficient D. useful

Choose the most appropriate of the four alternatives according to your knowledge and the information gained from *New Today's Guide to the United Nations*.

56. The name "United Nations" was suggested by
A. Trygve Lie, the first UN Secretary-General
B. Eric Drummond, the first League of Nations Secretary-General
C. John, D. Rockefeller, a renowned U.S. industrialist
D. Franklin D. Roosevelt, former U.S. President

57. United Nations Day is celebrated on 24 October to commemorate
A. the founding of the League of Nations
B. the adoption of the United Nations flag
C. the entry into force of the U.N. Charter
D. the completion of the U.N. headquarters in New York

58. The General Assembly appoints the Secretary-General on the recommendation of

A. the Security Council

B. the Trusteeship Council

C. the Secretariat

D. the International Court of Justice

59. In the selection of 15 judges for the International Court of Justice,

A. none of them should be re-elected

B. no two judges can be nationals of the same State

C. some of them can assume other positions in the U.N.

D. more than half of them must be from English-speaking countries

60. The "Act on Cooperation with UN Peacekeeping Operations and Other Operations" was established in

A. 1945　　B. 1956　　C. 1984　　D. 1992

Ⅷ. Read each of the following passages and answer the questions that follow.

[Passage 1: Questions 61 to 63]

(A) The recently issued Second World Ocean Assessment confirmed that many of the benefits that the global ocean provides to humankind are being undermined by our own actions.

Our seas are choking with plastic waste, which can be found from the remotest atolls to the deepest ocean trenches. Overfishing is causing an annual loss of almost $90 billion in net benefits—which also heightens the vulnerability of women, who are vital to the survival of small-scale fishing businesses. **(B)**

The theme of this year's observance, "The Ocean: Life and Livelihoods," underscores the importance of oceans for the cultural life and economic survival of communities around the world. **(C)** More than three billion people rely on the ocean for their livelihoods, the vast majority in developing countries.

(D) This will be critical to achieving the Sustainable Development Goals, keeping within reach the 1.5-degree target of the Paris Agreement, and ensuring the health of our oceans for today's and future generations.

61. Choose the best place from among (A), (B), (C), and (D) where the following sentence can be inserted:

As we strive to recover from COVID-19, let's end our war on nature.

62. Choose the best place from among (A), (B), (C), and (D) where the following sentence can be inserted:

This year's observance of World Oceans Day falls as the world wrestles with the COVID-19 pandemic, a climate crisis and humankind's continuing assault on oceans, seas and marine resources.

63. Choose the best place from among (A), (B), (C), and (D) where the following sentence can be inserted:

Carbon emissions are driving ocean warming and acidification, destroying biodiversity and causing sea level rise that threatens heavily inhabited coastlines.

[Passage 2: Questions 64 to 70]

The World Health Organization and the International Labour Organization have called for **(64)** measures to be put in place to protect workers' health while teleworking.

A new technical brief to healthy and safe teleworking, published by the two UN agencies, outlines the health benefits and risks of teleworking and the changes needed to **(65)** accommodate the shift towards different forms of remote work arrangements brought on by the COVID-19 pandemic and the digital transformation of work.

Among the benefits, the report says, there can be improved work-life balance, opportunities for flexible working hours and physical activity, reduced traffic, and time spent commuting and a decrease in air pollution—all of which can improve physical and mental health and **(66)** social well-being. Teleworking can also lead to higher productivity and lower operational costs for many companies.

However, the report warns that without proper planning and organization and without health and safety support, the impact of teleworking on the physical and mental health and social well-being of workers can be **(67)** significant. It can lead to isolation, **(68)** burnout, depression, home violence, musculoskeletal and other injuries, eye strain, increase in smoking and alcohol consumption, prolonged sitting and screen time and unhealthy weight gain.

The report outlines the roles that governments, employers, workers and health services at workplaces should play in promoting and protecting health and safety while teleworking.

"The pandemic has led to a **(69)** surge of teleworking, effectively changing the nature of work **(70)** practically overnight for many workers," said Dr Maria Neira, Director, Department of Environment, Climate Change and Health, World Health Organization.

64. In this context, the word "measures" is closest in meaning to

A. actions B. needs
C. scales D. funds

65. In this context, the word "accommodate" is closest in meaning to

A. inform B. prevent
C. support D. verify

66. In this context, the phrase "social well-being" is closest in meaning to

A. respectable social status
B. meaningful human relationships
C. psychologically healthy conditions
D. ability to communicate effectively

67. In this context, the word "significant" is closest in meaning to

A. interesting B. valuable
C. meaningful D. serious

68. In this context, the word "burnout" is closest in meaning to

A. electrical device failure B. physical or mental exhaustion
C. personal bankruptcy D. acute heart attack

69. In this context, the word "surge" is closest in meaning to

A. sudden increase B. emotional reaction
C. continuing popularity D. different variety

70. In this context, the word "practically" is closest in meaning to

A. effortlessly B. reasonably
C. almost D. however

IX. Read the following passage and answer the questions that follow.

([1] ~ [10] indicate paragraph numbers.)

[1] Twenty-five years ago, world leaders from 189 countries signed the Beijing Declaration and launched the Platform for Action, a bold roadmap for women's equal participation in every facet of society and life.

[2] Today, as we observe International Women's Day, no single country is on track to achieve the Sustainable Development Goal of gender equality by 2030. Despite hard-won gains over last quarter century, we are still 100 years from closing the gender gap. For girls and women today, that is as good as never.

[3] To be sure, there has been progress: girls' enrolment rates have doubled in the past 25 years. The global gap between the number of girls and boys in school has narrowed to near or full parity, and in some places, girls now outnumber boys in some levels of education. UNESCO estimates that since 2000 the number of girls not getting any education has dropped substantially from 205 million to 129 million.

[4] But 129 million is an appallingly large number of girls who are being denied their fundamental right to a quality education and to the future that learning unlocks. Moreover, the challenge to girls' education does not stop when girls get into the classroom. They are up against entrenched social, economic and cultural barriers that mean that for 6 out of 10 girls in low-income countries, primary schooling is the end of their educational road, and barely 1 in 10 will graduate from high school. The odds are worse for the most marginalized: refugees, girls living with disabilities and girls from poor families and rural areas.

[5] Just as appalling is that millions of girls who are in school are not learning the skills they need. In some countries, as few as 2 in 10 girls can read and understand a simple story by the time they finish primary school. Even when girls do go all the way to higher education, they are grossly under-represented in science, technology, engineering and mathematics, the very fields that are shaping the economies and societies of the future. This is a sheer waste of talent and potential.

[6] Clearly, we need a profoundly new approach. But this will happen only when leaders and their citizens recognize—and dismantle—power inequities in their societies that uphold the status quo.

[7] Progress in education is proof that this is possible. When countries make and follow through on concrete commitments to change, they can accelerate the velocity of gender equality progress. About 85% of the developing countries the Global Partnership for Education works with included gender equality in their long-term education plans. That means they are doing more to lower the common barriers to girls' education: by enrolling and retaining girls, making sure they get good quality learning materials, reducing sexual harassment and violence in and around school, installing proper menstrual hygiene facilities and boosting the number of female teachers who can motivate and relate to girls.

8 These approaches work. Ethiopia, for example, has made girls' education a priority in recent years. The result: more girls are going to, staying in and improving their performance in school, and the wide gap between the number of girls and boys who completed primary school has all but disappeared. Kenya has also invested intensively in girl-friendly interventions — especially in more remote areas — and as a result, girls' grade 1 enrolment has increased, and they are outperforming boys in math. Likewise, Nepal's efforts have, among other indicators, increased girls' enrolment in and completion of school in Nepal, even exceeding boys'.

9 The Beijing Platform for Action recognized that equal access to education is vital if more women are to become agents of change. That's why we and the organizations we represent are joining the Generation Equality campaign, which is mobilizing people of all ages and genders to reinvigorate the aspirations articulated in Beijing 25 years ago.

10 An equal generation is an educated generation. We must play our part to ensure that all girls and women everywhere have the knowledge and skills they need to lead the charge and break down the barriers to gender equality for good.

71. Which of the following is mentioned in Paragraph 1?

A. World leaders form 189 countries established an organization in Beijing.
B. The Platform of Action had a legal power to control participating countries.
C. The Beijing Declaration's expectations were too high to achieve.
D. A quarter century has passed since the Beijing Declaration was ratified.

72. Which of the following is mentioned in Paragraph 2?

A. No single country has done anything to promote gender equality.
B. The rate of progress in achieving gender equality is too slow.
C. It will take another century for people to start working on gender equality.
D. Today is the best chance for girls and women to close the gender gap.

73. Which of the following is mentioned in Paragraph 3?

A. The number of girls who have jobs has doubled during the last 25 years.
B. Most of the schools in the world have now become co-educational.
C. Globally the ratio gap of girls and boys in school has mostly been closed.
D. 205 million girls in the world are still not getting any education.

74. Which of the following is mentioned in Paragraph 4?

A. Providing a quality education to girls continues to be a big challenge.

B. The number one priority now is to get girls into the classroom.

C. Six out of ten girls in the world are studying in low-income countries.

D. Refugee girls suffer the most in receiving high school education.

75. Which of the following is mentioned in Paragraph 5?

A. Millions of girls fail to learn vocational skills in elementary school.

B. In some countries, 20 percent of girls are not taught how to read and write.

C. In higher education, large gender gaps exist in fields of study.

D. Girls are wasting their talent by not choosing to study science in college.

76. Which of the following can be inferred from Paragraph 6?

A. The author is content with the current approach to ensure gender equality.

B. The author believes that eliminating power inequities in society is the key.

C. The author is certain that being aware of gender inequalities will solve the problem.

D. The author hopes that power inequities among nations will be resolved soon.

77. Which of the following is mentioned in Paragraph 7?

A. Concrete commitments to change enable faster progress in gender equality.

B. About 85% of the world's developing countries are members of the Global Partnership for Education.

C. The Global Partnership for Education offers long-term education plans to developing countries.

D. Providing good quality learning materials motivates students to learn.

78. Which of the following is mentioned in Paragraph 8?

A. Ethiopia succeeded in eliminating the gender gap in academic grades.

B. Kenya focused on math education for girls in primary school.

C. Nepal managed to increase the number of girls who enter and finish school.

D. Ethiopia, Kenya, and Nepal received subsidies for their gender equality projects.

79. Which of the following can be inferred from Paragraph 9?

A. The Beijing Platform for Action is the conceptual foundation of the Generation Equality campaign.

B. The Beijing Platform for Action states that women are more capable of ensuring social change.

C. The Generation Equality campaign is a short-term event that celebrates the 25th anniversary of the Beijing Declaration and Platform of Action.

D. The Generation Equality campaign has been active around the world for the past 25 years.

80. Which of the following best summarizes the message of Paragraph 10?

A. We must be more aware that gender equality leads to creating more female world leaders.

B. We must remember that an educated generation can solve the problem of gender inequality.

C. We must help girls and women in the world to engage in activities that promote world peace.

D. We must take action to ensure gender equality and build an educated generation.

X. Write a short essay of around 80-100 words in English to answer the following question:

What is one social problem Japan faces and how can it be solved?

(You do not need to write down the number of words.)

マークシート記入例

東京の本会場でB級を受験する、国連 太郎さん、受験番号が「東京01-30001」、生年月日が「1980年10月24日」の場合の記入例です。

【受験番号/氏名】
それぞれ受験票の記載通りに記入してください。

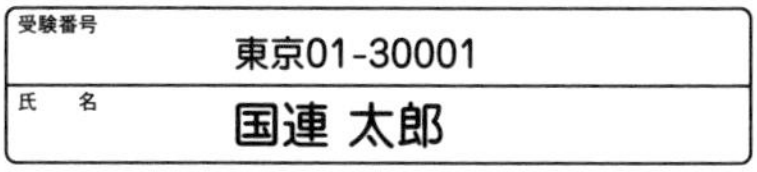

【受験地区】
下段の都道府県部分を塗りつぶしてください。

【会場番号】
都道府県部分に続く2桁の数字を塗りつぶしてください。

【受験番号】
ハイフン（−）以降の5桁の数字を塗りつぶしてください。

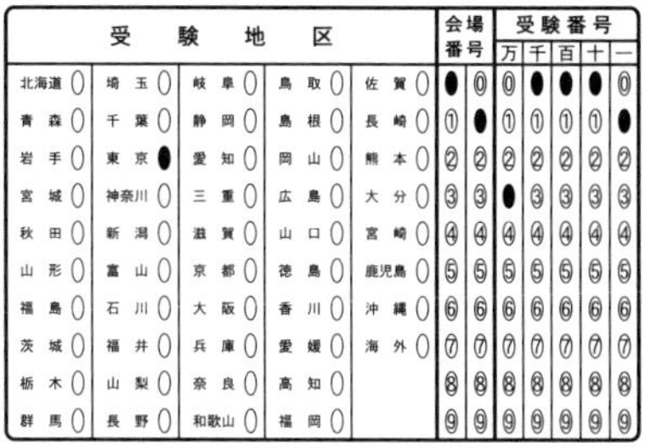

【受験級】
「B」と記入し、下段のB級部分を塗りつぶしてください。

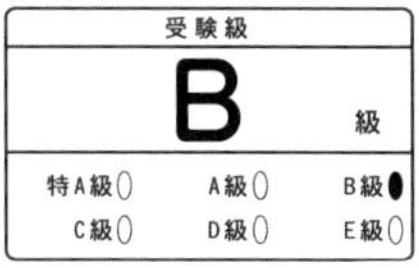

【生年月日】
4桁の西暦・月・日を塗りつぶしてください。
10未満の月・日の十の位は、「0」を塗りつぶしてください。

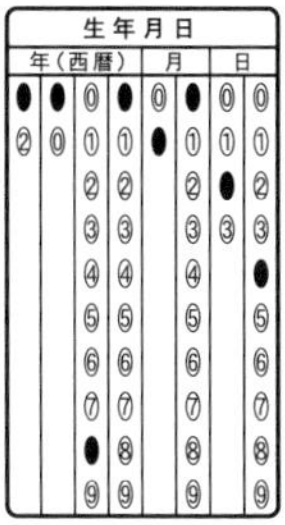

※HB以上の鉛筆を用いてマークをしてください。

※他の地区から会場を変更して受験する場合でも、受験票に記載されている受験地区・会場番号をマークしてください。

2022年
第1回試験

解答・解説

2022年　国連英検B級第1回試験
解答・解説

I　疑問文を含む英文が10題読まれます。
それぞれの英文に対して，最も適切な対応文を選びなさい。

1.　解答：B

解説　客が飲食店で尋ねている状況が推測されるので，Bの “Unfortunately not. (あいにくございません) が最も適切。

ナレーション　Do you have any vegetarian burgers?
「ベジタリアンバーガーありますか」

A. いくらですか。　B. あいにくございません。
C. ご注文よろしいですか。　D. それは感動的です。

2.　解答：B

解説　Do you have the time? は What time is it? の意味なのでBが適切。ちなみに，Do you have time? だと「いま時間ありますか」の意味である。

ナレーション　Excuse me. Do you have the time?
「すみません。時間教えてもらえますか」

A. はい，持っています。　B. 10時半です。
C. 5分後です。　D. いますぐではありません。

3.　解答：C

解説　面接がうまくいったかどうかを聞いている。過去のことを聞いているので，Bは不適切である。CのDon’t remind me.は「(いやなことを) 思い出させないで」の意味なのでこれが適切である。

ナレーション　How did the interview go?
「面接はどうだった？」

A. 例えば？　B. それは絶対うまくいかないよ。
C. 思い出させないで。　D. 何人？

4. 解答：D

解説 cover for ～ は，仕事などの場面で「～の代理をする」という意味。シフト制で交代するような仕事などの場合，仕事仲間（アルバイト仲間）の間でこうした会話が交わされることが多い。選択肢の中で最も適切なのは，D である。

ナレーション Can you cover for me tomorrow?

「あした私の代わりやってもらえる？」

A. ここにいたんだね。　B. 誰ですか。

C. はいどうぞ。　D. 何時（のシフト）？

5. 解答：D

解説 Would you mind ～ing? は相手に何かをして欲しいときに使う表現だが，英語では「～するのを気にしますか」（「～してもらうのはご迷惑ですか」）という聞き方をする。したがって，日本語で「はい」と言うべきところを，英語では「全く気にしません」（「全く迷惑などではありません」）となるので正解は D である。

ナレーション Would you mind giving me a hand with these boxes?

「この箱を運ぶのを手伝ってもらえますか」

A. いや，そうでもないです。　B. はい，そう思います。

C. はい，ここにあります。　D. もちろん。

6. 解答：C

解説 相手のお礼に対する応答なので C（大したことないです＝とんでもないです）が正解である。A の Will do! は，Have a good day! などと言われて，I will. の代わりに言う表現である。

ナレーション I really can't thank you enough.

「本当に何てお礼を言ってよいか」

A. そうします！　B. それはつまらない。

C. とんでもない。　D. それは場合による。

7. 解答：B

解説 I was thinking we could ～ は少し控えめに相手を誘う表現で，「もしかしたら～できるかなと思っていたんだけれど」という程度のニュアンスである。How about going on a road trip this weekend? と同じ意味である。したがって，誘いに OK する意味の応答である B. Yeah! Why not? (なぜしないの？　しようよ) が正解となる。

ナレーション I was thinking we could go on a road trip this weekend.
「今週末ドライブに行くのはどうかなぁと思っていたんだけど」
A. なんて綺麗なんだ！　B. うん，そうしよう。
C. いえ，それで全部です。　D. それはどこだった？

8.　解答：A

解説 相手ががっかりして落ち込んでいるので，それに対する勇気づけの応答として，A (少なくとも終わったんだから) が正解となる。

ナレーション That presentation did not go well.
「あのプレゼンはうまく行かなかった」
A. 少なくとも終わったんだから。　B. 他には何か？
C. 早いほどよい。　D. コピーとった？

9.　解答：D

解説 大学生が教授に助言を求めているので，応答として適切なのは，「どうしたのかな？」の意味の D が正解である。

ナレーション Professor, I'd like your advice on something.
「先生。ご助言をいただきたいことがあるのですが」
A. 好きにしなさい。　B. 確かに君の言う通りだ。
C. 私はどうなるのかな？　D. どうしたのかな？

10.　解答：A

解説 ASAP は as soon as possible の略。何らかの依頼を受けた人が「確認して連絡します」と言っているのだから，応答として適切なのは，Thank you. の意味の A である。

ナレーション I'll check on that and get back to you ASAP.
「すぐに調べて折り返し連絡します」
A. ありがとう。　B. やってみよう。
C. たしかにその通り。　D. 何て言ったのですか。

II

10題の対話文が読まれます。
その後に読まれるそれぞれの質問に対して最も適切な答えを選びなさい。

11. 解答：D

解説 女性は，自分の店のパートの従業員を確保できず，その理由として大手企業が出しているほどの給料が払えないと話しているので，正解はDとなる。

A. 店が小さすぎる。　B. 店の賃貸料が高すぎる。
C. 十分な時間がない。　D. 大手企業に勝てない。

ナレーション

Woman: It's so hard to find part-time employees these days.
Man: Well, maybe you'd have better luck if you offered them a higher wage.
Woman: I'm already doing the best I can but my tiny store can't compete with the wages offered by these big companies.
Question　What is the woman's problem?

(女)：最近はパートの人を探すの大変なのよ。
(男)：給料を上げれば少し状況はよくなるかもしれないよ。
(女)：努力はしているんだけど私の小さな店では大手の給料にはかなわないのよ。
質問　女性は何に困っているのですか。

12. 解答：A

解説 We're trying to talk him out of it.（そうしないように説得しようとしている）とあるのでAが正解である。

A. 息子の考えを変える　B. 息子の学費を払う
C. 家の近くの大学を探す　D. 子どもが高校を卒業できるよう助ける

ナレーション

Man: What will John be doing after high school?
Woman: He said he's going to join the military. We're trying to talk him out of it but no luck whatsoever. My husband even said we'll pay for all of his college tuition.
Man: Well, look on the bright side. At least he's clear on what he wants to do.

Question　What is the woman trying to do?

(男)：高校卒業後ジョン君はどうするんだい？

(女)：軍隊に入隊するって言ったのよ。私たちはやめるように説得しているんだけど言うことをきかないの。夫は大学なら学費は全部出すとまで言ったのだけど。

(男)：まあ，よい面もあるんじゃないかな。少なくともジョン君はやりたいことがはっきりしているんだから。

質問　女性はどうしようとしているのですか。

13.　解答：B

解説　女性は，自分の娘が初めはスポーツに興味がなかったのに，オリンピックを見て興味を持ったことを述べ，You never know. Maybe you can find ... (わからないわよ，あなただって……) と言っていることから，B が正解となる。

A. 新しいスポーツを始めること

B. オリンピックの競技を見ること

C. アーティスティックスイミングの競技を見ること

D. 自分の娘ともっと時間を過ごすこと

ナレーション

Woman: Have you been following the Olympic Games? Our family has been watching the highlights every day. My daughter is obsessed with artistic swimming now.

Man: Oh, I'm not a big sports fan.

Woman: Oh, neither was my daughter. She never used to watch sports but I guess there's just something about artistic swimming that really spoke to her. You never know. Maybe you can find your favorite Olympic event too.

Question　What does the woman suggest the man do?

(女)：オリンピック見てる？　うちの家族はハイライト番組を毎日見ているわ。娘はアーティスティックスイミングに夢中なの。

(男)：僕はあまりスポーツに興味ないからな。

(女)：あら，娘もそうだったわ。以前はスポーツ番組なんか見なかったのに，なぜかアーティスティックスイミングは本当に興味を持ったみたい。わからないわよ。あなたもお気に入りのスポーツを見つけるかも。

質問　女性は男性に何を勧めているのですか。

14.　解答：B

解説 Definitely not in our lifetimes. (僕たちの生きているうちは絶対無理) と男性は言っているので，B が正解である。

A. お金の無駄だ。　B. 生きているうちは不可能だ。

C. 環境に悪い。　D. あまりにも大勢が宇宙に行くだろう。

ナレーション

Woman: I wonder how long it would take for regular people like us to be able to travel to space.

Man: Definitely not in our lifetimes.

Woman: Unless we somehow manage to become billionaires.

Question　Which of the following best describes how the man feels about space travel?

(女)：私たちのような一般人が宇宙に行けるのはいつかしら。

(男)：僕たちの生きている間には実現しないだろうね。

(女)：私たちが億万長者か何かになれば別かもしれないけれどね。

質問　宇宙旅行についての男性の気持ちを最もよく表しているのはどれでしょうか。

15.　解答：C

解説 男性が言及していたのは，新車を買いに行った際ディーラーに来年まで納車ができないと言われたことだから，C が正解となる。through the roof は比喩表現で，数値などが「飛び抜けて高い」を意味する。

A. 生活費がかかりすぎる。

B. 家の屋根が壊れた。

C. 新車が届くまで長く待たなければならない。

D. 必要な自動車の部品が品切れである。

ナレーション

Woman: My living expenses are through the roof right now because of inflation.

Man: And we also have the supply chain crisis. It's so hard to get anything nowadays. I recently went to a car dealership to buy a new car and they said they won't get new shipments until next year!

Woman: I wonder how long this global crisis is going to continue.

Question Why is the man upset?

(女)：インフレのおかげで生活費は上がりっぱなしよ。

(男)：サプライチェーンの危機だね。いまでは何を手に入れるのも難しい状況だよ。最近車を買いにディーラーに行ったけど，来年まで新車の納車ができないんだって。

(女)：いつまでこの世界的危機が続くのかしら。

質問 なぜ男性は腹を立てているのでしょうか。

16. 解答：D

解説 Your being late shows that you don't respect me. や I've already let you waste enough of it (= my time). とあることから正解は D である。

A. 給料が安い。

B. 自分の芸術作品を女性が侮辱したと感じている。

C. 女性がしつこく質問をし過ぎている。

D. 自分や自分の時間を女性が尊重していないと感じている。

ナレーション

Man: That's the third time you're late this week!

Woman: I'm sorry. It won't happen again, I promise.

Man: Your being late shows that you don't respect me. Do that again and we are done with these lessons. I have a life outside of you and I've already let you waste enough of it.

Question Why is the man so angry?

(男)：今週遅刻 3 回目ですよ。

(女)：すみません。二度とないようにします。

(男)：遅刻というのは私に対する尊敬の気持ちが欠如しているということです。もし今度遅刻したら，レッスンは中止にします。あなたを教える以外に私にはやることがたくさんあるのに，既にもう相当な時間をムダにしたのですから。

質問　なぜ男性は怒っているのでしょうか。

17.　解答：C

解説　Most of the kids in my class don't even attend anymore. とあり，女性（母親）が，I know how much you hate your online classes but ... とあることから，C が正解となる。B への言及はなく，D は会話の中で言われている 30%と矛盾する。

A. 授業は対面である。

B. 授業は一週間に一度ある。

C. オンライン授業は学生たちに不評である。

D. 授業への出席は成績の 20%を占める。

ナレーション

Woman: Get out of bed honey or you'll be late for class.

Boy: What's the point? The class is recorded anyway. I'll just watch it later. Most of the kids in my class don't even attend anymore.

Woman: Honey, I know how much you hate your online classes but you still need to be there, even if it's virtually. Attendance is 30% of your grade.

Question　Which of the following statements is true based on this conversation?

(女)：　起きないと授業に遅れるわよ。

(少年)：なんで？　授業は録画だよ。あとで見るよ。クラスのほとんどの人がもう出席なんかしてないよ。

(女)：　ねえ，オンライン授業が嫌なのはわかるけど，たとえバーチャルでの参加であってもきちんと出席しないとだめでしょ。出席は成績の 30%を占めているし。

質問　この会話に基づいて正しいのはどれですか。

18.　解答：A

解説　男性が「ニュースを見ない方が精神衛生上よい」と述べたのに対して，女性が，I sometimes feel stressed covering these stories. と述べていることから，A が正解である。

A. レポーター　B. 政治家　C. 警察官　D. 店の経営者

ナレーション

Woman: Did you hear about the huge protests that happened over the weekend?

Man: No. I rarely watch the news these days. It's all so negative and divisive. I feel my mental health is much better when I don't focus on what's happening in the world.

Woman: That's a fair point. I sometimes feel stressed covering these stories but it's a necessary part of my job.

Question　What most likely is the woman's job?

(女)：週末に起こった抗議運動のこと聞いた？

(男)：いいや。最近ニュース見ないからなぁ。ニュースときたらあまりにもネガティブで分断をあおるものばかりだし。世界の出来事を知らない方が精神衛生上いいよ。

(女)：確かにそうね。こういう話をニュースにするのはときどきストレスを感じるわ。でもこれも仕事のうちなのよ。

質問　女性の仕事はおそらく何でしょうか。

19.　解答：C

解説　男性が，「歯のクリーニングは最後にいつしてもらったか」と聞いたり，「多くの働く母親が同じことを言っている」と述べたりしていることから，Cだとわかる。

A. カフェテリア　B. 託児所　C. 歯科医院　D. 心療内科

ナレーション

Man: When was the last time you had your teeth cleaned?

Woman: To be honest, I don't remember. I've been so busy with work and taking care of my family. I haven't had time to take care of myself. I probably wouldn't have made an appointment if the pain wasn't so bad.

Man: Yes, I often hear that from other busy working mothers like yourself.

Question　Where does this conversation most likely take place?

(男)：最後に歯のクリーニングをしてもらったのはいつですか。

(女)：正直覚えていません。仕事や家事で忙しくて。自分のことをする時間がずっとなかったんです。歯の痛みがなかったら予約は入れなかったかもしれません。

(男)：そうですね。あなたのように忙しく働く母親は皆そう言いますね。

質問　この会話が交わされているのはおそらくどこでしょうか。

20. 解答：A

解説　男性がアナの父親であり，「家に帰ったら2人に埋め合わせをする」と女性に言っていることから，アナは2人の娘であり，2人は夫婦だと推測するのが最も妥当なので，Aが正解である。

A. 夫婦　B. 監督と役者　C. 親と先生　D. 上司と社員

ナレーション

Man: Hey, I don't think I'll be able to make it in time for Anna's school play.

Woman: Oh don't give me that. You know how much this means to her. She's been telling her friends all month that her famous movie producer dad will be there!

Man: I know. But something just came up at the office and I'm the only one who can deal with it. I promise I'll make it up to both of you when I get home.

Question　What most likely is the relationship between the man and the woman?

(男)：ねえ。アナの学校の演劇会に間に合いそうにないんだけど。

(女)：えーっ，やめてちょうだい。どれだけ彼女にとって大切なものか知っているでしょ。アナはずっと，友達に，有名な映画プロデューサーの父親が来るって言っていたのよ！

(男)：わかってる。でも会社で問題が起こって，私しかそれに対応できる人間はいないんだ。君とアナには帰って来てから埋め合わせするよ。

質問　男性と女性の関係はおそらく何でしょうか。

III

5つの対話文が読まれます。各対話文の後で，それに対する質問が2つ読まれます。各質問に最も適切な答えを選びなさい。

Conversation 1

21. 解答：C

解説 男性が「具合の悪いときには出勤すべきではない」と言っているのに対し，女性はI know. But ... と，働けなくなったら経済的に困るという趣旨の発言をしていることから，正解はCとなる。

A. 仕事が好きだから。　B. 仕事を失うから。

C. 給料が必要だから。　D. 重要な締め切りがあるから。

22. 解答：C

解説 男性が，“I'll personally pay for your rent and help you take care of your daughter.” と述べていることから，Cが正解となる。

A. 彼女の仕事を引き継ぐ。　B. 上司と話す。

C. 彼女の生活費を支払う。　D. 締め切りに間に合うよう助ける。

ナレーション

Man: Hey, are you okay? You look super pale and you've been coughing the entire morning.

Woman: To be honest, I think I'm coming down with something.

Man: You know we're not supposed to come to work these days if you're not feeling well.

Woman: I know. But what if one of the managers tells me not to come to work for two weeks? You know I can barely afford to pay my rent and care for my daughter right now.

Man: If that happens, I'll personally pay for your rent and help you take care of your daughter, okay? You have my word. The important thing right now is that you get yourself to the doctor's office.

Questions 21. Why does the woman want to come to work?

22. What does the man promise to do for the woman?

(男)：ねえ大丈夫かい？　顔が真っ青だし午前中ずっと咳してたよ。

(女)：実は，風邪か何かにかかったみたいなの。

(男)：最近は具合が悪いときは出社しないということになっているよ。
(女)：わかっているの。でも２週間休めって言われたらどうなると思う？
いま家賃も子どもの養育費も出すのがやっとなのよ。
(男)：もしそんなことになったら，私が個人的に君の家賃と養育費を払うから。約束するよ。いま大事なのは，医者に行くことだよ。
質問　21. なぜ女性は出勤したいのですか。
22. 男性は女性に何をすると約束していますか。

Conversation 2

23.　解答：D

解説　女性がまず話題提供者として，現代がunprecedented peace and prosperity（過去に例を見ない平和と繁栄）の時代だと述べたのに対し，男性が反論し，女性がそれに対してさらに反論している。女性の主張もアジアや世界全体についての言及であるところから，Dが正解である。
A. 中東の紛争　　B. アジアの健康達成度
C. 人口減少　　D. 世界の繁栄

24.　解答：D

解説　統計数値が言及されているのは，話の順に，平均寿命，貧困率，紛争による死亡者数，である。したがって言及されていないのはDとなる。
A. 貧困率　　B. 戦争による死者数　　C. 平均寿命　　D. 幼児死亡率

ナレーション

Woman: I know it's hard to believe but we are actually living in a period of unprecedented peace and prosperity.
Man: That's definitely not what I'm seeing when I put on the TV or read the newspaper.
Woman: I'm just stating the facts. For example, life expectancy for people living in Asia was just 41 years in 1950 but in the 21st century, it's now 72 years. In 1990, 36% of the world's population lived in extreme poverty. Now it's less than 10%.
Man: Yeah, but what about the wars and conflicts? It feels like countries are fighting and bombing each other every month.

Woman: But if you take a bird's-eye view of the past 500 years, the number of deaths from battles and other conflicts has also decreased.

Questions 23. What is the main topic of this conversation?

24. Which statistic does the woman NOT mention?

(女)：信じ難いでしょうけど，私たちはこれまでにないほどの平和と繁栄の時代を生きているのよ。

(男)：テレビを見たり新聞を読んだりする限り，そうは絶対に見えないね。

(女)：私は事実を言っているだけよ。例えば，1950年にはアジアに住む人の平均寿命は41才だったけど，21世紀のいまは72才よ。1990年に極貧生活をしていた人は世界人口の36%だったわ。でもいまは10%未満よ。

(男)：そうか。でも戦争や紛争はどうなんだい？　毎月のようにいろいろな国が互いに戦ったり爆弾を落としたりしているように感じるんだけど。

(女)：でも，過去500年を眺めてみると，戦闘などの紛争による死者数も減っているのよ。

質問　23. この会話の主な話題は何ですか。

24. 女性が言及していない統計数値は何ですか。

Conversation 3

25.　解答：B

解説　女性が最初に "the new employee in the admin (= administration) office" に会ったことがあるかを男性に聞いており，その後2人はこの人物のことを話しているので，Bが正解。

A. ホームレスの人　　B. 新入社員

C. 自分たちの親友　　D. 以前の上司

26.　解答：B

解説　タイラー氏について，会話からは，働き始めて3カ月であること，以前はホームレスだったがいまはホームレスのためのシェルターに暮らしていること，アパートを借りるためにお金を貯めている最中であること，がわかる。したがって選択肢の中で正しいのはBとなる。
A. タイラーはアパートを所有している。
B. タイラーはお金を貯めている。
C. タイラーは2カ月働いた。
D. タイラーはゴミ出しをしない。

ナレーション

Woman: Have you met the new employee in the admin office? He's such a hard worker and has a great attitude. Where did the company find someone like him?

Man: You mean Tyler? Oh yeah, he's amazing. You won't believe this but he told me that he's living in a homeless shelter right now. Just three months ago, he said he was wandering the streets and going through the trash to look for food.

Woman: What?! No way. Wow, I would have never guessed that from just looking at him!

Man: Right? He said this job is helping him get back on his feet. He's trying to save up enough money to rent an apartment.

Woman: Wow, good for him! It's nice to hear these sorts of stories.

Questions 25. Who are the man and woman talking about?
26. Which of the following statements is true based on this conversation?

(女)：管理センターの新人に会ったことある？　彼ってとても働き者で，勤務態度もいいのよ。会社はどこで彼のような人を見つけたのかしら？

(男)：タイラーのこと？　そうそう，彼はすごくいいね。信じられないかもしれないけど，彼はいまホームレス・シェルターで暮らしているそうなんだ。つい3カ月前までは，街をさまよい，ゴミ箱をあさって食べ物を探していたんだって。

(女)：えっ！　まさか。うわぁ，彼を見ただけじゃ，そんなこと想像もつかなかったわ。

(男)：でしょ？　この仕事で立ち直れると言ってたよ。アパートを借りられるだけのお金を貯めようとしているんだ。

(女)：わあ，よかったわね。こうい話を聞けるのはうれしいね。

質問　25. 男性と女性は誰のことを話しているのですか。

26. この会話の内容として正しいのはどれですか。

Conversation 4

27. 解答：D

解説 会話から，女性はアイスクリームサンドイッチの個人事業を始めたばかりだとわかるので，D が正解となる。

A. 管理アシスタント　B. カフェのバリスタ

C. スーパーのレジ係　D. 事業経営者

28. 解答：C

解説 男性は女性の話を聞いて，個人経営が楽な仕事ではなく "grueling job"（厳しい，ハードな仕事）だと述べているので C が正解。

A. 楽しいと思っている。　B. 簡単だと思っている。

C. 難しいと思っている。　D. 退屈だと思っている。

ナレーション

Man: It's been a while since we've all gotten together.

Woman: I know. I've been so busy with the new business I barely go out these days.

Man: Yeah, I remember you said you were starting your own ice cream sandwich business. How's that going?

Woman: Super stressful and busy. In the beginning, it was just me and my sister. We make everything at home from scratch and deliver to local cafés and supermarkets every morning. But we just hired a new employee last week to manage the administrative side, so hopefully, I'll finally be able to take weekends off.

Man: I've always assumed that being your own boss means your schedule would be much more flexible but after hearing from you, it sounds like a grueling job.

Questions　27. What is the woman's job?

28. What does the man think about the woman's job?

(男)：2人で会うのは久しぶりだね。

(女)：そうね新しいビジネスで忙しくて，私も最近はほとんど外に出ていないのよ。

(男)：そうだ，そういえば，アイスクリームサンドイッチの商売を始めるって言ってたね。うまくいってる？

(女)：ストレスだらけで忙しいわ。最初は私と妹だけだったのよ。家で一から全部作って，毎朝地元のカフェやスーパーマーケットに配達したりする感じで。でも，先週，管理部門を担当する新しい従業員を雇ったばかりなので，ようやく週末は休みが取れるようになるのよ。

(男)：個人ビジネスって，もっとフレキシブルにスケジュールが組めるものだと思っていたけど，話を聞くと，相当ハードな仕事のようだね。

質問　27. 女性の職業は何ですか。

28. 女性の仕事について男性はどう思っていますか。

Conversation 5

29.　解答：A

解説　男性の発言から，自分の娘がスマートフォンを欲しがっているが不安もあることがうかがえるので，A が正解である。

A. 娘がスマートフォンを欲しがっている。

B. 娘がスマートフォン中毒になっている。

C. 娘がいつもパスワードを忘れてしまう。

D. 娘がオンラインで見知らぬ人と話している。

30.　解答：C

解説　女性が，"Kids these days are much better at technology than we are." と述べているところから，C が正解である。

A. アプリの使い過ぎだと思っている。

B. 物事を疑うところがあまりないと思っている。

C. テクノロジーに長けていると思っている。

D. あまり外出しないと思っている。

ナレーション

Man: My teenage daughter is asking me for a smartphone because all of her friends have one.

Woman: I wouldn't do it if I were you. Having a smartphone is extremely harmful for teens. Those social media sites will destroy her confidence and self-esteem. And you also risk the possibility of her meeting strangers online.

Man: But if I know all her passwords and monitor what she sees on her phone, it won't be a problem, right?

Woman: Do you really think you can control everything she does on her phone? Kids these days are much better at technology than we are. They can use certain functions in the apps to hide what they don't want us to see.

Man: Wow, they can do that?

Questions 29. Why is the man worried?

30. What does the woman think of the younger generation?

(男)：10代の娘が，友達がみんなスマートフォンを持っているからと言って，スマートフォンを欲しがっているんだよ。

(女)：私だったら買わないわ。スマートフォンを持つことは，10代の子どもにとってはとても有害よ。ソーシャルメディアサイトはお嬢さんの自信や自尊心を壊したりするのよ。それに，お嬢さんがネット上で見知らぬ人に会う可能性もあるわ。

(男)：でも，僕が彼女のパスワードを全部知っていて，彼女がスマホで何を見るか監視していれば，問題ないだろ？

(女)：お嬢さんが携帯ですることを全部管理できると本当に思ってるの？最近の子どもたちは，私たちよりもずっとテクノロジーに長けているわ。アプリの特定の機能を使って，私たちに見せたくないものを隠すことができるのよ。

(男)：へえ，そんなことができるんだ？

質問 29. なぜ男性は悩んでいるのですか。

30. 若者たちについて女性はどう思っていますか。

IV （初めに）2つの短いナレーションが読まれ，そのナレーションの後にそれぞれ5つの質問文が読まれます。最も適切な答えを選びなさい。

Talk 1

31. 解答：B

解説 話の流れから，話し手は，ある人の家（屋敷）を案内しているところだとわかるのでBが正解である。

A. シェフ　B. ツアーガイド　C. 学生　D. レストランのオーナー

32. 解答：A

解説 話し手とツアー客は，Mr. Gearという個人の家のkitchen（厨房）にいることが想像できるのでAが正解である。

A. 家の厨房　B. 学校の厨房

C. 会社の厨房　D. レストランの厨房

33. 解答：C

解説 "Right above the kitchen was the housing for ..."（厨房の真上には…がある）の…の部分に入るのは「ここで働く男性や女性」であるので，Cが正解である。

A. 貯蔵庫　B. 学生宿舎　C. 従業員宿舎　D. 事務所

34. 解答：D

解説 聞き慣れない単語だが，"Monel is a nickel-copper alloy." と説明があるので，Dが正解である。

A. 一種の食べ物　B. 一種の通貨

C. 一種のテーブル　D. 一種の金属

35. 解答：A

解説 テーブルの下のパイプについて "hot water running through the pipes" と説明があるのでAが正解である。

A. 熱いお湯　B. 炭　C. 電気　D. たきぎの煙

ナレーション

Now, I'm going to take you to the kitchen. Here we are at the entrance of the kitchen. Right above the kitchen was the housing for the women and men who worked here. The women lived on the second floor and the men lived on the third floor.

This here is the pantry area. It's where the staff would prepare the food to bring into the dining room.

This is a warming table. The surface of this table is made of monel. Monel is a nickel-copper alloy. It looks like stainless steel but it is much more durable and highly resistant to water damage. Of course, it is also much more expensive but since Mr. Gear only wanted the best, and he also had all the money in the world, his architect, Ms. Julies, chose monel as the surface for this table.

There are copper pipes underneath this warming table and in the past, they would have hot water running through the pipes to warm the plates so that when the staff was plating everything, all the food would stay nice and hot.

Questions 31. Who most likely is the speaker?
32. Where is the speaker speaking?
33. What is located above the kitchen?
34. What is monel?
35. What kept the table warm?

語句 pantry: 食料貯蔵室，ホテルなどの配膳室（ここでは後者の意味で使われている） alloy: 合金　durable: 耐久性のある　all the money in the world: 有り余るほどのお金

訳例　では次に厨房をご紹介します。ここは厨房の入り口です。厨房の真上には，ここで働く女性・男性従業員の住居がありました。女性は２階，男性は３階に住んでいました。

こちらは配膳室です。食堂に運ぶ食材を準備する場所です。

これは保温テーブルです。このテーブルの表面はモネルでできています。モネルはニッケルと銅の合金です。見た目はステンレスに似ていますが，耐久性に優れ，水による影響にも強いのが特徴です。もちろん，モネルの方がはるかに高価ですが，ギア氏は最高のものを求めていましたし，あり余るほどのお金を持っていましたので，担当建築家のジュリエス氏はこのテーブルの表面にモネルを選びました。

このウォーミングテーブルの下には銅のパイプがあり，昔はこのパイプにお湯を流してお皿を温めていたので，スタッフがすべての料理を運んでいるとき

も，すべての料理がおいしく温かいままだったのです。

質問　31. 話しているのはおそらく誰でしょうか。

32. 話し手はどこで話しているのでしょうか。

33. 厨房の上には何がありますか。

34. モネルとは何ですか。

35. テーブルを暖かくしていたのは何ですか。

Talk 2

36.　解答：D

解説　話の概要から，話者は難病を患い，臨床試験での治療の結果，健康を取り戻したということがわかるので，D が正解である。

A. 看護士　　B. 医師　　C. 研究者　　D. 元患者

37.　解答：A

解説　話の冒頭に健康の大切さを述べているが，全体としては個人の体験を聞いてもらい，あとは聴衆にそこから何かを学んでもらうというスタンスであるので，話の目的としては，A が正解となる。

A. 自分の体験を共有すること

B. 新薬の宣伝をすること

C. より安価な治療を提唱すること

D. 医療ケアの不平等に抗議すること

38.　解答：A

解説　話し手は，multiple sclerosis という病気とそれによる身体機能の低下，特に歩く能力と手で物をつかむ能力を失ったと述べているので，正解は A である。

A. 歩けなくなること

B. 近くの高校を見つけること

C. 臨床試験を受けることを拒否されること

D. 医療費がかさみ破産すること

39.　解答：B

解説　治療として，注射や投薬について言及されているが，話し手を快方に導いたのは「幹細胞移植」の治験である。D の chemotherapy（化学療法）にも注射は含まれるが主としてがん治療の文脈で使われる。したがって正解は B となる。

A. 心理療法　　B. 幹細胞移植　　C. 臓器移植　　D. 化学療法

40. 解答：C

解説 話し手は，話の最後で，hope for the future が人間にとって最も大切だと述べているので，C が正解である。

A. お金　　B. 家族　　C. 希望　　D. 勇気

ナレーション

A person with health has a million dreams. A person without it only has one-- to become healthy again.

When I was 15, I was diagnosed with multiple sclerosis or MS. Over the course of two years, I was gradually losing my ability to walk and grab things with my hands. I suffered from major fatigue so I couldn't even get out of bed. I ended up leaving high school in the middle of the year and had to be homeschooled. In addition to all that, I had all these side effects from the injections and drugs I was taking to stop the MS.

Back then, I felt like I had no future. Fortunately, my mom found out about Dr. Kurt's research on using stem cell therapy to treat MS patients and I was lucky enough to be able to participate in the clinical trial. After getting the stem cell transplant, my life changed completely. I was able to go back to school. I didn't need a wheelchair to get around. Before, all I could focus on was this disease. But now, I feel like I have my body and life back. I have also gained back the most important thing a person could have– hope for the future.

Questions 36. Who most likely is the speaker?

37. What is the purpose of the talk?

38. According to the talk, which of the following did the speaker have to deal with?

39. Which treatment is mentioned in the talk?

40. What does the speaker say is the most important thing for a person to have?

語句 be diagnosed with ～: ～と診断される　multiple sclerosis: 多発性硬化症　end up ～ ing: 結局～することになる　be homeschooled: 家で教育を受ける　side effects: 副作用（ワクチン接種による影響の場合には「副反応」という日本語が使われている）　clinical trial: 臨床試験　stem cell transplant: 幹細胞移植

訳例　健康な人には100万の夢がある。健康でない人が持つ夢はただ1つ，「健康になること」です。

15歳のとき，私は多発性硬化症（MS）と診断されました。2年以上かけて，私は徐々に歩く能力と手で物をつかむ能力を失っていきました。私は極度の疲労のためベッドから出ることさえできませんでした。結局，高校は途中で退学し，家で学ばねばなりませんでした。さらに，MSの進行を止めるための注射や飲んでいた薬による副作用もありました。

当時は，自分には未来がないように感じていました。幸いなことに，母が幹細胞療法によるMS患者の治療に関するカート博士の研究について知り，私は幸運にも臨床試験に参加することができました。幹細胞移植を受けた後，私の人生は完全に変わりました。学校に戻れるようになったのです。移動に車椅子を必要としなくなったのです。以前は，この病気のことばかり考えていました。でもいまは，自分の身体と人生を取り戻したような気がします。そして，人が持つ最も大切なもの，未来への希望も取り戻しました。

質問　36. 発言者は誰ですか？
37. 講演の目的は何ですか？
38. 講演によると，講演者は次のどれに直面したのでしょうか。
39. 講演では，どのような治療法について言及されていますか。
40. 講演者は，人が持つべき最も大切なものは何だと言っていますか。

V 4つの選択肢の中から，
以下のそれぞれの英文の（　　　）に入る最も適切なものを選びなさい。

41.　解答：C

解説 spending 12 days（12日間滞在したこと）がこの3つの単語の最も自然な順番であり，残るafterの位置を考えるとCが正解となる。

訳例　日本の億万長者，前澤友作氏が12日間の国際宇宙ステーションでの滞在を終え，月曜日に地球に帰還した。

42. 解答：A

解説 almost all が自然なつながりであるので，正解は A となる。

訳例 世界中で急増しているオミクロンの変種は，毎日報告される新しい症例のほとんどすべてを占めている。

43. 解答：D

解説 be on standby で「待機状態である」の意味であるから D が正解となる。

訳例 太平洋地域の国連事務所はトンガの状況を注視しており，要請があれば支援を提供できるよう待機している。

44. 解答：B

解説 not able to keep up (with the demand)「(需要に) 追いつくことができない」と考えると，B が正解となる。

訳例 世界のガス需要が拡大し，供給が追いつかないため，天然ガス価格は今期過去最高水準に達した。

45. 解答：B

解説 the urgent need for the Security Council to ～ の後には動詞が来るべきなので，B を選ぶ。impose ～ on ... は「～を…に課す」の意味である。

訳例 国連専門担当官は，安全保障理事会がミャンマー軍に対する武器禁輸を課し，軍事政権に対する財政圧力を大幅に高めることが緊急に必要であることを改めて強調した。

VI

下線を引いた単語または語句の中から，
文法的もしくは慣用的に不適切なものを選びなさい。

46. 解答：B

解説 (B) when の次は主語＋動詞が来て when they use となるか，when using と動名詞が来る必要がある。

訳例 国際電気通信連合 (ITU) が実施した調査によると，より多くの子どもや若者がオンラインでの時間を過ごす中，インターネット使用時の安全性について最も懸念されるのは「ネットいじめ」である。

47. 解答：C

解説 vaccinate は「～にワクチンを接種する」の意味の他動詞であるから，「ワクチン接種を受けた観光客」の意味にするには（C）は vaccinated でなければならない。

訳例 フィリピンは金曜日，パンデミックからの経済回復を加速させるため，2月10日からワクチン接種が完了した観光客の受け入れを開始すると発表した。

48. 解答：D

解説 working (D) world peace を文脈上意味の通る表現にするには，(D) を for にして「平和のために努力すること」とする必要がある。

訳例 オリンピック休戦は，大会期間中の選手の安全な通行の確保と，長期的には世界平和のために努力するという考えを促進することを目的としている。

49. 解答：A

解説 sense of ～ の～には名詞が来る必要があるので（A）は safety and security とする必要がある。

訳例 国連開発計画（UNDP）の新しいデータと分析によると，人々の安全・安心感はほとんどすべての国で低くなっており，世界の7人に6人が不安感に悩まされている。

50. 解答：C

解説 (C) could have prevented は，could have been prevented とすることで，「(適正な対処をしたならば）予防されていたはずの」と文法的に正しい形（受動態の仮定法過去完了）になる。

訳例 世界保健機関（WHO）の推計によると，世界で少なくとも10億人が，予防できたはずの，あるいは未対処の状態の近視または遠視の視覚障害を持っている。

VII-A 『新 わかりやすい国連の活動と世界』から得た知識に基づき，(A)～(D) から空欄を埋めるのに最も適切なものを選びなさい。

51. 解答：B

解説 国連加盟の申請書には，国連憲章遵守の旨の声明（declaration）が付帯していなければならない。

A. 結論　B. 声明　C. 提出　D. 翻訳

52. 解答：D

解説 国連加盟は，最終的に総会の３分の２以上の多数 (majority) をもって認められる。

A. 選挙　　B. 数値　　C. 人口　　D. 多数

53. 解答：A

解説 a Babel of tongues は旧約聖書に記された「バベルの塔」に由来する表現で「言葉の混乱」の意味である。国連の公用語は，この混乱を避ける (avoid) ためのものである。

A. 避ける　　B. 守る　　C. 築く　　D. 習得する

54. 解答：B

解説 国連事務局が日常業務で使うのは，英語とフランス語 (French) である。

A. 中国語　　B. フランス語　　C. ロシア語　　D. スペイン語

55. 解答：C

解説 国連専門職員は，６つの公用語のうち最低２カ国語に堪能である (proficient) 必要がある。

A. 気づいて　　B. 確信して　　C. 堪能で　　D. 便利で

訳例　国連は，国連憲章の義務を受け入れ，その義務を履行する能力と意志があると認められるすべての平和愛好国に開放されている。加盟を望む国は安全保証理事会に，憲章に記された義務を受け入れるという (51) 声明書を含む申請書を提出する。安全保証理事会が新規加盟の勧告を行い，総会の３分の２以上の (52) 多数により加盟が決定される。加盟は，総会が加盟を決定した日をもって発行する。

国連職員の話す言語は，約 170 種類に及ぶ。言語の混乱を (53) 避けるため，数カ国語が「公用語」あるいは「常用語」として指定されている。

総会で使用される言語は，アラビア語，中国語，英語，フランス語，ロシア語，スペイン語の６言語で，演説や文書はすべてこの６言語に翻訳される。事務局が日常の業務で使用する言語は英語と (54) フランス語で，職員はどちらかの言語で文書を作成することになっている。専門職員は，公用語のうち少なくとも２言語に (55) 堪能であることが強く求められる。

『新 わかりやすい国連の活動と世界)』p.45

Ⅶ-B 『新 わかりやすい国連の活動と世界』から得た知識に基づき，４つの選択肢から空欄を埋めるのに最も適切なものを選びなさい。

56. 解答：D

解説 「国際連合」の命名者はフランクリン・ルーズベルト元米国大統領である。

A. 初代国連事務総長トリグブ・リー

B. 初代国際連盟事務局長エリック・ドラモンド

C. 著名な米国実業家ジョン D. ロックフェラー

D. 元米国大統領フランクリン D. ルーズベルト

『新 わかりやすい国連の活動と世界』p.43 参照

57. 解答：C

解説 10 月 24 日の国連デーは，国連憲章発効を祝した記念日である。

A. 国際連盟の発足　　B. 国連旗の採択

C. 国連憲章の発効　　D. ニューヨーク国連本部の完成

同上 p.44 参照

58. 解答：A

解説 国連総会は安全保障理事会の勧告に基づき事務総長を任命する。

A. 安全保障理事会　　B. 信託統治理事会

C. 事務局　　D. 国際司法裁判所

同上 p.61 参照

59. 解答：B

解説 国際司法裁判所の 15 名の裁判官の選出における規定は，同一国の国民から２名を選出することはできないということである。

A. 裁判官の再選をすることはできない。

B. 同一国の国民から２名を選出することはできない

C. 何人かは国連の別の職務に就くことができる。

D. 半数以上が英語圏出身者でなければならない。

同上 p.60 参照

60. 解答：D

解説 「国際連合平和維持活動等に対する協力に関する法律」（PKO 法）が成立したのは，1992 年である。

A. 1945 年　　B. 1956 年　　C. 1984 年　　D. 1992 年

同上 p.168 参照

Ⅷ-A 以下の各英文を読み，下記のそれぞれの質問に答えなさい。
下記の英文を挿入するのに最も適した箇所を，(A)～(D) から選びなさい。

Passage 1

61. 解答：D

解説 聴衆に向けた環境保護への強いアピールをしており，メッセージの後半であることが予想される。(D) の次の This will be critical ... にも論理的につながることから，D が正解となる。

62. 解答：A

解説 World Oceans Day が行われることや，人間の海に対する破壊行為が問題となっていることが述べられている。話の導入部分だと予想され，さらに (A) の次の文で，人間の破壊行為が海の恩恵を損なっていることに言及されており論理的につながることから，A が正解である。

63. 解答：B

解説 この文は，carbon emissions (二酸化炭素排出) が海洋環境にどう影響しているかを述べている。第２パラグラフが，plastic waste, overfishing, など，海洋環境への影響を具体的に述べたパラグラフであり，さらにそれぞれの文が which や who などを用いて説明している文体であることなどから，この文の位置として B が正解となる。

語句 assault on ～: ～への破壊行為　being undermined: 損なわれている　choke: 窒息する　atoll: 環礁　ocean trench: 海溝　overfishing: (海での) 乱獲　vulnerability: 脆弱性《ぜいじゃくせい》　acidification: 酸性化　observance: (式典を) 祝うこと　underscore ～: ～を強調する　1.5-degree target: 世界の平均気温の上昇を産業革命以前と比べて＋ 1.5℃に抑えようという目標

訳例　(A) 今年の「世界海洋デー」は，世界が COVID-19（新型コロナウイルス感染症）の大流行，気候危機，そして人類による海洋，海域，海洋資源への継続的な破壊行為と闘っている最中に開催されます。先日発表された「第２次世界海洋アセスメント」では，世界の海洋が人類にもたらす恩恵の多くが，私たち自身の行動によって損なわれていることが確認されました。

私たちの海はプラスチック廃棄物に苦しんでおり，その兆候ははるか遠くの環礁から最も深い海溝に至るまでで見られます。乱獲により，年間約900億ドルの純益が失われており，小規模漁業の存続に欠かせない女性の弱い立場をさらに悪化させています。(B) 炭素排出は海洋の温暖化と酸性化を促進し，生物多様性を破壊し，多くの人間が生活している沿岸地域の海面上昇を引き起こしています。

今年の開催テーマである「海：生命と暮らし」は，世界中のコミュニティの文化的生活と経済的生存にとって海が重要であることを強調するものです。30億人以上の人々が生活の糧を海に依存しており，その大半は発展途上国の人々です。

(D) COVID-19からの回復に努めるとともに，自然に対する戦争行為にも終止符を打とうではありませんか。これは，持続可能な開発目標を達成し，パリ協定の1.5℃の目標を達成し，現在および将来の世代のために海洋の健全性を確保するために不可欠なことです。

Ⅷ-B

Passage 2

64. 解答：A

解説 この文脈における measures は「対策」（を講じる）の意味であるから A が最も近い。

A. 行動　B. 必要　C. 規模　D. 資金

65. 解答：C

解説 この文脈における accommodate は「（新たな状況など）に適した対応をする」意味，ここでは具体的に、「リモートワークへのシフトに必要な対応や支援をする」となるので C が最も近い。

A. 通知する　B. 防ぐ　C. 支援する　D. 立証する

66. 解答：B

解説 social well-being とは，社会生活をする上で人間関係において幸福な状態であることを意味するのでBが正解である。

A. 高い社会的地位　　B. 意味のある人間関係

C. 献身的に健康な状態　　D. 効果的にコミュニケーションを行う能力

67.　解答：D

解説　この文脈における significant は「(危惧されるほど状況が) 重大な」ことを意味しているので，D が正解である。

A. 興味深い　　B. 貴重な　　C. 意義深い　　D. 重大な

68.　解答：B

解説　ここでは，brunout は「(身体的・精神的に) 燃え尽きた状態」を意味しているので，B が正解である。

A. 電気系統の故障　　B. 肉体的精神的疲弊

C. 個人破産　　D. 急性心不全

69.　解答：A

解説　surge of teleworking の surge は「(大波が押し寄せるような) 急激な増加」を意味するので，A が正解である。

A. 急増　　B. 感情的な反応　　C. 変わらぬ人気　　D. 異なる種類

70.　解答：C

解説　ここでの practically overnight の practically は「(本当はそうではないにしても) ほとんどそう言ってよいくらいに」という意味であるから，C が正解である。

A. たやすく　　B. ほどほどに　　C. ほとんど　　D. しかしながら

語句　technical brief: 専門家の助言などを含む概説　brought on by ～: ～によってもたらされた　operational cost: (事業運営に必要な) 業務コスト　musculoskeletal: 筋骨に関する　prolonged: 長時間の

訳例　世界保健機関 (WHO) と国際労働機関 (ILO) は，テレワーク中の労働者の健康を保護するための (64) 対策を講じるよう呼びかけています。

この2つの国連機関が発表した健康的で安全なテレワークのための新しい技術概説では，テレワークの健康上の利点とリスク，および COVID-19 (新型コロナウイルス感染症) の流行と仕事のデジタル変革がもたらすさまざまな遠隔勤務形態へのシフト (65) に対応するために必要な変化について概説されています。

報告書によると，利点として，ワークライフバランスの改善，柔軟な勤務時間や運動の機会，交通量の減少，通勤時間の短縮，大気汚染の減少などが挙げられ，これらはすべて身体的，精神的健康や (66) 良好な社会生活を向上させることができます。また，テレワークは多くの企業にとって，生産性の向上と業務コストの削減につながります。

しかし，適切な計画や組織，安全衛生面でのサポートがなければ，テレワークが労働者の身体的・精神的健康や良好な社会生活に与える影響は (67) 重大なものになる可能性があると，報告書は警告しています。孤立，(68) 燃え尽き症候群，うつ病，家庭内暴力，骨や筋肉の怪我，眼精疲労，喫煙やアルコール摂取の増加，長時間座り続けたり画面を見続けたりする習慣，不健康な体重増加などにつながる可能性があります。

この報告書は，テレワーク中の健康と安全を促進・保護するために，政府，雇用者，労働者，職場の保健サービスが果たすべき役割について概説しています。

世界保健機関 (WHO) 環境・気候変動・保健局長のマリア・ネイラ博士は，「パンデミックによってテレワークが (69) 急増し，多くの労働者にとって (70) ほとんど一夜にして仕事の性質が変わってしまった」と述べています。

IX 以下の英文を読み，下記のそれぞれの質問に答えなさい。

【長文問題の解答対策】

英語の長文を読む際の基本的アプローチについては，2021 年度の解説を参照していただき，ここでは，問題 IX に出題される英文の特徴に即した読み方について言及したい。問題 IX で用いられる英文の多くは，国際連合が取り組んでいる世界の諸問題について，それに取り組んでいる当事者（国連関係者）あるいはそれらの諸問題に精通している専門家やジャーナリストが書いた英文やスピーチスクリプトが多い。

これらの英文の文体的特徴として，主張とその理由や背景，事例から得られた分析結果や示唆，事象間の因果関係などについて述べる文が多く，どうしても一文が長くなる傾向がある。文が長いということは，複数の情報が 1 つの文にまとめられているということなので，それらの情報間の関係を捉えられるようにすればよいのだが，ここが難しい。特に日本人が苦手とする，関係詞節や前置詞句をはじめとする後置修飾（名詞のあとからその名詞の説明をする表現が付属する構造），コンマやコロンのあとに説明が追加される場合，挿入句など，文を複雑にする要素が満載である。基本的には経験が物を言うのだが，困ったときは，「いったい何が（誰が）どうしたのか」を読み取ってみるとよい。つまり，その文の中心的な主語と動詞を探すのである。主語は関係詞節などで長くなっていることがあるが，動詞は（動詞句になっても）1〜2語なので見つけやすい。

また，内容的特徴としては，国連が取り組む諸問題，特にSDGs関連のトピックに関する内容が多いので，そういったトピックに関する英字新聞やニュースの記事，国連ホームページから閲覧できる報告書や資料などを読んでおくのもよいだろう。その中で重要と思われるキーワードや英文をメモしたり，あるいは表計算ソフトなどに入力してデータベースを作成したりするのもよいだろう。そうした表現の中には，Xの課題作文問題で使えるものもあるかもしれない。

こうした学習経験の積み重ねに基づき，実際の試験において英文を読む際には，まずトピックは何か，誰が何のために書いているのか（スピーチスクリプトの場合は誰がどのような場で話しているのか）を想像し，パラグラフごとの要点を捉えながら読み進めるのである。

今回の英文は，冒頭に，Twenty-five years ago とあり，その際 the Beijing Declaration が何らかの行動指針を発信し，それは社会における男女平等を推進しようとしたものだったとわかる。そしてその指針の目指したものが今日どうなっているかを，International Women's Day に当たり振り返る，という論考であると推察できる。

71. 解答：D

解説 25年前に世界189カ国のリーダーが北京宣言に調印したとある。正確には調印のあと批准という手続きになるが，選択肢の中ではDが筆者の意図を表している。

第1パラグラフで述べられているのは次のどれか。

A. 189カ国の世界の指導者が北京である組織を設立した。

B. 行動綱領は，参加国を統制する法的な力を持っていた。

C. 北京宣言の期待するものは高すぎて達成できなかった。

D. 北京宣言の批准から四半世紀が経過した。

72. 解答：B

解説 no single country in on track to achieve ～ by 2030（2030 年までに～を達成しそうな国は 1 つもない）とは，進展の歩みが遅いことを述べているので，B が正解である。

第 2 パラグラフで述べられているのは次のどれか。
A. 男女平等を推進するために，どの国も何もしてこなかった。
B. 男女平等の達成の進歩は歩みが遅すぎる。
C. 男女平等に取り組み始めるにはあと 1 世紀はかかるだろう。
D. 今日こそが少女と女性が男女の格差を縮める最良のチャンスだ。

73. 解答：C

解説 このパラグラフの第 2 文（The global gap between ...）に，女子と男子の格差は「ほぼ，あるいは完全に同じになった」とあるので，C が正解である。

第 3 パラグラフで述べられているのは次のどれか。
A. 仕事を持つ女子の数は過去 25 年の間で倍増した。
B. 世界のほとんどの学校は共学になった。
C. 世界の学校における女子と男子の比率はほぼ差が解消された。
D. 世界では 2 億 500 万人の少女がまだ教育を受けていない。

74. 解答：A

解説 このパラグラフの第 1 文に，多くの女子が質の高い教育（a quality education）を与えられていない，と述べられているので，A が正解である。

第 4 パラグラフで述べられているのは次のどれか。
A. 女子に質の高い教育を提供することは，依然として大きな課題である。
B. いま一番優先すべきことは，女子に授業を受ける機会を与えることである。
C. 世界の女子の 10 人のうち 6 人は低所得国で学んでいる。

D. 難民の女子は高校教育を受けるのに最も苦しんでいる。

75. 解答：C

解説 このパラグラフ4行目で，教育における男女格差の問題の中で，特に科学技術や数学などの分野で女子が，“they are grossly under-represented”（その占める割合に関して著しく低い）ことを述べているので，Cが正解である。Dは科学に限ってそう断言しているわけではないので不適である。

第5パラグラフで述べられているのは次のどれか？

A. 何百万人もの少女が，小学校で職業技術を学ぶことができない。

B. ある国では，20%の女子が読み書きを教わっていない。

C. 高等教育では，学問の分野において大きな男女格差が存在する。

D. 女子は，大学で科学を学ばないことで才能を無駄にしている。

76. 解答：B

解説 筆者は，「男女不平等の現状を容認するそれぞれの社会にはびこる力の不平等」(power inequalities in their societies that uphold the status quo）が問題の根底にあると述べているのでBが正解である。

第6パラグラフから推測されることは次のどれか。

A. 筆者は男女平等を実現するための現在のアプローチに満足している。

B. 筆者は，社会における力の不平等をなくすことが重要だと考えている。

C. 筆者は，男女間の不平等を意識することが問題を解決することになると確信している。

D. 筆者は国家間の力の不平等が早く解決されることを望んでいる。

77. 解答：A

解説 このパラグラフの第2文（When countries ...）に選択肢Aと同じ趣旨の内容が示されている。85%という割合はグローバル・パートナーシップに加盟している途上国を100%としたときの割合なのでBは不適切。CやDに関する言及はこのパラグラフにはない。

第 7 パラグラフで述べられているのは次のどれか。

A. 変化への具体的なコミットメントが，男女平等のより早い進展を可能にする。

B. 世界の途上国の約 85%が教育のためのグローバルパートナーシップに加盟している。

C. 教育のためのグローバル・パートナーシップは，開発途上国に長期的な教育計画を提供する。

D. 良質な教材を提供することは，生徒の学習意欲を高める。

78.　解答：C

解説　エチオピアが成功したのは就学者の男女差の解消，ケニアが力を入れたのは僻《へき》地《ち》における女子教育であるので A, B は不適である。また D については言及されていない。このパラグラフで言及されているのは C である。

第 8 パラグラフで述べられているのは次のどれか。

A. エチオピアは学業成績における男女差をなくすことに成功した。

B. ケニアは小学校の女子への算数教育に力を入れた。

C. ネパールは学校に入学し卒業する女子の数を増やすことに成功した。

D. エチオピア，ケニア，ネパールは男女共同参画事業に対して補助金を受けた。

79.　解答：A

解説　このパラグラフの第 1 文（北京行動綱領の趣旨）と第 2 文（That's why ...）との関係から A の内容が推測できる。B, C, D についてはこのパラグラフからは読み取れない。

第 9 パラグラフから推測されることは次のどれか。

A. 北京行動綱領は，平等を目指す全ての世代キャンペーンの概念的基盤である。

B. 北京行動綱領は，女性の方が社会変革を確実にする能力が高いとしている。

C. 平等を目指す全ての世代キャンペーンは，北京宣言と行動綱領の 25

周年を記念する短期間のイベントである。

D. 平等を目指す全ての世代キャンペーンは，過去 25 年間，世界中で行われてきた。

80. 解答：D

解説 このパラグラフにおける強いメッセージは，We must play our part to ensure ... に込められている。読者に対して「我々はそれぞれが役目を果たさねばならない」としているので，その趣旨に最も適するのは行動を起こすことを求めるメッセージとなっている D である。

第 10 パラグラフのメッセージを最もよく表しているのは次のどれか。

A. 男女平等がより多くの世界の女性リーダーを生み出すことにつながるということを，私たちはもっと認識する必要がある。

B. 私たちは，教育を受けた世代が男女間の不平等の問題を解決できることを忘れてはならない。

C. 私たちは，世界の少女と女性が世界平和を促進する活動に従事するのを助けなければならない。

D. 私たちは，男女平等を実現し，教育を受けた世代を育てるために行動を起こさなければならない。

語句 the Beijing Declaration:（1995 年 9 月に第 4 回世界女性会議で採択された）北京宣言　the Platform for Action:（北京宣言とともに採択された）行動綱領　International Women's Day: 国際女性デー（国連が制定した記念日で毎年 3 月 8 日となっている）　parity: 同等　appallingly: 驚くほど　unlock ～: ～を開放する　entrenched: 強固な　marginalized: 追いやられた，取り残された　grossly under-represented: 著しく（占める）割合が低い　profoundly new approach: 根本的に新しいアプローチ　dismantle ～: ～を取り除く　status quo: 現状　follow through on ～: ～をやり遂げる　velocity: 速度　menstrual hygiene facilities: 生理用衛生設備　reinvigorate ～: ～を再び活性化する　articulate ～: ～を明言する　for good: 永遠に

訳例

1. 25 年前，189 カ国の世界の指導者たちが北京宣言に署名し，社会と生活のあらゆる場面で女性が平等に参加するための大胆なロードマップであるプラットフォーム（行動綱領）を立ち上げました。
2. 国際女性デーを迎えたきょう，2030 年までに男女平等という持続可能な開発目標を達成できそうな国は 1 つもありません。過去四半世紀の間に苦労

して勝ち取った成果にもかかわらず，私たちは男女の格差を縮めるのにまだ 100 年かかるという現状です。今日の少女と女性にとって，それは永遠に実現しないのと同じことなのです。

3. 確かに，進展はありました。女子の就学率は過去 25 年間で 2 倍になりました。学校に通う女子と男子の数の世界的な格差は，ほぼあるいは完全に同程度にまで狭まり，地域によっては，教育段階により女子が男子より多くなっているところもあります。ユネスコの推計によると，2000 年以降，教育を受けられない女子の数は 2 億 500 万人から 1 億 2,900 万人へと大幅に減少しています。
4. しかし，1 億 2,900 万人という数字は，質の高い教育を受ける基本的な権利と，学習が切り開く未来に対する権利を否定されている少女の数として，驚くほどの数です。さらに，女子の教育に対する課題は，女子が学校に入学したら終わりではありません。少女たちは，社会的，経済的，文化的な根強い障壁に直面しており，低所得国の少女 10 人のうち 6 人は初等教育が教育の終着点となり，高校を卒業するのは 10 人に 1 人がやっとという状況です。難民，障害のある少女，貧しい家庭や農村部の少女など，最も取り残された人々にとっては，その割合はさらに低くなります。
5. 同様に恐ろしいことは，学校に通っている何百万人もの少女たちが，必要なスキルを学んでいないことです。国によっては，小学校を卒業するまでに簡単な物語を読んで理解できる少女は 10 人に 2 人というところもあります。女子が高等教育まで進んだとしても，将来の経済や社会を形成する科学，技術，工学，数学の分野では，女子の割合が著しく低くなっています。これは，才能と可能性の無駄遣いと言えます。
6. 明らかに，私たちは根本的に新しいアプローチを必要としています。しかし，それは指導者とその市民たちが，現状を容認する社会的地位の不平等を認識し，それを解消したときにのみ実現するものです。
7. 教育の進歩は，それが可能であることを証明しています。各国が変革に向けた具体的なコミットメントを表明し，それを実行するとき，男女平等の進展を加速させることができるのです。教育のためのグローバル・パートナーシップが協働する開発途上国の約 85%は，長期教育計画にジェンダーの平等を盛り込んでいます。つまり，女子教育に対する共通の障害を減らすために，より多くの取り組みを行っているのです。その取り組みには，女子の入学と卒業までの確実な支援，良質な教材の提供，学校内や周辺でのセクハラや暴力の削減，適切な生理用衛生設備の設置，女子の意欲を向上させ共感力を持った女性教師の増員などがあります。
8. こうしたアプローチは有効です。例えば，エチオピアは近年，女子教育を優先課題としています。その結果，より多くの少女が学校に通い，在籍し，成績も向上し，初等教育を修了した女子と男子の数の大きな差はほぼなくなりました。ケニアもまた，特に遠隔地における女子に優しい教育改革に集中的に投資し，その結果，女子の1学年への就学率が上昇し，数学の成績が男児を上回っています。同様に，ネパールの取り組みも，他の指標と比較して，女子の就学率および修了率が上昇し，男子を上回っています。

9. 北京行動綱領は，より多くの女性が変革の担い手となるためには，教育への平等なアクセスが不可欠であることを確認しました。私たちや私たちが代表する団体が平等を目指すすべての世代（Generation Equality）キャンペーンに参加しているのはこのためです。このキャンペーンは，あらゆる年齢と性別の人々を動員し，25年前に北京で明確にされた願いを再び活性化させることを目的としています。

10. 平等な世代とは，教育を受けた世代です。私たちは，世界中のすべての少女と女性が，ジェンダー平等を主導し，永久に障壁を取り除くために必要な知識と技能を確実に身につけられるよう，それぞれの役割を果たす必要があります。

X

以下の質問に対して，80 〜 100 語の短いエッセイを英語で書きなさい。

質問：日本が直面する社会問題の1つは何か？　どう解決できるか？

（語数を記入する必要はありません）

【Essay writing 問題の解答対策】

英語で意見文を書く力を高めるための基本的学習法については，2021年度の解説を参照していただき，ここでは，指定された語数（B級では80–100語前後）で意見文を書く力を養う際のポイントを3つ挙げる。まず，回答する際の「分量バランス」に慣れることである。例えば，課題への回答として主張を一言で記述するIntroductionに1〜2文，それを説明・支持するBodyに3〜4文，主張を再度まとめるConclusionに1〜2文，といったバランス感覚を養いながら練習することである（文の数は目安であり一文の長さにより増減する）。次に，課題への回答である主張を考える際，その理由や根拠をセットで考えるようにする。言い換えれば，理由や根拠が容易に思い浮かべられるような主張をするということである。最後に，英文を書く際は，主張を的確に表現するために必要なキーワードやキーフレーズを英語で思い浮かべられるかを自問することである。言いたいことが優れていても，必要な英語表現が書けなければ相手には伝わらない。これら3つのポイントを同時に考慮することで，読み手に伝わる英文を書くことができる。伝えたいことと伝えられることのバランスを考えながら，明確な論理構成で英文を書くことで，高評価が得られるだろう。そのために，普段から，さまざまなトピックについて自分の意見を持ち，言いたいことを日本語ではなく英語で考え英語で書く訓練が必要となる。

解答例 Japan's aging population crisis brings with it a host of social problems, one of which is the issue of "akiya," or vacant homes. As the number of akiya increases, so do other social problems such as a decline in property value for surrounding homes and health and safety concerns.

One way to help solve this problem is for the government to change current property laws and make it easier for local governments to seize an akiya if it has been clearly abandoned for more than a certain amount of time. This can help decrease the number of akiya.

Akiya is a unique social problem in Japan and it is imperative that the government act quickly to solve this issue. (119 words)

構成 ① Introduction: 質問に対する回答を明確に述べる。ここでは次のようになっている。

- 高齢化社会がもたらす数ある社会問題の中で，「空き家」の問題がある。
- 空き家があると，周辺の家の不動産価値が下がる上，特に災害時には健康や安全上の問題を引き起こす。

② Body: 短めのエッセイ課題の場合できるだけ簡潔に論を展開する。ここでは，次のようになっている。

- 1つの方法は，物権法を改正して地方自治体が一定期間使われていない空き家を差し押さえることを容易にすることである。
- それにより空き家は減るだろう。

③ Conclusion: 質問への回答（とその重要性）を再度端的にまとめる。

- 空き家対策に政府が早急に対応することが重要だ。

2022年B級第1回試験　正解一覧

I

1. B　2. B　3. C　4. D　5. D　6. C　7. B　8. A　9. D　10. A

II

11. D　12. A　13. B　14. B　15. C　16. D　17. C　18. A　19. C　20. A

III

21. C　22. C　23. D　24. D　25. B　26. B　27. D　28. C　29. A　30. C

IV

31. B　32. A　33. C　34. D　35. A　36. D　37. A　38. A　39. B　40. C

V

41. C　42. A　43. D　44. B　45. B

VI

46. B　47. C　48. D　49. A　50. C

VII -A

51. B　52. D　53. A　54. B　55. C

VII -B

56. D　57. C　58. A　59. B　60. D

VIII -A

61. D　62. A　63. B

VIII -B

64. A　65. C　66. B　67. D　68. B　69. A　70. C

IX

71. D　72. B　73. C　74. A　75. C　76. B　77. A　78. C　79. A　80. D

2022年
第2回試験
問題

Ｂ級試験問題用紙

Ｂ級

外務省後援

２０２２年度第２回国際連合公用語

英語検定試験（120分）

受験上の注意

1. 問題用紙は試験開始の合図があるまで開いてはいけません。その間に、この**受験上の注意を熟読しておいてください。**
2. **受験番号と氏名を２枚の解答用紙（マークシートと作文用紙）**に記入してください。
3. 解答用紙の配布は１人１部のみです。複数の配布は致しません。
4. 試験開始前は、答案への解答記入は禁止です。
5. マークシートの記入は、１～100までの記入箇所がありますが、この級では１～80までを使います。
6. マークシートの記入は、必ずＨＢ以上の濃い鉛筆を使って該当箇所を黒く塗りつぶしてください。書き間違いの場合は「アト」が残らないように消してください。マークシートは絶対に折ったり曲げたりしないでください。
7. 受験級、受験地区、会場番号、受験番号のマークシートへの記入は監督者の指示に従い、間違いなく記入してください。**(裏表紙の「マークシート記入例」参照)**
8. 作文は、⑴ 読みやすい文字をペン、ボールペンまたはＨＢ以上の濃い鉛筆で書いてください。⑵ 使用語数の80～100語を目安にしてください。
9. 試験問題についての質問は、印刷が不鮮明な場合を除き、一切受けつけません。
10. 中途退室の際は、マークシートと作文用紙を持って監督者に渡し、他の受験者の迷惑にならないように静かに退室してください。中途退室後の再入室はできません。
11. 試験中は他の受験者の妨げとなる行動は慎んでください。また携帯電話等の電源はお切りください。
12. マークシートと作文用紙は監督者に提出し、問題用紙はご自由にお持ち帰りください。

＊試験問題の複製や転載、インターネットへのアップロード等、いかなる媒体への転用を禁止します。

リスニングテストについて

1. リスニングテストは試験開始後、合図があってから実施されます。(40問あります)
2. リスニングテストが始まる前にリスニング問題の指示と内容を読んで、どういう形式のテストなのか、概要をつかんでおいてください。
3. テスト中の発言は、放送機器の具合が悪く放送された英語の聴き取りができない場合を除いて、しないようにしてください。

試験結果について

1. 試験の結果は2022年11月24日㈭頃に受験申込書に記載された住所に郵送で通知します。
2. その間に住所変更をされた方は、郵便局へ住所変更の届け出を忘れずに行ってください。
3. 発表前の試験結果のお問合せには応じられません。

UNA-JAPAN
公益財団法人 日本国際連合協会
http://www.unaj.or.jp/

I. Directions: You will hear 10 statements or questions. For each statement or question, choose the most appropriate response and mark your answer on your answer sheet.

1. A. I think I do. B. I'm a lawyer.
C. Why don't you? D. How do you do?

2. A. Have a nice trip! B. She's amazing.
C. There you go. D. It was awful.

3. A. Nice! I'm so happy for you. B. Where are you going?
C. Oh, I'm so unlucky. D. OK, how much is that?

4. A. No, that's not mine. B. I'm planning to go next year.
C. It's fine as it is, thank you. D. Here's the update.

5. A. No worries! We'll be here. B. Just on time!
C. Are you tired yet? D. I think I'm good.

6. A. Since it's so hot. B. I've been there a few times.
C. For my parents. D. Almost twenty years.

7. A. Aren't you hot? B. It's a bit small.
C. Really? How come? D. No. I don't have any money.

8. A. Nice talking to you! B. I'd like a glass of water.
C. It's almost time for lunch! D. Sorry, maybe another time.

9. A. Do you smell smoke? B. It's that area over there.
C. Wow. What a nice place! D. Oh, I didn't know that. My bad.

10. A. Don't mention it. B. What do you think?
C. You're welcome to come! D. I was thinking the same thing.

II. Directions : You will hear 10 short conversations. Choose the best answer for each follow-up question and mark your answer on your answer sheet.

11. A. Clean his home　　B. Treat his illness
C. Pay for his meal　　D. Cook him a meal

12. A. Early retirement　　B. The man's investments
C. Exchange rates　　D. High-return stocks

13. A. A writer　　B. A bookstore owner
C. A publisher　　D. A librarian

14. A. Classmates　　B. Best friends
C. Priest and churchgoer　　D. Strangers

15. A. A robbery　　B. A car accident
C. A street fight　　D. An earthquake

16. A. Her dessert order　　B. Her takeout order
C. Her check　　D. Her restaurant

17. A. Having kids　　B. Graduating college
C. Studying abroad　　D. Learning Japanese

18. A. Unenthusiastic　　B. Unsafe
C. Excited　　D. Happy

19. A. To order more chairs
B. To make an appointment
C. To ask about her recent order
D. To change her shipping address

20. A. She thinks he is very logical.
B. She thinks he is well-prepared.
C. She thinks he is irrationally anxious.
D. She thinks he spends too much money.

Ⅲ. Directions : You will hear five conversations. After each conversation, you will hear two follow-up questions. Choose the best answer for each question, and mark your answer on your answer sheet.

[Conversation 1]

21. A. At a call center   B. At a hair salon
C. At a restaurant   D. At city hall

22. A. Book a different tour.
B. Reschedule to Tuesday
C. Keep her appointment
D. Cancel her appointment

[Conversation 2]

23. A. Post online   B. Interview applicants
C. Contact references   D. Ask for a resume

24. A. She likes the idea.
B. She hates the idea.
C. She wants him to help her.
D. She thinks it's too troublesome.

[Conversation 3]

25. A. The woman is a local politician.
B. The man is a climate change activist.
C. The man denies climate change exists.
D. The woman is worried about climate change.

26. A. Heat waves   B. Typhoons
C. Hurricanes   D. Floods

[Conversation 4]

27. A. They're expensive.   B. They're violent.
C. They're fun.   D. They're addicting.

28. A. When he is at work
B. When he has money
C. When he has free time
D. When he is with his friends

[Conversation 5]

29. A. At a school
B. At a non-profit organization
C. At a refugee processing center
D. At a government research institute

30. A. She was surprised.
B. She agreed with him.
C. She was sympathetic.
D. She didn't believe him.

IV. Directions : You will hear two short talks. After each talk, you will hear five follow-up questions. Choose the best answer for each question, and mark your answer on your answer sheet.

[Talk 1]

31. A. A business owner B. A mover
C. A design teacher D. A real estate agent

32. A. By pursuing her passion
B. By having great mentors
C. By learning from her failures
D. By completing many successful projects

33. A. On her blog B. On a video sharing site
C. In her book D. On an Internet forum

34. A. Studying design B. Knowing many people
C. Not making mistakes D. Not having a Plan B

35. A. Selling her house B. Moving to a different place
C. Focusing on work D. Taking time off work

[Talk 2]

36. A. A teacher trainer B. A high school student
C. A sports coach D. A foreign policy specialist

37. A. University students B. Teachers
C. Bureaucrats D. Athletes

38. A. Every time I wash my car, it rains the next day.
B. When I eat pork cutlets before a test, I always pass.
C. When I wear a certain color, my favorite team always wins.
D. Every time I have a presentation at work, my kid gets sick.

39. A. Foreign diplomats
B. Politicians
C. Professors
D. Sports therapists

40. A. The bandwagon fallacy
B. The slippery slope fallacy
C. The no true Scotsman fallacy
D. The Texas sharpshooter fallacy

V. Choose from among the four alternatives the one that best completes each of the following sentences.

41. "But when we talk about war crimes, we cannot forget that (   ) war itself," Mr. Guterres said.
A. crimes of the worst are
B. worst of the crimes is
C. the crimes of worst are
D. the worst of crimes is

42. Twenty Ukrainians, (   ) not have family or friends in Japan, arrived at Haneda Airport on Tuesday on a government aircraft.
A. some of whom do
B. of whom do some
C. whom some of do
D. do some of whom

43. The number of babies born in Japan in 2021 fell by 29,231, or 3.5%, from the previous year (   ) of 811,604, the Ministry of Health, Labour and Welfare said Friday.
A. record to a low
B. low a record to
C. to a record low
D. a low record to

44. The UK recorded temperatures rising above 40 degrees Celsius (   ) its 350 years of climate records.
A. in the first time for
B. the first time in for
C. for the first time in
D. first in the time for

45. At an annual memorial in Hiroshima, António Guterres (　　　　　　) posed by crises in Ukraine, the Middle East, and the Korean Peninsula.

A. risk the warned of　　　　B. warned of the risk

C. of the risk warned　　　　D. the risk warned of

Ⅵ. Choose from among the underlined words or phrases the one that is grammatically or idiomatically incorrect.

46. Japan (A) was elected as a non-permanent member of the United Nations Security Council (UNSC) at the elections (B) of the UN General Assembly and (C) served a two-year term in the UNSC (D) starting from January 1, 2023.

47. During a ceremony in Brussels on July 5, NATO ambassadors (A) signing the (B) accession protocols that will (C) move Finland and Sweden a step closer to (D) joining the alliance.

48. The UN human rights office urged Morocco and Spain (A) to ensure that migrants' human rights were protected (B) in their joint border, and that border officers refrain (C) from any use (D) of excessive force.

49. Nearly one billion people worldwide suffer from some (A) form of mental disorder, according to (B) late UN data — a staggering figure that is even more (C) worrying, if you consider that it includes (D) around one in seven teenagers.

50. A new milestone in (A) mobility has been (B) reached with the adoption of a (C) proposal to extend automated driving in certain traffic (D) environment from the current limit of 60 km/h to up to 130 km/h.

Ⅶ. Choose the best answer from the choices marked (A), (B), (C), and (D) to fill in the blanks based on the knowledge gained from *New Today's Guide to the United Nations.*

The International Court of Justice, whose seat is at The Hague, Netherlands, is the principal **(51)** __________ organ of the United Nations. The Court's functions are defined in its Statute, which is an integral part of the United Nations Charter and is based on the Statute of the Permanent Court of International Justice, which functioned at the time of the League of Nations.

The jurisdiction of the Court covers all questions which States **(52)** ________ to it, and all the matters provided for in the Charter of the United Nations or in treaties or conventions in force. States may bind themselves in advance to accept the jurisdiction of the Court in special cases, either by **(53)** ________ a treaty or convention which provides for reference to the Court or by making a special declaration to that effect. Such declaration accepting compulsory jurisdiction may exclude certain classes of cases.

The Court consists of 15 judges elected by the General Assembly and the Security Council, voting **(54)** ________. They are chosen on the basis of their qualifications, not on the basis of nationality, and care is taken to ensure that the principal legal systems of the world are represented in the Court. No two judges can be **(55)** ________ of the same State. The judges serve for a term of nine years and may be re-elected. They cannot engage in any other occupation during their term of office.

51. A. commercial B. political
C. social D. judicial

52. A. refer B. lead
C. consent D. object

53. A. avoiding B. challenging
C. signing D. vetoing

54. A. collaboratively B. independently
C. unanimously D. tentatively

55. A. criminals B. scholars
C. nationals D. leaders

Choose the most appropriate of the four alternatives according to your knowledge and the information gained from *New Today's Guide to the United Nations*.

56. Among the seven threats to world peace that Secretary-General António Guterres mentioned in his address to the General Assembly on 19 September 2017, he first mentioned

A. terrorism
B. nuclear peril
C. human mobility
D. climate change

57. The Charter of the United Nations was signed on 26 June 1945 in

A. Amsterdam

B. London

C. Paris

D. San Francisco

58. The official seal and emblem of the United Nations is a map of the world, seen from

A. the equator

B. the U.K.

C. the North Pole

D. the South Pole

59. The Human Rights Council is made up of

A. 36 Member States

B. 47 Member States

C. 120 Member States

D. 193 Member States

60. The United Nations Association of Japan was established in

A. 1947 B. 1956 C. 1962 D. 1975

Ⅷ. Read each of the following passages and answer the questions that follow.

[Passage 1: Questions 61 to 63]

Mangroves are tropical marine forests with huge potential. They protect coastlines from erosion and storm surge; and provide food and shelter for a diverse array of wildlife, and nursery habitats for commercially important fish and shellfish. **(A)**

They also fight climate change: the UN Environment Programme (UNEP) estimates that global mangrove forests sequester within their roots, trunks, and in the soil as much as 22.8 million tons of carbon each year.

(B) Along with climate change impacts such as rising sea levels and temperatures, mangrove forests are being depleted because their wood is valuable and prized by coastal communities as a prime source of timber for construction, fuel, and even medicines. Rampant coastal urbanization, and unsustainable agriculture and aquaculture practices round out the long list of challenges.

(C) Sometimes, innovative partnerships can lead to sustainable solutions. Over the past three years, UN agencies, the Kenyan Government and other key partners have joined forces to launch several community-based conservation projects. **(D)**

61. Choose the best place from among (A), (B), (C), and (D) where the following sentence can be inserted:

But all hope is not lost!

62. Choose the best place from among (A), (B), (C), and (D) where the following sentence can be inserted:

They aim to help tackle poverty and deliver climate, biodiversity and local-level benefits to communities on the Kenyan coast.

63. Choose the best place from among (A), (B), (C), and (D) where the following sentence can be inserted:

While they provide valuable services for people and the planet, mangroves are in trouble.

[Passage 2: Questions 64 to 70]

Almost 8 million children under 5 in 15 crisis-hit countries are at risk of death from severe **(64)** wasting unless they receive immediate therapeutic food and care—with the number rising by the minute, UNICEF warned today as world leaders prepare to meet at the G7 summit.

Since the start of the year, the **(65)** escalating global food crisis has forced an additional 260,000 children—or one child every 60 seconds—to suffer from severe wasting in 15 countries **(66)** bearing the brunt of the crisis, including in the Horn of Africa and the Central Sahel. This rise in severe wasting is in addition to existing levels of child undernutrition that UNICEF warned amounted to a 'virtual tinderbox' last month.

"We are now seeing the **(67)** tinderbox of conditions for extreme levels of child wasting begin to catch fire," said UNICEF Executive Director Catherine Russell. "Food aid is **(68)** critical, but we cannot save starving children with bags of wheat. We need to reach these children now with therapeutic treatment before it is too late."

Soaring food prices driven by the war in Ukraine, persistent drought due to climate change in some countries, at times combined with **(69)** conflict, and the ongoing economic impact of COVID-19 continue to drive up children's food and nutrition **(70)** insecurity worldwide, resulting in catastrophic levels of severe malnutrition in children under 5. In response, UNICEF is scaling up its efforts in 15 most affected countries.

64. In this context, the word "wasting" is closest in meaning to

A. abusing B. poisoning
C. weakening D. yearning

65. In this context, the word "escalating" is closest in meaning to

A. appearing B. floating
C. promising D. intensifying

66. In this context, the phrase "bearing the brunt of" is closest in meaning to

A. becoming the cause of
B. suffering the impact of
C. taking the responsibility of
D. wishing for the end of

67. In this context, the word "tinderbox" is closest in meaning to

A. something dangerous B. something expensive
C. something unknown D. something immoral

68. In this context, the word "critical" is closest in meaning to

A. negative B. risky
C. serious D. vital

69. In this context, the word "conflict" is closest in meaning to

A. argument B. disagreement
C. war D. yelling

70. In this context, the word "insecurity" is closest in meaning to

A. ambition B. crisis
C. doubt D. humility

IX. Read the following passage and answer the questions that follow.

([1] ~ [10] indicate paragraph numbers.)

[1] As Secretary-General of the United Nations, I spend much of my time speaking with world leaders and taking the pulse of global trends. It's clear to me that we are at a defining moment in international relations. Global decision making is plagued by gridlock—and a fundamental paradox lies at the heart of it. On the one hand, many of today's global leaders recognize our common threats—COVID, climate, the unregulated development of new technologies. They agree that something needs to be done about them. Yet that common understanding is not matched by common action.

[2] Indeed, divides keep deepening. We see them everywhere: in the unfair and unequal distribution of vaccines; in a global economic system rigged against the poor; in the utterly inadequate response to the climate crisis; in digital technology and a media landscape that profit from division; and in growing unrest and conflict around the world. So if the world agrees on the diagnosis of these common problems, why is it unable to effectively treat them? I see two fundamental reasons.

[3] First, because foreign policy often becomes a projection of internal politics. As a former Prime Minister, I know that despite good intentions, international affairs can be hijacked by domestic politics. Perceived national interests can easily trump the larger global good. This impulse is understandable, even if it is wrong-headed in instances where solidarity is in a country's self-interest.

[4] Vaccines are a prime example. Everyone understands that a virus like COVID-19 does not respect national borders. We need universal vaccination to reduce the risk of new and more dangerous variants emerging and affecting everyone, in every country. Instead of prioritizing vaccines for all through a global vaccination plan, governments have acted to safeguard their people. But that is only half a strategy. Of course, governments must ensure the protection of their own people. But unless they work simultaneously to vaccinate the world, national vaccination plans could be rendered useless as new variants emerge and spread.

[5] Second, many of today's global institutions or frameworks are outdated or simply weak and the necessary reforms are impeded by geo-political divides. For example, the authority of the World Health Organization is nowhere near what is required to coordinate the response to global pandemics. At the same time, international institutions with more power are either paralyzed by division—like the Security Council—or undemocratic—like many of our international financial institutions. In short, global governance is failing at precisely the moment when the world should be coming together to solve global problems.

[6] We need to act together in the national and global self-interest, to protect critical global public goods, like public health and a livable climate, that support humanity's well-being. Such reforms are essential if we are to deliver on common aspirations

for our collective global goals of peace, sustainable development, human rights and dignity for all.

7 This is a difficult and complex exercise that must take into account questions of national sovereignty. But doing nothing is not an acceptable option. The world desperately needs more effective and democratic international mechanisms that can solve people's problems. As the pandemic has taught us, our fates are tied. When we leave anyone behind, we risk leaving everyone behind. The most vulnerable regions, countries and people are the first victims of this paradox in global policy. But everyone, everywhere is directly threatened.

8 The good news is that we can do something about our global challenges. Problems created by humanity can be solved by humanity. Last September, I issued a report on these issues. *Our Common Agenda* is a starting point; a roadmap to gather the world together to tackle these governance challenges and reinvigorate multilateralism for the 21st century. Change won't be easy, nor will it happen overnight. But we can begin by finding areas of consensus and moving in the direction of progress. This is our greatest test because so much is at stake.

9 We are already seeing the consequences. As people start to lose trust in the ability of institutions to deliver, they also risk losing faith in the values that underlie those institutions. In every corner of the world, we see an erosion of trust and what I fear is the emergence of a twilight of shared values. Injustice, inequality, mistrust, racism and discrimination are casting dark shadows across every society.

10 We must restore human dignity and human decency and respond to people's anxieties with answers. In the face of growing interconnected threats, enormous human suffering, and shared risks, we have an obligation to speak up and act to put out the fire.

71. Which of the following is mentioned in Paragraph 1?

A. Leaders in the world have been collaborating to tackle global issues.
B. The COVID-19 pandemic has caused worldwide armed conflicts.
C. The development of new technologies is worsening gender inequality.
D. Many global leaders are not taking action to address their common threats.

72. Which of the following is mentioned in Paragraph 2?

A. Vaccines are not being provided in a fair and equal manner.
B. A global economy depends on the people in developing countries.
C. Efforts have been made to tackle the issue of climate crisis.
D. The media are profiting by using advanced digital technology.

73. Which of the following can be inferred from Paragraph 3?

A. The author condemns world leaders for prioritizing domestic interests.
B. The author doubts that world leaders will ever reach an agreement.
C. The author understands why world leaders focus on national interests.
D. The author believes that a nation's solidarity is of utmost importance.

74. Which of the following is mentioned in Paragraph 4?

A. The impact of the COVID-19 pandemic varies from country to country.
B. Worldwide vaccination will slow the spread of dangerous variants.
C. Governments have contributed to universal vaccination for a long time.
D. National vaccination should take priority to minimize the global risk.

75. Which of the following is mentioned in Paragraph 5?

A. The WHO has more global influence than the Security Council.
B. The world's response to global pandemics has been well-coordinated.
C. Many of the UN's financial institutions are favoring developing countries.
D. Reform in global governance has never been needed so urgently as now.

76. Which of the following can be inferred from Paragraph 6?

A. The author believes that ensuring global human welfare is a goal shared by all UN members.
B. The author thinks that the national and global interests are separate matters.
C. The author assumes that human rights are being protected in most countries in today's world.
D. The author worries that many world leaders will not collaborate in the long run.

77. Which of the following is mentioned in Paragraph 7?

A. National sovereignty is secondary to international well-being.
B. The world needs leaders who can establish a new global institute.
C. The pandemic is proof that people's fates are interconnected.
D. The most vulnerable regions, countries, and people should be saved first.

78. Which of the following is mentioned in Paragraph 8?

A. Humans have caused numerous irreversible environmental problems.
B. *Our Common Agenda* includes proposals for global collaboration.
C. The sooner the reforms are made, the better results are gained.
D. World leaders should start by tackling the toughest challenges.

79. Which of the following is mentioned in Paragraph 9?

A. Negative impacts of the world's failure to collaborate are emerging.

B. People's faith in the value of the world's institutions is still strong.

C. Shared values are beginning to grow among people in the world.

D. Every society rejects injustice, inequality, racism, and discrimination.

80. Which of the following would be the best title for this article?

A. Problems Facing the World Today

B. The Role of the United Nations

C. Protecting Human Rights and Dignity

D. The Need for Collaborative Action

X. Write a short essay of around 80-100 words in English to answer the following question:

What should the government do to make Japan a more gender-equal society?

(You do not need to write down the number of words.)

マークシート記入例

東京の本会場でB級を受験する、国連 太郎さん、受験番号が「東京01-30001」、生年月日が「1980年10月24日」の場合の記入例です。

【受験番号/氏名】
それぞれ受験票の記載通りに記入してください。

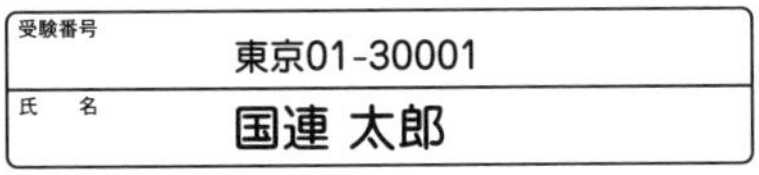

【受験地区】
下段の都道府県部分を塗りつぶしてください。

【会場番号】
都道府県部分に続く2桁の数字を塗りつぶしてください。

【受験番号】
ハイフン（－）以降の5桁の数字を塗りつぶしてください。

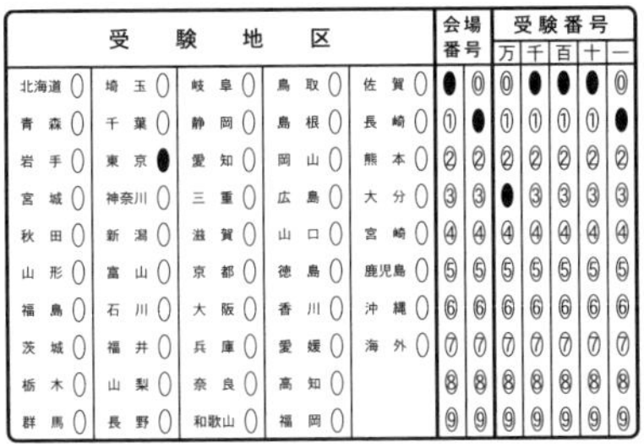

【受験級】
「B」と記入し、下段のB級部分を塗りつぶしてください。

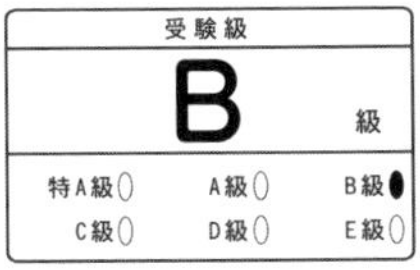

【生年月日】
4桁の西暦・月・日を塗りつぶしてください。
10未満の月・日の十の位は、「0」を塗りつぶしてください。

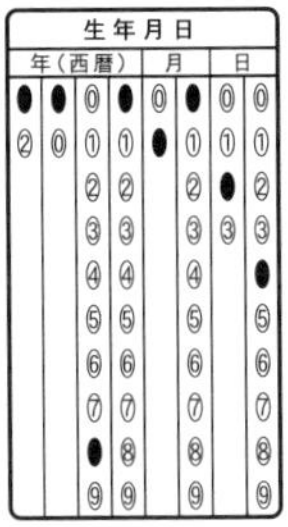

※HB以上の鉛筆を用いてマークをしてください。

※他の地区から会場を変更して受験する場合でも、受験票に記載されている受験地区・会場番号をマークしてください。

2022年

第2回試験

解答・解説

2022年　国連英検B級第2回試験
解答・解説

I　疑問文を含む英文が10題読まれます。
それぞれの英文に対して，最も適切な対応文を選びなさい。

1. 解答：B

解説 What do you do? は相手の職業を聞く表現である。What are you doing?（何をしているの？）とは全くニュアンスが異なることに注意する。正解はBとなる。

ナレーション　What do you do?
「仕事は何ですか」
A. そう思います。　B. 私は弁護士です。
C. あなたもやったら？　D. はじめまして。

2. 解答：D

解説 旅行の感想を聞いているので，Dが正解となる。awful は「恐ろしい」の意味もあるがここでは「最悪の」の意味になる。There you go. は「どうぞ」「できたね」など複数の意味があるが，ここでの応答としては不適切。

ナレーション　How was your trip to Italy?
「イタリア旅行はどうでしたか」
A. 旅行，楽しんで来て！　B. 彼女は素晴らしい。
C. できたできた。　D. 最悪だった。

3. 解答：A

解説 無料チケットが当たったと言って喜んでいるのだから，応答として適切なのは，Aである。I'm so happy for you. は日本語では「よかったね」の意味。

ナレーション　I just won free tickets to Hawaii!

「ハワイへの無料旅行券当たったんだ！」

A. いいね。よかったね。　B. どこに行くの？

C. あー，私は運が悪い。　D. わかりました，いくらですか。

4. 解答：C

解説　何らかのサブスクリプションサービスのプラン変更の勧誘なので，適切な応答は，C となる。fine as it is は「いまのままでよい」の意味である。

ナレーション　Would you like to update to our premium plan?

「プレミアムプランへのアップデートはいかがですか」

A. いいえ，私のではありません。　B. 来年行くつもりです。

C. いまのままで結構です。　D. これがアップデートです。

5. 解答：A

解説　待ち合わせに遅れそうなので，電話で遅れると連絡している状況である。したがって応答として適切なのは，「大丈夫（心配しないで），待っているよ（私たちはここにいるよ）」の意味の A である。

ナレーション　Sorry I'm running a bit late!

「ごめん，少し遅れてる」

A. 大丈夫！　待ってるよ。　B. 時間ピッタリだ！

C. もう疲れた？　D. 私は大丈夫です。

6. 解答：D

解説　How long ～？と期間を聞いているので，正解は D となる。A の Since it's so hot. には since が含まれるので紛らわしいがここでは「～以来」の意味ではなく「～なので」の意味となる。

ナレーション　How long have you been living in the States?

「アメリカにはどれくらい住んでいるのですか」

A. 暑すぎるから。　B. 数回行ったことがあります。

C. 両親のためです。　D. ほぼ 20 年になります。

7. 解答：C

解説　オンラインショッピングが好きではない，というコメントに対する応答であるから C が適切である。

ナレーション I'm not a big fan of shopping online.
「オンラインショッピングはあまり好きではありません」
A. 暑くないですか。　B. 少し小さいです。
C. 本当？　どうして？　D. いいえ。お金がありません。

8. 解答：D

解説 飲み会への誘いに対する応答であるから，Dが正解である。Nice talking to you! は「お話できてよかったです！」が文字通りの意味であるが，人との別れ際に言う表現である。

ナレーション Let's go for a few rounds of drinks tonight.
「今晩少し飲みに行こうよ」
A. ではまた！　B. 水をください。
C. もうお昼の時間だ！　D. ごめん，また今度ね。

9. 解答：D

解説 禁煙だと知らずに注意されたときの応答であるからDが適切である。Aに含まれるsmell smokeは「焦げ臭い」「(火事などの) 煙の臭いがする」の意味で，I smell smoke. (焦げ臭い)，They smelled smoke and left the building. (焦げ臭いにおいがして建物から非難した) のように使う。

ナレーション Sir, this is a no-smoking area.
「お客様，ここは禁煙でございます」
A. 焦げ臭いですか。　B. それは向こうです。
C. わー，いいところだね。　D. あ，知りませんでした。ごめんなさい。

10. 解答：A

解説 お礼を言っている相手への返答であるから，Aが正解である。Don't mention it. の文字通りの意味は「それは言うに及びません」であるが日本語では「どういたしまして」に近い意味である。

ナレーション I don't know how to thank you.
「何とお礼を申してよいのか」
A. どういたしまして。　B. どう思う？
C. ぜひ来てください！　D. 私も同じことを考えていました。

II 10題の対話文が読まれます。
その後に読まれるそれぞれの質問に対して最も適切な答えを選びなさい。

11. 解答：C

解説 レストランなどで，bill（勘定書）を見て，Let me get this. と言えば「私が払います」の意味となる。また，it's my treat は「私のおごりです」の意味。C が正解である。

A. 家を掃除する　　B. 病気を治す
C. 食事代を払う　　D. 食事を作ってあげる

ナレーション

Woman: Let me get this. You're here visiting us so it's my treat.
Man: Oh really? Wow, thank you so much. I really appreciate it.
Woman: Of course! I hope you enjoyed the meal!
Question　What is the woman going to do for the man?

(女)：ここは私に払わせて。私たちに会いに来てくれたんだから，私が払います。
(男)：本当？　ありがとう。本当にありがとう。
(女)：当然のことよ！　食事，気に入ってくれたらうれしいわ。
質問　女性は男性に何をしてあげるのですか。

12. 解答：B

解説 Portfolio とはもともとは書類入れの意味だが，お金に関する話題の場合には「投資やその結果の状況をまとめた書類」を意味する。女性が your investments などと言っていることからも，B が正解である。

A. 早期退職　　B. 男性の投資　　C. 外国為替レート　　D. 高利回り株

ナレーション

Man: The economy has been doing so badly that I'm scared to look at my portfolio each morning.
Woman: If your investments are in long-term funds, you shouldn't be too worried.
Man: But I'm planning to retire in five years. I'm afraid the stock market won't recover by then.
Question　What is the main topic of this conversation?

(男)：経済が本当に悪化しているので毎朝ポートフォリオ（有価証券明

細）を見るのが怖いよ。

(女)：あなたの投資が長期のファンドなら，それほど心配はないわよ。

(男)：でもあと５年で退職なんだよ。それまでに株式市場は回復しないんじゃないかと心配なんだ。

質問　この会話の主な話題は何でしょう。

13. 解答：B

解説 女性が「私たちのお客様が」と言い，I'll make sure we dedicate a whole shelf over there just for you.「あなたのためだけにあそこの棚全部を捧げます」と言っていることから，B が正解となる。

A. 作家　B. 書店の店主　C. 出版社の人　D. 図書館員

ナレーション

Woman: How's your book going? A lot of our customers have been asking me when you're coming out with the new one.

Man: I'm almost done. I just sent my publisher the final chapter yesterday.

Woman: That's great! Can't wait to read it! I'll make sure we dedicate a whole shelf over there just for you.

Question　What is most likely the woman's job?

(女)：本のご執筆の方はどうなっていますか？　新作はいつ出るのかと読者のみなさんから質問が多く寄せられています。

(男)：もうすぐでき上がります。昨日最終章の原稿を出版社に送ったところですよ。

(女)：それはよかったです！　待ち遠しいです！　先生のためだけの棚を用意しておきますね。

質問　女性の仕事はおそらく何でしょう。

14. 解答：D

解説 「あのう，すみません，写真撮ってもらえますか」と，カジュアルかつ丁寧に頼んでいるところから，D が最も妥当な答えである。

A. クラスメート　B. 親友

C. 神父と教会に通う人　D. 知らない人同士

ナレーション

Man: Excuse me. Hi. Could you take a picture for me and my friend over there?

Woman: Sure. I'm not good with these types of cameras so you'll have to show me. What do I do?

Man: Okay, so to take the picture, press this button halfway first to focus. And when you see on this screen that our faces are in focus, then press the button down all the way. Oh, and could you take it vertically to get all of the church in the background?

Question What is the relationship between the man and the woman?

(男)：あのう，すみません。そこのところで，私と友人の写真を撮ってもらってもいいですか。

(女)：もちろん。このタイプのカメラはあまり得意ではないので，使い方，教えてもらえますか。どうすればよいのですか。

(男)：はい。まず写真を撮るには，このボタンを半分押して焦点を合わせます。そしてこのモニター画面で私たちの顔に焦点が合ったところで，最後までボタンを押してください。あっ，それから後ろの教会が全部写るようにタテで撮ってもらえますか。

質問 男性と女性の関係はおそらく何でしょう。

15. 解答：B

解説 男性が，You do know this is a one-way street. と言い，女性が，No, no I didn't. に続けて「1 人での運転は昨日から」と述べていることから，B が正解である。

A. 強盗　B. 自動車事故　C. 路上のけんか　D. 地震

ナレーション

Woman: Is everyone okay? Are you guys hurt? I'm so sorry. I didn't see you coming out of there.

Man: We're okay. You do know this is a one-way street, right?

Woman: No, no I didn't. I am so sorry. I just started driving by myself from yesterday. Anyway, could you call the police? My phone got stolen a few days ago so I don't have a phone on me right now.

Question　Which of the following just happened to both the man and the woman?

(女)：みなさん大丈夫ですか？　けがは大丈夫ですか？　本当にごめんなさい。そこから出てくるとは思わなかったので。

(男)：大丈夫です。ここ一方通行だって知ってますよね。

(女)：えっ，いいえ知りませんでした。すみません。昨日から1人で運転を始めたばかりなので。とにかく，警察を呼んでもらえますか。携帯を数日前に盗まれて，いま電話がないんです。

質問　男性と女性に起きた出来事は次のどれでしょう。

16. 解答：A

解説　女性が，"but um ... we ordered dessert a while ago. Is that coming soon?" と言っていることから，A が正解である。

A. デザートの注文　　B. 持ち帰りの注文

C. お勘定　　D. 自分のレストラン

ナレーション

Man:　I hope your meal is going well. I'm just going to leave the check right here. Is there anything else I can get you? Maybe a box for the pasta?

Woman: Everything is delicious. Thank you. We don't need a box for the pasta but um ... we ordered dessert a while ago. Is that coming soon?

Man:　Let me go and check on that for you.

Question　What did the woman ask the man about?

(男)：お食事は大丈夫でしょうか。お勘定書きはここに置かせていただきますね。他に何かご注文はございますか。パスタ用のお持ち帰り用箱をお持ちしましょうか。

(女)：みんなおいしいです。ありがとう。箱はいりませんけど……しばらく前にデザートをオーダーしたんですが。すぐ来ますか。

(男)：確認して参ります。

質問　女性は男性に何について尋ねましたか。

17. 解答：C

解説 最終的にあきらめたのは，trying to go (to Japan) であるから C が正解である。A については put off having kids とあるが完全にあきらめたとは言っていないし，B や D についてはこの会話からはわからない。

A. 子どもを持つこと　　B. 大学を卒業すること

C. 留学すること　　D. 日本語を勉強すること

ナレーション

Man: So, when are you going to Japan? Weren't you planning on studying there?

Woman: Oh, don't remind me. I spent two whole years learning Japanese and my husband and I put off having kids just so I could go and study in Japan. I waited for a whole year and even after all that, the government still wouldn't issue me a student visa because of the pandemic. So I just finally gave up on trying to go.

Man: Oh wow. I had no idea. That must have been so disappointing.

Question　What did the woman give up on?

（男）：で，日本に行くの？　日本で勉強する計画じゃなかったかい？

（女）：あらもう思い出させないで。丸２年日本語を勉強した上に日本で勉強するために子どもを持つのも延期にしたのよ。それでまた丸１年待って，それでも政府はコロナのせいで学生ビザを発給しようとしないのよ。それで結局行くのをあきらめたの。

（男）：えー。なんて言ったらよいか。本当に残念だったね。

質問　女性は何をあきらめたのでしょうか。

18. 解答：A

解説 ペットと離ればなれになるし出張中は忙しいので，"I'm so not looking forward to it at all." と女性が話していることから A が正解である。

A. 喜んでいない　　B. 不安だ　　C. 楽しみだ　　D. うれしい

ナレーション

Woman: You look happy! What's the occasion?

Man: I'll finally be able to take a day off next week. I've been so busy these past couple of months that I haven't had any rest at all. I heard you're traveling soon?

Woman: Yeah, I have a business trip to the UK next week. I'll be away from my dog for three months, and I probably won't get any time off while I'm there. I'm so not looking forward to it at all.

Question How does the woman probably feel?

(女)：うれしそうだね。何かあったの？

(男)：来週やっと休暇がとれるんだ。ここ3カ月本当に忙しくて，全く休めてないんだ。君は近々旅行に行くんだって？

(女)：そうよ。来週イギリスに出張だわ。3カ月ワンちゃんと離ればなれになるし，向こうにいる間は全く休めないわ。全く楽しみじゃないの。

質問 女性はおそらくどのような気持ちでしょうか。

19. 解答：C

解説 20脚注文したはずの椅子が12脚しか届かなかった件で，担当のアンダーソン氏と話がしたい，というのが女性の要望なので，Cが正解である。

A. 椅子を追加注文するため

B. 会う約束をするため

C. 最近の注文について問い合わせるため

D. 送り先住所を変更するため

ナレーション

Man: ABC Corporation. This is Ryan speaking.

Woman: Hi, I'm Alice Walker from Tomorrow Innovations. I'd like to speak with Mr. Anderson regarding a recent shipment I received from him. I ordered twenty chairs but he only sent me twelve.

Man: I'm afraid Mr. Anderson is not in the office today. I'll have him contact you as soon as he gets back. Could I get your phone number?

Question Why did the woman call?

(男)：ABCコーポレーション，ライアンと申します。

(女)：もしもし，トゥモローイノベーションのアリス・ウォーカーです。

先日届けていただいた荷物の件で，発送担当のアンダーソンさんとお話がしたいのですが。20 脚の椅子を注文したのですが，届いたのは 12 脚だったものですから。

(男)：あいにく本日，アンダーソンは留守にしておりまして。戻りましたらすぐに連絡を差し上げるようにいたします。お電話番号をいただいてよろしいでしょうか。

質問　女性はなぜ電話をしたのですか。

20. 解答：C

解説 非常用の水や缶詰を買い込んできた男性に，女性が「世紀末予測ビデオの見過ぎよ！」と言っていることから，C が正解である。

A. 非常に論理的だと思っている。

B. 準備周到だと思っている。

C. むやみに心配性だと思っている。

D. お金の使い過ぎだと思っている。

ナレーション

Woman: Why did you order so much water and canned foods? Do we have enough space to store all this?

Man: You never know when a food shortage might be coming. I just want to be well-prepared.

Woman: I think you've been watching too many end-of-the-world prediction videos online.

Question　What does the woman think about the man?

(女)：なぜそんなにたくさんお水と缶詰を注文したの？　こんなにたくさん入れておく場所ある？

(男)：いつ食糧難が起きるかわからないんだよ。十分な備えをしておくためだよ。

(女)：あなた，オンラインで世紀末予測についてのビデオを見過ぎだわ。

質問　女性は男性についてどう思っていますか。

III　5つの対話文が読まれます。各対話文の後で，それに対する質問が2つ読まれます。各質問に最も適切な答えを選びなさい。

Conversation 1

21.　解答：B

解説　女性が，a bang trim（前髪のカット）と full color（ヘアカラー）の予約について電話しているのでBが正解である。ちなみに，salon はヘアサロンなどの「サロン」，似た単語で saloon は「酒場」の意味である。

A. コールセンターで　　B. ヘアーサロンで

C. レストランで　　D. 市役所で

22.　解答：D

解説　女性が，「明日の予約はキャンセル」して「別の機会にまた予約を入れます」と言っているので，Dが正解である。

A. 別のツアーを予約する　　B. 火曜日に予定を変更する

C. 予約をそのままにする　　D. 予約をキャンセルする

ナレーション

Man:　City Center Salon. How may I help you?

Woman: Hi. I have an appointment with Lisa tomorrow at 3p.m. for a bang trim and full color. Unfortunately, something suddenly came up so I need to reschedule to sometime next week.

Man:　Sure thing. Let me check Lisa's schedule really quickly. Okay, so next week, Lisa is only available on Tuesday after 4p.m. or on Thursday at noon.

Woman: Hmm ... I'm not available at any of those times. Can you just cancel my appointment for tomorrow and I'll book Lisa again another time?

Man:　Of course. Okay, you're all set. We hope to hear from you soon!

Questions　21. Where is the man probably working?

22. What did the woman decide to do for now?

(男)：シティーセンターサロンです。いつもありがとうございます。

(女)：こんにちは。明日午後3時にリサさんに前髪のカットとフルカラーの予約をしているのですが。あいにく，急に予定が入ってしまったので，来週に変更したいのですが。

(男)：もちろんです。いますぐにリサのスケジュールを確認します。来週は，火曜日の午後４時以降か，木曜日の正午しか空いていませんね。

(女)：うーん，その時間だとだめだわ。明日の予約をキャンセルしてもらえますか。それで別の機会にまたリサさんを予約します。

(男)：もちろんです。では，またのご連絡をお待ちしております。

質問　21. 男性はおそらくどこで働いているのでしょうか。

22. いまのところ女性はどうしようと決めましたか。

Conversation 2

23.　解答：B

解説　男性の助言には，オンライン募集，履歴書の要求，身元照会先に連絡する (contact references) ことは含まれるが，直接応募者と面接することには触れていないので，B が正解である。references とは履歴書などに記載する「身元照会先」で，志願者のことをよく知り問い合わせにも答えられる人物を意味している。

A. オンラインで募集する　　B. 応募者を面接する

C. 身元照会先に連絡する　　D. 履歴書を提出してもらう

24.　解答：D

解説　女性が最後に「面倒だからその方法は今度にする」という趣旨の発言をしていることから，D が正解である。男性の助言が「嫌だ」とまでは言っていないので B は不適である。

A. よい考えだと思っている。

B. それは嫌だと思っている。

C. 男性に助けて欲しいと思っている。

D. それは面倒すぎると思っている。

ナレーション

Woman: The daycare we usually put our daughter in is closed so I'm looking for someone who can babysit for me next week from

Monday to Friday while I'm working from home.

Man: Why don't you try posting an advertisement online? I'm sure you can find someone easily that way.

Woman: Is it safe though? How will I know if I can trust a random stranger I find online?

Man: Ask the applicants to submit a resume with their background and work experience. Oh, and ask for references and then contact them.

Woman: That sounds like so much work and it would take so much time. Maybe I'll try doing that next time when I'm not in such a hurry to find someone.

Questions 23. Which of the following does the man NOT suggest to the woman?

24. What does the woman think about the man's suggestion?

(女)：いつも娘を預けている保育園が閉園しちゃって，来週，月曜から金曜まで私が家からオンラインで仕事をしている間，誰かベビーシッターをしてくれる人を探しているの。

(男)：インターネットに広告を出してみたら？　きっと簡単に見つかると思うよ。

(女)：でも大丈夫？　ネットで見つけた見ず知らずの人を信用できるかどうか，どうやって判断したらいいの？

(男)：応募者に経歴や職歴を書いた履歴書を提出してもらうんだよ。それと，身元紹介先も書いてもらってそこに連絡してみるんだよ。

(女)：それってすごく大変そうだし，時間もかかりそうね。今度，そんなに急ぎでないときにそうするわ。

質問　23. 次のうち男性が女性に助言していないのはどれですか。

24. 女性は男性の助言についてどう思っていますか。

Conversation 3

25.　解答：D

解説　会話の内容から，2人とも気候変動については否定していないが，女性は気候変動への政治家の対応を危惧しているのに対し，男性は，実際には気候変動活動家が警告しているほどの極端な深刻さはないと言っている。こうした内容と矛盾しないのはDである。

A. 女性は地元の政治家である。
B. 男性は気候変動活動家である。
C. 男性は気候変動の存在を否定している。
D. 女性は気候変動について危惧している。

26. 解答：A

解説 女性は heat waves（熱波）と wild fires（山火事）について言及しているので，選択肢の中では A が正解である。

A. 熱波　B. 台風　C. ハリケーン　D. 洪水

ナレーション

Woman: There have been high temperature records all over the world and our leaders are still not taking climate change seriously.

Man: I think the problem is the climate change side always warns about the consequences of climate change but then nothing extremely serious actually happens so it's hard for people to take these warnings seriously.

Woman: Are unprecedented natural disasters like heat waves and wildfires not serious enough?!

Man: Well obviously not, right? Climate change just isn't as important to regular people as it is to climate activists.

Woman: What is more important than whether humanity can exist or not?

Questions 25. Which of the following is probably true based on this conversation?

26. Which natural disaster does the woman specifically mention?

(女)：世界中で最高気温の記録が更新されているのに，指導者たちはまだ気候変動に真剣に取り組んでいないわね。

(男)：問題は，気候変動の危険を主張する側がいつも気候変動の悪影響について警告しているのに，実際には極端に深刻なことが起きないから，人々がこれらの警告を真剣に受け止められないことだと思うんだ。

(女)：熱波や山火事といった前例のない自然災害は十分に深刻ではないのかしら？

(男)：明らかに深刻じゃないだろ？　気候変動は，一般の人々にとっては，気候変動活動家ほど重要ではないんだ。

(女)：人類が存在できるかどうかよりも重要なことってあるの？

質問　25. この会話の内容からして正しいのは次のどれですか。

26. 女性は特にどの自然災害について話していますか。

Conversation 4

27.　解答：A

解説　女性がスマートフォンのゲームについて述べている箇所は，話の順に，“so much fun,” “addicting,” “mindless and violent” である。この中に含まれないのは A である。

A. 値段が高い。　B. 暴力的だ。　C. 楽しい。　D. 中毒性がある。

28.　解答：C

解説　男性がスマートフォンでゲームをするのは “only when I have time to kill”（暇つぶしの時間があるときだけ）と述べているので，C が正解である。

A. 仕事中　B. お金があるとき

C. 暇な時間があるとき　D. 友人と一緒のとき

ナレーション

Man: I've been really into this game lately. It's so much fun.

Woman: I try to stay away from smartphone games. They're so much fun that they become addicting. Also, aren't most of them just super mindless and violent?

Man: Mindless maybe. But they're not always violent. I spend a lot of time playing games but I also have a busy social life. It's all about balance. I play them only when I have time to kill.

Woman: I admit I might be a bit biased because of all the bad stuff I see on TV about video game addiction.

Man: Fair enough, but like I said, if you just play it in your free time, I don't see anything wrong with it. I've seen some of my coworkers play games on their phone at work though. Now that's a problem.

Questions 27. What does the woman NOT say about smartphone games?

28. When does the man play smartphone games?

(男)：最近，このゲームにすごくハマっているんだ。すごく楽しいよ。

(女)：スマートフォンのゲームには手を出さないようにしているの。楽しすぎて中毒になりそう。それに，ほとんどのゲームが頭をつかわないし，暴力的じゃない？

(男)：頭をつかわないって言われればそうかもしれないけど。でも，いつも暴力的というわけじゃないよ。僕は長時間ゲームをするけど，社会生活も忙しく送っているよ。バランスが大事なんだ。時間があるときだけゲームをすることにしているんだ。

(女)：テレビでゲーム中毒について悪いことばかり言っているので，私は少し偏見があるかもね。

(男)：そうだね。でも，さっきも言ったように，暇なときにやるだけなら，何も問題ないと思うよ。でも，同僚が仕事中に携帯電話でゲームをしているのを見たことがあるけど，それはそれで問題だよね。

質問 27. スマートフォンのゲームについて女性が言っていないのはどれですか。

28. 男性はいつスマートフォンのゲームをしますか。

Conversation 5

29. 解答：B

解説 冒頭の女性と男性のやり取りから，女性が難民支援のための募金活動をしており，男性も女性の所属している団体をNGOと認識しているいることが伺えるから，Bが正解である。

A. 学校で　　B. 非営利団体で

C. 難民認定処理センターで　　D. 政府研究機関で

30.　解答：C

解説 募金の多くが非営利団体の運営に回されてしまうのではないかとの男性の懸念に対し，女性が，“I totally hear you.”（= I totally understand.）と反応しているので，C が正解である。女性は男性の発言（募金がきちんと支援につながらない）に対して賛成しているわけではないので B は不適である。

A. 驚いた。　　B. 彼の考えに賛成した。

C. 共感した。　　D. 彼の言葉を信じなかった。

ナレーション

Woman: Hi, are you interested in donating to help refugees displaced by the war?

Man: Umm ... sure. Can I ask how much of the money actually goes to helping refugees? No offense but I've heard that a lot of these NGOs actually spend much of the money on administrative and fundraising costs, so not all the money goes to the actual cause.

Woman: I totally hear you. At International Refugees Fund, 90% of the money we receive will go directly to helping refugees. Here is a detailed breakdown of how and where we spend the money.

Man: Hmm ... okay. Wow that's impressive. Sorry if I sounded a little cynical. Can I donate 20 dollars?

Woman: Of course. Thank you so much! We'll definitely put it to good use!

Questions　29. Where does the woman probably work?

30. How does the woman react to the man's concern?

（女）：こんにちは，戦争で避難している難民を助けるために寄付にご協力いただけますか。

（男）：うーん……いいですよ。でも，その寄付金のうち，実際に難民を助けるために使われるのはどれぐらいなんですか。気を悪くしたらすみません，でもこういったNGOの多くは，実際には管理費や資金調達費にお金の多くを費やして，すべてのお金が実際の目的に使われるわけではない，と聞いたことがあるんです。

(女)：おっしゃることはよくわかります。でも国際難民基金では，受け取ったお金の9割が難民支援に直接使われます。どこにどのようにお金を使うか，詳しい内訳はこちらです。

(男)：ふーん……なるほど。ああ，確かにすごいですね。ちょっと皮肉っぽく聞こえたらすみませんでした。20ドル寄付してもいいですか。

(女)：もちろんです。本当にありがとうございます。ぜひ有効に使わせていただきます。

質問　29. 女性はおそらくどこで働いているでしょうか。
　　　30. 男性の心配に対して女性はどう反応していますか。

IV

（初めに）2つの短いナレーションが読まれ，そのナレーションの後にそれぞれ5つの質問文が読まれます。最も適切な答えを選びなさい。

Talk 1

31.　解答：A

解説　話し手はインテリアデザイン事業を一から立ち上げたときの体験談を語っているので，Aが正解である。

A. 事業主　　B. 宅配業者　　C. デザインの教師　　D. 不動産

32.　解答：C

解説　自信の源は“learning from failures”だったと語っていることから，Cが正解となる。

A. 情熱を追い続けることによって
B. すばらしい指導者を持つことによって
C. 失敗から学ぶことによって
D. 多くのプロジェクトに成功したことによって

33.　解答：A

解説　“Oh, and I also shared a lot of my failures with the audience on my blog ...”と話していることから，Aが正解である。

A. ブログで　　B. ビデオ共有サイトで
C. 自らの本で　　D. インターネットのフォーラムで

34. 解答：D

解説 自分の成功の要因について，“There was no Plan B.” つまり成功以外の選択肢を残さないように自分を追い込んだと述べている。D が正解となる。
A. デザインを学んだこと　　B. 多くの人と人脈があったこと
C. 間違いをしなかったこと　　D. 第 2 の選択肢を持たなかったこと

35. 解答：D

解説 話し手は，自らを追い込むために家を売り，別の場所に引っ越し，すべての時間と労力を新しい事業に費やしたと言っている。言及されていないのは D である。
A. 家を売ったこと　　B. 引っ越したこと
C. 仕事に集中したこと　　D. 仕事を休んだこと

ナレーション

I think there were two things I did that helped me take my interior design business from a one-person side job in my bedroom to what it is today.

First, I built up my confidence by learning from my failures. I didn't study design. I was a self-taught designer so a lot of what I was doing was just trial and error. And trust me, I failed a lot. But I didn't let my mistakes stop me from moving forward. I filed away every mistake as a learning experience for what not to do in the future. Oh, and I also shared a lot of my failures with the audience on my blog so they could learn from my mistakes as well. I think that really helped me build trust with them.

Second, I forced myself to focus on my goal by not giving myself any option to turn back. I sold my house, moved to a different state, and put all my time, money and energy into the business. There was no Plan B. I didn't have an exit strategy so I had to succeed. I don't know if that was the smartest decision, but at that time, that was the right decision for me.

Questions　31. What is most likely the speaker's job?

32. What did the speaker say helped her gain confidence?

33. Where did the speaker share stories of her failures?

34. What does the speaker attribute her success to?

35. Which of the following did the speaker NOT mention doing?

語句　self-taught: 独学の　trial and error: 試行錯誤　And trust me: 本当に，真面目な話　force oneself to ～: 自分に鞭《むち》打って～する　put ～ into ... : ～（時間や労力など）を…に注ぐ　exit strategy: 出口戦略（プロジェクトがうまくいかなかったときに最小限の損害でそれから撤退する方法）

訳例　インテリアデザインの仕事を，寝室で１人でやっていた副業から，いまのような形にすることに成功した要因として，私は２つのことがあったと思います。

１つ目は，失敗から学ぶことで自信をつけたこと。私はデザインの勉強をしたわけではありません。独学でデザインを学び，試行錯誤を繰り返してきました。もちろん，失敗もたくさんしました。でも，失敗を恐れて前に進めないということはありませんでした。すべての失敗を，今後やってはいけないことの学習経験としてファイルしました。また，私の失敗談をブログで紹介し，そこからブログの読者に学んでもらうようにしました。そうすることで，読者との信頼関係を築くこともできたと思います。

次に，後戻りする選択肢を自分に与えないことで，目標に集中するように自分を追い込みました。家を売り，別の州に移り住み，時間，お金，エネルギーをすべてビジネスに注ぎました。プランＢはなく，出口戦略もなかったので，成功するしかなかった。それが最も賢明な判断であったかどうかはわかりませんが，当時はそれが私にとって正しい判断だったのです。

質問　31. 話し手の仕事はおそらく何でしょうか。

32. 話し手は，何が自信につながったと言っていますか。

33. 話し手は，失敗談をどこで共有しましたか。

34. 話し手は，成功の要因は何だと言っていますか。

35. 次のうち，話し手が言及しなかったものはどれですか。

Talk 2

36. 解答：A

解説 “In order to help your students think deeply ...” とあることから，話し手は，教員を相手に講義をしているとわかるので，A が正解である。

A. 教員研修のトレーナー　B. 高校生

C. スポーツのコーチ　D. 外交政策の専門家

37. 解答：B

解説 話し手が教員研修のトレーナーであるらしいことや，他の選択肢の聴衆に向けて話している可能性は低いので，B が正解である。

A. 大学生　B. 教師　C. 官僚　D. 運動選手

38. 解答：C

解説 「誤った原因の誤謬《ごびゅう》」つまり，因果関係に関する誤りの例として，「赤い服を着ると必ず自分の応援しているチームが勝つ」という主張が挙げられていたので，C が正解である。

A. 洗車するたびに翌日は雨になる。

B. とんかつを食べるといつも合格する。

C. ある色の服を着ると応援チームがいつも勝つ。

D. 仕事でプレゼンをすると必ず子どもが病気になる。

39. 解答：B

解説 Ad hominem attack は，正当な主張に対して真っ向から立ち向かいたくない政治家が使うと述べているので B が正解である。

A. 外交官　B. 政治家　C. 教授　D. スポーツセラピスト

40. 解答：B

解説 話し手が挙げていたのは，順に，false cause, ad hominem, No true Scotsman, Texas sharpshooter, bandwagon であるので，選択肢の中で言及されていないのは B である。ちなみにこの the slippery slope fallacy は，確たる裏付けもなく「○○○しないと（すると）×××になる」などと連鎖反応によって大変なことが起こると主張する論法である。

A. バンドワゴンの誤謬　B. 下り坂論法の誤謬

C. 真のスコットランド人の誤謬　　D. テキサスの狙撃手の誤謬

ナレーション

Logical fallacies are mistakes that people make in the reasoning process. In order to help your students think deeply, they need to know about the different types of logical fallacies.

Here's an example. You might hear someone claim, "Whenever I wear red, my favorite sports team always wins." That means if they wear red every day for the rest of their life, their team will never lose another game! This argument is a false cause fallacy. A happens, then B happens. So you assume that A caused B. Maybe, but maybe not.

Another logical fallacy that's quite common is the ad hominem attack, which is when someone attacks the person instead of the argument. For instance, you say something like, "I don't think our government should be so aggressive when dealing with China," and the other person replies with, "Well, you never graduated college so you don't know what you're talking about." Ad hominems are horrible for debate but they are often used by politicians who don't want to directly address a legitimate argument.

There are many other logical fallacies like the "No true Scotsman fallacy," the "Texas sharpshooter fallacy," the "bandwagon fallacy," etc. I can go on and on but the main point here is in order to help your students make strong arguments, you should teach them about logical fallacies.

Questions 36. Who most likely is the speaker?

37. Who is the speaker most likely speaking to?

38. Which example does the speaker give to explain the false cause fallacy?

39. Who does the speaker say often use ad hominem attacks?

40. Which of the following logical fallacies did the speaker NOT mention?

語句 logical fallacy: 論理的誤謬（ごびゅう）　reasoning process: 推論過程

claim: ～と主張する（「クレームを言う」の意味ではないので要注意） false cause fallacy: 誤った原因による誤謬　ad hominem attack: 人身攻撃（ラテン語で to the person を意味する） No true Scotsman fallacy: 真のスコットランド人論法の誤謬（全ての○○は～だ，と一般化して言いたい場合，そうでない例が出てきても，いやそれは真の○○ではないのだ，と一般化を弁護する論法） Texas sharpshooter fallacy: テキサスの狙撃兵の誤謬（狙撃兵が銃弾をたくさん打ち込んだ後から的を描いて自分がすぐれた狙撃手だと主張するように，都合のよいデータを強調して論理構築しようとする誤謬）
bandwagon policy: 衆人に訴える論法の誤謬（皆がそう信じているので正しい，といった誤謬。bandwagon はパレードなどの楽隊車の意味で，「人気のある側」を比喩的に示している）

訳例　論理的誤謬とは，人が推論する過程で犯す間違いのことです。生徒が深く考えるためには，さまざまな種類の論理的誤謬について知っておく必要があります。

例を挙げてみますね。例えば，「赤い服を着ると，好きなスポーツチームがいつも勝つ」と主張する人がいるとします。つまり，もしその人が一生，毎日赤い服を着ていたら，そのチームは二度と試合に負けることはない，ということになります。この主張は，false cause fallacy（誤った原因による誤謬）です。A が起きると，B が起きる。だから，A が B を引き起こしたと仮定しているわけです。

もう一つの論理的誤謬は，よくあることですが，ad hominem attack（人身攻撃）です。これは，誰かがその人の議論ではなく，その人自身を攻撃することです。例えば，あなたが「中国を相手にするとき，政府はそれほど攻撃的になるべきではないと思う」と言って，相手が「大学を出ていないのだから，君はものがわかっていないのだ」と言うような場合です。Ad hominems は議論としてはひどいものなのですが，正当な議論に直接立ち向かいたくない政治家がよく使います。

他にも，「真のスコットランド人論法の誤謬」「テキサスの狙撃兵の誤謬」「衆人に訴える論法の誤謬」など，多くの論理的誤謬があります。まだまだありますが，ここで重要なのは，生徒が説得力のある議論をするのを助けるためには，論理的誤謬について教えるべきだということです。

質問　36. 話し手はおそらく誰ですか。

37. 話し手はおそらく誰に向かって話していますか。

38. 話し手は，どのような例を挙げて，誤った原因の誤謬を説明していますか。

39. 話し手は，人身攻撃をよく使うのは誰だと言っていますか。

40. 次の論理的誤謬のうち，話し手が触れていないものはどれですか。

V 4つの選択肢の中から,
以下のそれぞれの英文の（　　　　）に入る最も適切なものを選びなさい。

41. 解答：D

解説 worst には the が付きやすいことを考えると，the worst of 〜「〜の中で最悪のもの」という表現が自然だとわかる。D が正解である。

訳例 「しかし，戦争犯罪について語るとき，最悪の犯罪は戦争そのものであることを忘れてはならない」とグテーレス氏は述べた。

42. 解答：A

解説 「20 人のウクライナ人」を説明する表現が来る。ここでは，「そのうちの何人かは日本に家族や友人がいない」ということで，some of whom do not ... とつながるので A が正解である。

訳例 日本に家族や友人がいない人も含め，ウクライナ人 20 人が火曜日，政府専用機で羽田空港に到着した。

43. 解答：C

解説 fell by ... from A to B という構造を見つけられれば「A（前年）から…だけ減少し B（過去最低の○人）に至った」という意味だとわかる。C が正解となる。

訳例 厚生労働省が金曜日に発表したところによると，2021 年に日本で生まれた新生児の数は，前年から 29,231 人（3.5%）減少し，過去最低の 811,604 人となった。

44. 解答：C

解説 for the first time in 〜 は「〜（ある期間）の中で初めて」の意味の決まり文句である。したがって C が正解となる。

訳例 英国は 350 年にわたる気候の記録の中で初めて，40 度以上の気温を記録した。

45. 解答：B

解説 まず動詞が先に来るべきなので選択肢 A と B が候補に挙がるが，posed の前に来るのは，B. warned of the risk である。

訳例　アントニオ・グテーレス事務総長は，広島で行われた恒例の追悼式で，ウクライナ，中東，朝鮮半島の危機がもたらすリスクについて警告した。

VI

下線を引いた単語または語句の中から，
文法的もしくは慣用的に不適切なものを選びなさい。

46.　解答：C

解説　「選出された」(was elected) は過去形でよいが，「2023 年 1 月 1 日から 2 年間の任期を務める」のは記事が書かれた時点では未来のことであるから (C) は will serve とするのが正しい。

訳例　日本は，国連総会の選挙で国連安全保障理事会 (UNSC) の非常任理事国に選出され，2023 年 1 月 1 日から 2 年間の任期を務めることになった。

47.　解答：A

解説　NATO ambassadors がこの文の主語であり，文の後半にそれを受ける主動詞がないことから，(A) signing を signed とする必要がある。

訳例　7 月 5 日，ブリュッセルでの式典で，NATO の各国大使は加盟議定書に署名し，フィンランドとスウェーデンの加盟に一歩近づけた。

48.　解答：B

解説　「共同国境で」という場合，国境に設置された検問所の場所を指しているので (B) in は at とするのが適切である。(注：モロッコ内にはスペイン領のいわゆる飛び地が 2 カ所あり，ヨーロッパに渡る中継地としてモロッコ領からスペイン領の飛び地に越境しようとして移民が警備隊と衝突する事件が起きたりする。)

訳例　国連人権局はモロッコとスペインに対し，共同国境において移民の人権が守られるよう，また国境職員が過剰な力の行使を控えるよう促した。

49.　解答：B

解説　(B) late (遅れた) を latest (最新の) とすることで文脈上意味の通る英文になる。

訳例　国連の最新データによると，世界で約 10 億人が何らかの精神障害に苦しんでいる。この驚くべき数字は，10 代の若者の約 7 人に 1 人が含まれていることを考えると，さらに憂慮すべきものである。

50. 解答：D

解説 「特定の交通環境における」を英語では in certain traffic ... と表現しており，certain の前に a がないことから，「特定のいつくか想定される環境における」と考えねばならないので，(D) は environments と複数にする必要がある。

訳例 特定の交通環境における自動運転を，現在の時速 60km から 130km まで拡大する案が採択されたことで，人間の交通手段における新たな進展が得られた。

Ⅶ-A

『新 わかりやすい国連の活動と世界』から得た知識に基づき，(A)～(D) から空欄を埋めるのに最も適切なものを選びなさい。

51. 解答：D

解説 国際司法裁判所は国連の司法 (judicial) 機関である。

A. 商業の　B. 政治の　C. 社交の　D. 司法の

52. 解答：A

解説 国際司法裁判所は，加盟国が裁判所に付託する (refer) すべての問題を管轄する。

A. 付託する　B. つながる　C. 同意する　D. 反対する

53. 解答：C

解説 加盟国は，あらかじめ国際司法裁判所の管轄権を義務として受け入れる手続きをすることができるが，その方法の 1 つが，条約や協定に調印すること (signing) である。

A. 避けること　B. 意義を唱えること

C. 調印すること　D. 拒否権を行使すること

54. 解答：B

解説 国際司法裁判所の裁判官の選出においては，総会と安全保障理事会が個々に (independently) 投票を行い，双方で投票の絶対多数を得た候補者が当選となる。

A. 共同で　B. 個々に　C. 全会一致で　D. 暫定的に

55.　解答：C

解説　国際司法裁判所の裁判官は，そのうちのいずれの２人も，同一国籍〔同一国の国民 (nationals)〕であってはならない。

A. 罪人　　B. 学者　　C. 国民　　D. 指導者

訳例　オランダのハーグにある国際司法裁判所は，国連の主要な (51) 司法機関である。この裁判所の機能は，国際連盟の時代の常設国際司法裁判所規程に基づいて作成され，現在の国連憲章の重要な一部をなす規程に定義されている。

国際司法裁判所の管轄権は，国が裁判所に (52) 付託するすべての問題，国連憲章または現行の条約や協定に定められたすべての事項に及ぶ。国は特別な事件の場合，裁判所への付託を条件とする条約や協定に (53) 調印するか，または同様の趣旨の特別宣言を行うことにより，事前に裁判所の管轄権を義務として受け入れることができる。このような義務管轄権を受け入れる宣言では，ある種の事件は除外されることがある。

裁判所は，総会及び安全保障理事会が (54) 個々に行う投票によって選出された 15 人の裁判官によって構成される。裁判官は，国籍によってではなく個々の資格によって選出されると同時に，世界の主要な法体系の代表が揃うよう配慮されている。同一国籍〔同一国の (55) 国民〕の裁判官が２人選出されることはない。裁判官の任期は９年で，再選されることもある。裁判官は任期中に他の職業に就くことはできない。

『新 わかりやすい国連の活動と世界』p.59

Ⅶ-B　『新 わかりやすい国連の活動と世界』から得た知識に基づき，４つの選択肢から空欄を埋めるのに最も適切なものを選びなさい。

56.　解答：B

解説　2017 年９月 19 日の国連総会でグテーレス事務総長は世界平和に対する７つの脅威について述べたが，最初に挙げられたのは核の危険だった。

A. テロリズム　　B. 核の危険　　C. 人間の移動　　D. 気候変動

『新 わかりやすい国連の活動と世界』p.24 参照

57.　解答：D

解説　国連憲章は 1945 年６月 26 日にサンフランシスコで調印された。

A. アムステルダム　　B. ロンドン　　C. パリ　　D. サンフランシスコ

同上 p.43 参照

58.　解答：C

解説　国連の公式の印章・標章は北極の上から見た世界地図である。

A. 赤道　B. 英国　C. 北極　D. 南極

同上 p.45 参照

59.　解答：B

解説　人権理事会は 47 加盟国から構成されている。

A. 36 加盟国　B. 47 加盟国　C. 120 加盟国　D. 193 加盟国

同上 p.59 参照

60.　解答：A

解説　日本国際連合協会は，日本が国連に加盟した 1956 年に先立ち，1947 年に設立された。

A. 1947 年　B. 1956 年　C. 1962 年　D. 1972 年

同上 p.170 参照

VIII-A　以下の各英文を読み，下記のそれぞれの質問に答えなさい。
下記の英文を挿入するのに最も適した箇所を，(A)～(D) から選びなさい。

Passage 1

61.　解答：C

解説　否定的な内容から，希望の光が見える内容へのつなぎの文であるから，第 3 パラグラフと第 4 パラグラフのつなぎとなる文であるとわかるので，C が正解である。

62.　解答：D

解説　They aim to ～ の They が何を指しているかを考える。They はケニア沿岸のコミュニティを助けるものだとわかるので，D が正解となる。

63.　解答：B

解説　「マングローブは人々に利益を与える一方で……」とあるので，その直前にマングローブの環境や人間への貢献について語っている (B) の位置に挿入するのが最適である。

語句 erosion: 浸食　storm surge: 高潮　nursery habitat:（稚魚などが安全に育つことのできる）生育場　sequester ～: ～を吸収する　be depleted: 枯渇する　rampant: 止まない　round out ～: ～を膨らませる

訳例　マングローブは，大きな可能性を秘めた熱帯海域の森林です。海岸線を浸食や高潮から守り，多様な野生生物の食料や避難場所を提供し，商業的に重要な魚介類の稚魚の生育場となっています。

マングローブは気候変動とも闘っています。国連環境計画（UNEP）は，世界のマングローブ林がその根や幹，土壌の中に毎年2,280万トンもの炭素を吸収していると推定しています。

(B) マングローブ林は，人と地球に貴重な恩恵を提供する一方で，危機に瀕《ひん》しています。海面や気温の上昇といった気候変動の影響に加え，マングローブ林は，その木材が建築用材，燃料，さらには医薬品の主要な供給源として沿岸地域の人々に珍重されているため，枯渇が進んでいるのです。さらに，沿岸部の都市化の進行，持続不可能な農業や養殖業など，さまざまな問題が山積しています。

(C) しかし，すべての希望が失われたわけではありません。革新的なパートナーシップは，持続可能な解決策につながる可能性があります。過去3年間，国連機関，ケニア政府，その他の主要なパートナーが力を合わせ，コミュニティを基盤とした保全プロジェクトをいくつか立ち上げてきました。(D) これらのプロジェクトは，貧困問題に対処するとともに，気候変動，生物多様性，地域レベルの利益をケニア沿岸のコミュニティに提供することを目的としています。

Ⅷ-B

Passage 2

64.　解答：C

解説 wasting はここでは死に至る子どもたちの健康状態，つまり消耗症（栄養失調で体力が極度に弱る状態）を指しているので，正解はCである。

A. 虐待　　B. 中毒　　C. 衰弱　　D. 切望

65.　解答：D

解説 escalate はここでは「深刻化する」の意味であるからDが正解である。

A. 顕在化する　　B. 浮遊している　　C. 有望な　　D. 激化する

66. 解答：B

解説 bear the brunt of ～ は「～の攻撃を受ける」の意味である。前後の文脈からも，B の意味であることが推測できる。

A. ～の原因となっている　　B. ～の影響を受けている
C. ～の責任をとっている　　D. ～の終わりを望んでいる

67. 解答：A

解説 tinderbox とは「(昔，火をおこすのに用いた) 火口《ほくち》を入れた箱」で一触即発の状態の比喩として用いられる。“begin to catch fire” とあることからも，A の意味だと推測できる。

A. 危険なもの　　B. 高価なもの　　B. 未知のもの　　D. 不道徳なもの

68. 解答：D

解説 この文脈においては，critical は「非常に重要な」の意味で用いられているので，正解は D である。

A. 否定的な　　B. 危険な　　C. 重大な　　D. 非常に重要な

69. 解答：C

解説 この文脈においては，conflict は「紛争」の意味で用いられているので，最も近いものは C である。

A. 議論　　B. 意見の相違　　C. 戦争　　D. 叫び

70. 解答：B

解説 insecurity は「不安」「不安定状態」の意味であり，ここでは，子どもたちへの食料・栄養調達の危機を意味しているので，B が最も適切である。

A. 野心　　B. 危機　　C. 疑念　　D. 謙遜

語句 theraputic: 治療を目的とした　the Horn of Africa: アフリカの角（エチオピア，エリトリア，ジブチ，ソマリア，ケニアを含む，“角” のように突き出たアフリカ大陸東部の地域の呼称）　dought: 干ばつ　drive up ～: ～に拍車をかける　catastrophic: 破壊的な

訳例　ユニセフは本日，G7 サミットでの協議を控えた各国首脳に対し，危機的状況にある 15 カ国の 5 歳未満の子どものうち，800 万人近くが，直ちに治療食

とケアを受けなければ重度の（64）消耗症で死亡する危険があり，その数は刻一刻と増加していると警告した。

今年に入ってから，（65）深刻化する世界的な食糧危機により，アフリカの角や中央サヘルなど，（66）危機の影響を受けている15カ国において，26万人（60秒に1人）の子どもたちが重度の消耗症に苦しんでいる。この重度の消耗症の増加は，ユニセフが先月「まさに事実上の火薬箱状態」だと警告した子どもの栄養失調の現状が，さらに悪化していることを示している。

ユニセフのキャサリン・ラッセル事務局長は，「私たちはいま，極度のレベルの子どもの消耗症という（67）火薬庫が燃え始めるのを目の当たりにしている」と述べ，さらに「食糧援助は（68）非常に重要だが，小麦の袋で飢餓に苦しむ子どもたちを救うことはできない。手遅れになる前に，いま，この子どもたちに治療薬を届ける必要がある」とした。

ウクライナ戦争による食糧価格の高騰，気候変動による持続的な干ばつが一部の国で発生し，それが時として（69）紛争と重なったこと，さらにコロナ禍の経済的影響が続いていることから，世界中で子どもたちの食糧・栄養（70）不安が続き，5歳未満の子どもたちの栄養不良は壊滅的なレベルになっている。これに対し，ユニセフは最も影響を受けている15カ国において，取り組みの規模を拡大している。

IX

以下の英文を読み，下記のそれぞれの質問に答えなさい。

【長文問題の解答対策】

英語の長文を読む際の基本的アプローチについては，2021年度の解説を参照していただき，ここでは，問題IXに出題される英文の特徴に即した読み方について言及したい。問題IXで用いられる英文の多くは，国際連合が取り組んでいる世界の諸問題について，それに取り組んでいる当事者（国連関係者）あるいはそれらの諸問題に精通している専門家やジャーナリストが書いた英文やスピーチスクリプトが多い。

これらの英文の文体的特徴として，主張とその理由や背景，事例から得られた分析結果や示唆，事象間の因果関係などについて述べる文が多く，どうしても一文が長くなる傾向がある。文が長いということは，複数の情報が1つの文にまとめられているということなので，それらの情報間の関係を捉えられるようにすればよいのだが，ここが難しい。特に日本人が苦手とする，関係詞節や前置詞句をはじめとする後置修飾（名詞のあとからその名詞の説明をする表現が付属する構造），コンマやコロンのあとに説明が追加される場合，挿入句など，文を複雑にする要素が満載である。基本的には経験が物を言うのだが，困ったときは，「いったい何が（誰が）どうしたのか」を読み取ってみるとよい。つまり，その文の中心的な主語と動詞を探すのである。主語は関係詞節などで長くなっていることがあるが，動詞は（動詞句になっても）1～2語なので見つけやすい。

また，内容的特徴としては，国連が取り組む諸問題，特にSDGs関連のトピックに関する内容が多いので，そういったトピックに関する英字新聞やニュースの記事，国連ホームページから閲覧できる報告書や資料などを読んでおくのもよいだろう。その中で重要と思われるキーワードや英文をメモしたり，あるいは表計算ソフトなどに入力してデータベースを作成したりするのもよいだろう。そうした表現の中には，Xの課題作文問題で使えるものもあるかもしれない。

こうした学習経験の積み重ねに基づき，実際の試験において英文を読む際には，まずトピックは何か，誰が何のために書いているか（スピーチスクリプトの場合は誰がどのような場で話しているのか）を想像し，パラグラフごとの要点を捉えながら読み進めるのである。

特に冒頭のパラグラフは，英文全体の理解に最も重要で，ここで概要を的確につかめるかどうかが，その後のパラグラフの理解のスピードや理解の深さに影響する。今回の英文は，冒頭に，As Secretary-General of the United Nations, I spend ... とあることから，国連事務総長の演説（原稿）であることがわかる。また3行目には“we are at a defining moment in international relations”とあり，事務総長の立場から現在の国際情勢の課題について考察する内容なのではないかと推察できる。

71．解答：D

解説 このパラグラフの最後の2文が話の中心的テーマとなっている。すなわち，世界のリーダーたちは，問題があることについてはagreeしているが，それに見合う共通の行動（common action）が見られないということで，Dが正解である。

第1パラグラフで述べられているのは次のうちどれか。

A. 世界の指導者たちは協力して地球規模の問題に取り組んでいる。

B. COVID-19（新型コロナウイルス感染症）の大流行が世界的な武力紛

争を引き起こした。
C. 新しいテクノロジーの発達が男女間の不平等を悪化させている。
D. 多くのグローバルリーダーたちは，共通の脅威に対処するための行動をとっていない。

72. 解答：A

解説 第2パラグラフで，事務総長は分断された世界の現状を語っており，選択肢の中で言及されているのはワクチン提供における不平等（unfair and unequal distribution of vaccines）であるから，A が正解である。

第2パラグラフで述べられているのは次のどれか？
A. ワクチンは公平，平等に提供されていない。
B. 世界経済は，発展途上国の人々に依存している。
C. 気候危機の問題への取り組みがなされている。
D. メディアは高度なデジタル技術を利用して利益を得ている。

73. 解答：C

解説 筆者（話し手である国連事務総長）は，このパラグラフで，国内の利益を優先しがちなリーダーの心情にも一定の理解を示している（This impulse is understandable ... とある）ので C が正解である。

第3パラグラフから推測されるのは次のどれか。
A. 筆者は国内の利益を優先する世界の指導者たちを非難している。
B. 筆者は世界の指導者たちが合意に達することができるかどうか疑っている。
C. 筆者は世界の指導者たちがなぜ国益を重視するのか理解している。
D. 筆者は国家内での連帯が最重要であると考えている。

74. 解答：B

解説 このパラグラフの中心的メッセージは，世界的なワクチン接種に協力することが，変異株の蔓延《まんえん》を遅らせ，自国の国民を守ることにつながるということであるので，B が正解である。

第4パラグラフで述べられているのは次のどれか。

A. COVID-19のパンデミックの影響は，国によって異なる。

B. 世界的なワクチン接種により，危険な変異株の蔓延を遅らせることができる。

C. 各国政府は長い間，国民全員へのワクチン接種に寄与してきた。

D. 世界的なリスクを最小化するために，国家内のワクチン接種が優先されるべきだ。

75. 解答：D

解説 このパラグラフで事務総長は，地政学的分断によりWHO，安全保障理事会などの国際機関がその力を発揮できていないことを述べ，最後にIn short, global governance is failing ... と，グローバル・ガバナンスができていない状況の重大さを訴えている。この点を要約しているのはDである。

第5パラグラフで述べられているのは次のうちどれか。

A. WHOは安全保障理事会よりも世界的な影響力を持っている。

B. パンデミックに対する世界の対応は協力体制が整っている。

C. 国連の金融組織の多くは発展途上国を優遇している。

D. グローバル・ガバナンス改革がこれほど緊急に必要とされる時はない。

76. 解答：A

解説 筆者（国連事務総長）は3行目Such reforms are essential if we are to ... 以下で，「我々が平和，持続可能な開発，人権，すべて人類の尊厳という地球規模の目標を達成するという共通の願望を実現するには」と述べていることから，加盟国がこうした目標を共有していることを前提として話をしていることが推測できるので，Aが正解となる。

第6パラグラフから推測されることは次のどれか。

A. 筆者は，地球規模の人類の福祉を実現することは，すべての国連加盟国が共有する目標であると信じている。

B. 筆者は，国家と地球全体の利益とは別問題だと考えている。

C. 筆者は，今日の世界のほとんどの国で人権が保護されていると考えている。

D. 筆者は，世界の多くの指導者が最終的には協力しないのではないかと心配している。

77. 解答：C

解説 このパラグラフの4行目に As the pandemic has taught us, our fates are tied. とあるので，Cが正解となる。AやDはこのパラグラフの内容と矛盾し，Bはこのパラグラフでは言及がないので不適である。

第7パラグラフで述べられているのは次のうちどれか。

A. 国家主権は国際的な幸福に比べれば二の次である。

B. 世界は新しい世界的組織を設立することができるリーダーを必要としている。

C. パンデミックは，人々の運命が相互に関連していることを証明している。

D. 最も脆弱《ぜいじゃく》な地域，国，そして人々をまず救うべきである。

78. 解答：B

解説 『私たちの共通の課題（Our Common Agenda)』が，課題解決に向けた道標（a roadmap）となると国連事務総長が言及しているのでBが正解である。Aの環境問題やCの改革の時期とその成果の関連については言及がなく，Dはこのパラグラフで述べられていることと矛盾する（同意できるところから着手しようと述べている）ので不適である。

第8パラグラフで述べられているのは次のうちどれか。

A. 人類は取り返しのつかない環境問題を数多く引き起こしてきた。

B.『私たちの共通の課題』には，世界的な協力のための提案が含まれている。

C. 改革が早ければ早いほど，よりよい結果が得られる。

D. 世界の指導者たちは，最も困難な課題に取り組むことから始めるべきだ。

79. 解答：A

解説 このパラグラフで「私たちは，すでにその影響を目の当たりにしています」という導入に続き，世界が協調できていないことの悪影響を例示している。B, C, D のような明るい内容についての言及はなく，A が正解である。

第 9 パラグラフで述べられていることはどれか？

A. 世界が協調できていないことによる悪影響が現れている。

B. 世界機関の価値に対する人々の信頼はまだ強い。

C. 世界の人々の間で，価値観の共有が進み始めている。

D. あらゆる社会は，不正，不平等，人種的偏見や差別を否定している。

80. 解答：D

解説 選択肢のトピックは直接的・間接的にこのスピーチで触れられているが，中心的なメッセージは，分断されて協調的行動ができない世界の国々が，互いに運命共同体であることを認識し協力すべきだ，ということであるので，D が正解である。

この記事のタイトルとして最も適切なものはどれか。

A. 今日の世界が直面する問題

B. 国連の役割

C. 人権と尊厳の保護

D. 協調的行動の必要性

語句 take the pulse of 〜: 〜の脈をとる，〜の動向を把握する　gridlock: 行き詰まり　rig 〜 against ...: 〜を…に不利となるよう操作する　unrest and conflict: 暴動や紛争　perceived national interests: 意識された国益　trump 〜: 〜を負かす　wrong-headed: 判断を誤った　render 〜 useless: 〜を無意味なものに変える　impede 〜: 〜を阻害する　geo-political divides: 地政学的な分断　sovereignty: 主権　reinvigorate 〜: 〜を再び活性化する　multilateralism: 多国間主義　deliver: 結果を出す

訳例 1. 国際連合事務総長として，私は世界の指導者たちと話をし，世界の動向を把握することに多くの時間を費やしています。いま，私たちは明らかに国際関係において岐路に立たされています。国際的な意思決定が行き詰まり，

その根底にあるのは根本的な矛盾です。すなわち，一方では，今日の世界のリーダーたちの多くが，COVID，気候，無秩序な新技術の開発など，共通の脅威を認識しています。そして，これらの脅威に対して何かをしなければならないことに同意しています。しかし，その共通の理解は，共通の行動と一致していないのです。

2. 実際，溝は深まるばかりです。不公平で不平等なワクチンの配給，貧しい人々に不利なグローバル経済システム，気候危機へのまったく不十分な対応，分裂から利益を得るデジタル技術とメディア環境，世界中で拡大する暴動と紛争など，私たちは至るところでそのような状況を目の当たりにしています。では，もし世界がこれらの共通の問題の診断に同意しているならば，なぜ効果的に対処することができないのでしょうか。私は２つの根本的な理由があると考えています。
3. 第１に，外交政策がしばしば内政の投影になってしまっているからです。元首相として，私は，善意にもかかわらず，国際情勢が国内政治に乗っ取られることがあることを知っています。国益を意識することが，より大きな世界的利益を簡単に無視する結果になるのです。連帯が自国の利益につながる場合に誤った判断をしてしまったとしても，このような衝動は理解できます。
4. ワクチンがその典型例です。COVID-19のようなウイルスが国境を問わず蔓延することは誰もが理解しています。より危険な新型ウイルスが出現し，あらゆる国のあらゆる人に影響を及ぼすリスクを減らすために，私たちは全ての人々へのワクチン接種を必要としています。そのとき各国政府は，世界的なワクチン接種計画を通じてすべての人々へのワクチンを優先する代わりに，自国民を保護するために行動してきました。しかし，それは戦略の半分に過ぎません。もちろん，政府は自国民の安全を確保しなければなりません。しかし，全世界のワクチン接種を同時に行わなければ，新型ウイルスの出現と蔓延により，各国のワクチン接種計画が無意味になる可能性があります。
5. 第２に，現在のグローバル規模の制度や枠組みの多くは時代遅れであるか，脆弱であるにもかかわらず，必要な改革が地政学的な隔たりによって妨げられていることです。例えば，世界保健機関（WHO）の権限は，世界的なパンデミックへの対応を調整するために必要なレベルにはほど遠い状態です。同時に，より大きな力を持つ国際機関は，安全保障理事会のように分裂によって麻《ま》痺《ひ》しているか，多くの国際金融機関のように非民主的なものになってしまっています。つまり，グローバル・ガバナンスは，世界が一丸となって地球規模の問題を解決すべき時に，破綻しているのです。
6. 私たちは，公衆衛生や住みやすい気候など，人類の幸福を支える重要な地球規模の公共財を守るために，国家と同時に世界の自己利益のために共に行動する必要があるのです。平和，持続可能な開発，人権，全ての人類の尊厳といった私たちの集団的な世界目標に向けた共通の願望を実現するためには，こうした改革が不可欠なのです。

7. これは，国家主権の問題を考慮に入れる必要のある，困難で複雑な取り組みです。しかし，何もしないことは容認できる選択肢ではありません。世界は，人々の問題を解決できる，より効果的で民主的な国際的メカニズムを切に必要としています。パンデミックが私たちに教えてくれたように，私たちの運命は互いにつながっています。誰かを置き去りにすれば，すべての人を置き去りにする危険性があるのです。最も脆弱な地域，国，人々が，グローバルな政策におけるこの矛盾の最初の犠牲者です。しかし，誰もが，どこでも，直接的に危険にさらされているのです。

8. 幸いなことに，私たちはグローバルな課題に対して打つ手を持っています。人類が生み出した問題は，人類が解決することができるのです。昨年9月，私はこれらの問題に関する報告書を発行しました。『私たちの共通の課題(Our Common Agenda)』はその出発点であり，世界を結集させてこれらのガバナンスの課題に取り組み，21世紀の多国間主義を再活性化するための道筋です。変革は容易ではないし，一夜にして実現するものでもありません。しかし，我々は合意できる分野を見つけ，前進の方向へ向かうことから始めることができるのです。これは我々の最大の試練であり，世界の運命の多くがかかっています。

9. 私たちは，すでにその影響を目の当たりにしています。人々は制度の実現能力に対する信頼を失い始めると，そうした制度の根底にある価値観に対する信頼も失う危険性があります。世界の至るところで，信頼の喪失が見られ，共有された価値観の喪失と私が懸念する状態が出現しているのです。不公平，不平等，不信，人種的偏見や差別がすべての社会で暗い影を落としています。

10. 私たちは，人間の尊厳と良識を取り戻し，人々の不安に答えを出さなければなりません。相互に結びついた脅威の増大，甚大な人的被害，そして共有のリスクに対し，私たちは声を上げ，火を消すために行動する義務があるのです。

X 以下の質問に対して，80～100語の短いエッセイを英語で書きなさい。

質問：日本をより男女平等社会にするために政府がすべきことは何か。

（語数を記入する必要はありません）

【Essay writing 問題の解答対策】

英語で意見文を書く力を高めるための基本的学習法については，2021年度の解説を参照していただき，ここでは，指定された語数（B級では80–100語前後）で意見文を書く力を養う際のポイントを3つ挙げる。まず，回答する際の「分量バランス」に慣れることである。例えば，課題への回答として主張を一言で記述するIntroductionに1～2文，それを説明・支持するBodyに3～4文，主張を再度まとめるConclusionに1～2文，といったバランス感覚を養いながら練習することである（文の数は目安であり一文の長さにより増減する）。次に，課題への回答である主張を考える際，その理由や根拠をセットで考えるようにする。言い換えれば，理由や根拠が容易に思い浮かべられるような主張をするということである。最後に，英文を書く際は，主張を的確に表現するために必要なキーワードやキーフレーズを英語で思い浮かべられるかを自問することである。言いたいことが優れていても，必要な英語表現が書けなければ相手には伝わらない。これら3つのポイントを同時に考慮することで，読み手に伝わる英文を書くことができる。伝えたいことと伝えられることのバランスを考えながら，明確な論理構成で英文を書くことで，高評価が得られるだろう。そのために，普段から，さまざまなトピックについて自分の意見を持ち，言いたいことを日本語ではなく英語で考え英語で書く訓練が必要となる。

解答例 Although it is not easy for the government to fix the problem of gender inequality, funding various childcare options may be one way to tackle ameliorate this problem.

Many working women opt for part-time or non-career track positions in order to take care of their children. However, if the government aggressively funded and developed more affordable childcare options, these working mothers could consistently and reliably use nurseries or afterschool programs, hire nannies or babysitters, according to their work schedule and childcare needs.

If the government provided more affordable and quality childcare options, working women would be able to choose to nurture both their careers and their children. (107 words)

構成 ① Introduction: 質問に対する回答を明確に述べる。ここでは次のようになっている。

- 男女間不平等の解消は難しい問題だが，子育てに関する経済支援がそれに対応する１つの方法である。

② Body: 短めのエッセイ課題の場合できるだけ簡潔に論を展開する必要がある。ここでは，次のようになっている。

- 多くの女性が子育てのために，パートタイムやノンキャリア職種を選んでいる。
- もし政府がより廉価な子育てサービスを予算化・実現すれば，働く女性たちは，自分たちの仕事のスケジュールや必要に応じて，継続的に安心して保育園や学童保育を利用したり，乳母やベビーシッターを雇ったりすることができるようになるだろう。

② Conclusion: 質問への回答を再度端的にまとめる。

- 廉価で質の高い子育てサービスの充実により，女性は子育てと仕事を両立する道を選べるようになるだろう。

2022年B級第2回試験　正解一覧

Ⅰ
1. B　2. D　3. A　4. C　5. A　6. D　7. C　8. D　9. D　10. A

Ⅱ
11. C　12. B　13. B　14. D　15. B　16. A　17. C　18. A　19. C　20. C

Ⅲ
21. B　22. D　23. B　24. D　25. D　26. A　27. A　28. C　29. B　30. C

Ⅳ
31. A　32. C　33. A　34. D　35. D　36. A　37. B　38. C　39. B　40. B

Ⅴ
41. D　42. A　43. C　44. C　45. B

Ⅵ
46. C　47. A　48. B　49. B　50. D

Ⅶ-A
51. D　52. A　53. C　54. B　55. C

Ⅶ-B
56. B　57. D　58. C　59. B　60. A

Ⅷ-A
61. C　62. D　63. B

Ⅷ-B
64. C　65. D　66. B　67. A　68. D　69. C　70. B

Ⅸ
71. D　72. A　73. C　74. B　75. D　76. A　77. C　78. B　79. A　80. D

国連英検実施要項

（2023 年度時点）

主　　催 問い合わせ先	公益財団法人 日本国際連合協会 国連英検事務局 〒 104-0031　東京都中央区京橋 3-12-4 MAOビル 4 階 TEL 03-6228-6831 ／ FAX 03-6228-6832 http://www.kokureneiken.jp/

※国連英検 D 級・E 級は 2023 年度より開催を休止中。最新の実施情報は国連英検ホームページ http://www.kokureneiken.jp/ で必ず確認すること。

<table>
<tr><td>試験日</td><td><table><tr><th></th><th>1 次試験</th><th>2 次試験</th></tr><tr><td>第 1 回</td><td>毎年 5 月下旬の日曜日</td><td>毎年 7 月中旬の日曜日</td></tr><tr><td>第 2 回</td><td>毎年 10 月下旬の日曜日</td><td>毎年 12 月中旬の日曜日</td></tr></table>※ 2 次試験は特 A 級・A 級のみ。</td></tr>
<tr><td>試験地</td><td>■ 1 次試験…札幌・仙台・さいたま・千葉・東京・神奈川・名古屋・神戸・京都・大阪・広島・福岡・鹿児島・那覇の予定
■ 2 次試験…特 A 級：東京・大阪
※特 A 級・A 級の併願者の 2 次試験はすべて東京・大阪で行なわれる。
A 級：札幌・仙台・東京・名古屋・大阪・福岡・那覇の予定
受験会場名，所在地は受験票に明示される。受験地の変更はできない。なお，1 次試験を特別会場で受験した受験者の 2 次試験は，最寄りの試験会場となる。
※開催最小人数に満たない会場は開催を中止する場合がある（1 次・2 次共）。</td></tr>
<tr><td>検定料
（税込）</td><td>特 A 級…13,200 円　　A 級…11,000 円
B 級…8,800 円　　C 級…5,500 円
※一度納入された検定料は返却できない。申し込み後の変更もできない。
※事務局が申込書を検定料の受領後，受付完了。</td></tr>
<tr><td>併願受験
検定料
（税込）</td><td>特 A 級＋A 級＝ 22,000 円　　A 級＋B 級＝ 17,600 円
B 級＋C 級＝ 13,200 円
※一度納入された検定料は返却できない。申し込み後の変更もできない。
※事務局が申込書を検定料の受領後，受付完了。</td></tr>
<tr><td>1 次試験の
開始時間</td><td>A 級　C 級……午前 10 時 30 分（集合時間午前 10 時）
特 A 級　B 級……午後 2 時（集合時間午後 1 時 30 分）</td></tr>
</table>

試験内容

■１次試験

級	試験方法	試験時間
特Ａ・Ａ	リーディング・英作文	120 分
Ｂ	リスニング・リーディング・英作文	120 分
Ｃ	リスニング・リーディング	100 分

■２次試験

※特Ａ級・Ａ級の１次試験合格者および１次試験免除者が対象。

※面接シートに事前に所要事項を英語で書き込み，外国人面接官などの質問事項に答える。

※Ａ級については会場によりSkype等によるオンライン面接になる場合もある。

※面接の内容は試験実施の品質向上と厳正さを担保することを目的に録音（オンラインの場合は録画）される。

合格発表

合格者には合格カードを発行

試験結果は郵送にて通知。

	１次試験	２次試験
第１回	毎年６月下旬	毎年８月中旬
第２回	毎年 11 月下旬	毎年１月中旬

受験申し込み要項

●併願の場合

午前午後で隣接する２つの級を同日に受験することができる。併願を希望する場合は「受験申込書」の併願欄に記入して申し込むこと。

●１次試験免除

前回または前々回の１次試験に合格し，２次試験に不合格または欠席した場合，申請により１次試験が免除され，２次試験のみ受験できる。申込書の所定欄にその旨を記入し申し込むこと。検定料は同じ。

受験票

申込書と検定料金の受理後，受験地の会場・所在地が記載された受験票が１次試験日の１週間前までに送付される。届かない場合は，必ず試験日の３日前までに国連英検事務局（03-6228-6831〈代表〉）へ問い合わせること。顔写真１枚（4センチ×３センチ）を試験日までに用意し受験票に貼り付けておくこと。試験当日は，受験票とともに身分証明書を持参すること。

受験申し込み方法

書店，郵送，インターネット（PC・スマートフォン）で申し込みができる。
詳細は国連英検ホームページ http://www.kokureneiken.jp/ で確認する。

申込受付期間

第１回　３月初旬～４月下旬　※翌日消印有効

第２回　８月初旬～９月下旬　※翌日消印有効

検定料のお支払い方法

電話で申し込む場合	国連英検事務局へ電話・FAXにて申し込みができる。申し込み受付後「コンビニ支払用紙」が郵送される。
郵送で申し込む場合	国連英検事務局に受験申込書を請求する。 ●支払方法：必ず受験者氏名で銀行または郵便局から振り込む。
インターネット（PC・スマートフォン）で申し込む場合	国連英検のホームページから申し込みができる。 （PC・スマートフォン）http://www.kokureneiken.jp/ ●支払方法：クレジットカード支払い，コンビニエンスストア支払い，銀行または郵便局から振り込む。

検定料の各種支払詳細

振込の場合	**●銀行からの振込** 銀行名：　三菱UFJ銀行　日本橋支店 口座名：　（公財）日本国際連合協会　国連英検事務局 口座番号：普通口座0010400 金額：　該当級の受験料 ※振込手数料は受験者負担。 ※現金・為替は取り扱い不可。 ※いずれも事務局が申込書と検定料の受領を確認後，受付完了。 ※インターネット（PC・スマートフォン）で申し込んだ受験者は，ご依頼人の前に「受付番号」（メールにて通知される）を記入する。
	●郵便局からの払込 郵便局設置の払込書（青票）にて以下の内容を記入の上，払い込む。 加入者名：（公財）日本国際連合協会 口座番号：00130-7-24670 金額：　該当級の受験料 ※振込手数料は受験者負担。 ※ご依頼人欄に受験者名，住所，電話番号を必ず記入する。インターネット（PC・スマートフォン）で申し込んだ受験者は，ご依頼人の前に「受付番号」（メールにて通知される）を記入する。 ※払込金受領書は必ず保管する。
クレジットカードの場合	**●インターネット（PC・スマートフォン）からの申し込みのみ可能** 入力フォームにて「クレジットカード払い」を選択し，カード番号，有効期限などを入力する。 ※利用可能クレジットカードは国連英検のホームページで確認のこと。
コンビニエンスストアの場合	●インターネット（PC・スマートフォン）からの申し込みの場合 入力フォームにて「コンビニ払い」を選択すると，払込票が送付される。 ●電話・FAXで申し込みの場合 申し込み受付完了後事務局より「コンビニ支払用紙」が郵送される。 ※全国の主要なコンビニエンスストアにて受験料を支払う。

著者・執筆協力者プロフィール

著　者

江 原 美 明（えはら・よしあき）
武蔵野大学特任教授，元神奈川県立国際言語文化アカデミア教授，教育学博士，国連英検指導検討委員会委員。著書に『基礎から学ぶ英語科教育法』（共著，松柏社）他。

Nguyen Thoa Thi（グエン・トアー・テイ）
神奈川県立総合教育センター非常勤講師，上智大学大学院修士課程（応用言語学）修了，国連英検指導検討委員会委員。

執筆協力者

服 部 孝 彦（はっとり・たかひこ）
大妻女子大学・同大学院教授。言語学博士。国連英検統括監修官。著書に『国連英検ベーシック・トライアル』（三修社）など多数。

リスニング問題の音声ダウンロードのご案内

リスニング問題の音声については、PC、スマートフォン等で以下の国連英検ウェブサイトから再生またはダウンロードして下さい。

【音声提供 URL】

http://www.kokureneiken.jp/dist/listening/

CD をご希望の場合

PC やスマートフォンでの音声データの取り扱いについてよく分からないという方は CD-R をお送りしますので国連英検事務局までお問い合わせ下さい。

【連絡先】

公益財団法人 日本国際連合協会 国連英検事務局 宛

TEL 03-6228-6831　FAX 03-6228-6832　URL http://www.kokureneiken.jp/

国連英検過去問題集《こくれんえいけんかこもんだいしゅう》［B級《びーきゅう》］〈2021-2022年度実施《ねんどじっし》〉

2023年7月31日　第1刷発行

編　者　　公益財団法人　日本国際連合協会
著　者　　江原美明　グエン・トアー・テイ
執筆協力　服部孝彦
発行者　　前田俊秀
発行所　　株式会社三修社
〒150-0001 東京都渋谷区神宮前2-2-22
TEL 03-3405-4511 FAX 03-3405-4522
振替 00190-9-72758
https://www.sanshusha.co.jp
印刷・製本　日経印刷株式会社
編集協力／大嶋晶代
装丁デザイン／仁井谷伴子

ISBN978-4-384-06075-1 C2082